HANDBOOK FOR A
POST-*ROE*
AMERICA

HANDBOOK FOR A
POST-*ROE*
AMERICA

ROBIN MARTY

Seven Stories Press
New York / Oakland / London

Seven Stories Press
140 Watt Street
New York, NY 10013
www.sevenstories.com

Library of Congress Cataloging-in-Publication Data

Names: Marty, Robin, author.
Title: Handbook for a post-Roe America / Robin Marty.
Description: New York : Seven Stories Press, [2019]
Identifiers: LCCN 2018050872| ISBN 9781609809492 (paperback) | ISBN
  9781609809508 (ebook)
Subjects: LCSH: Reproductive rights--United States--History. |
  Abortion--United States--History. | Abortion--Law and legislation--United
  States--History. | Pro life movement--United States--History. | Pro-choice
  movement--United States--History. | Social change--United States.
Classification: LCC HQ767 .M385 2019 | DDC 362.1988/800973--dc23
LC record available at https://lccn.loc.gov/2018050872

Book design by Jon Gilbert

Printed in the USA.

9 8 7 6 5 4 3 2 1

Contents

Why This Book?

For a large section of the US population, the 2016 presidential election was a turning point. It shook complacent mainstream Americans out of their stupor and alerted them to the danger that marginalized communities already knew: that as long as the financial and political power of the country remained concentrated in the hands of the rich, the white, the male, and the conservative, those outside that power structure would see their own rights dismantled at a rapid pace.

The realization brought millions to the streets on January 21, 2017, as the Women's March spurred women and their allies in cities throughout the US to protest President Donald Trump's inauguration. In commercial airports, people protested the administration's Muslim travel ban, while white allies joined the community of Standing Rock in their ongoing effort to stop the Dakota Pipeline project. Back in DC the March on Washington protested the lack of gun restrictions after a year full of mass shootings, and all along the border protestors gathered as asylum seekers and their children were ripped from each other's arms and deported simply for the crime of seeking safety in the United States.

It took the reality of a puppet-figure Republican president, a religious right-dominated Congress, and now the most conservative Supreme Court in modern history to finally push progressive Americans of privilege to take action. For cisgender, straight, white, middle- and upper-class women especially, the idea that legal abortion (and even birth control) could actually disappear, and that the restrictions could be vast enough to affect more than just those of color, those in low-population areas and the South, and the rural and urban poor has become a harsh reality. The announcement that Supreme Court justice Anthony Kennedy was retiring and that yet another Trump nomination would tip the court to the right for decades to come was a wake-up call that has thrown those not regularly engaged in reproductive-rights activism into action.

But what, exactly, should we be doing right now?

While this moment may feel like a crisis point, the truth is that for many communities this fight has been going on for decades, even centuries. Modern gynecology came about through experimentation on black slaves. Today's contraceptives were initially tested—often coercively and without any informed consent—on women of color. Our medical history is highlighted by periods of sterilization of those who were disabled, or too poor, or the wrong color, or who had what we considered "too many" children. The decades prior to *Roe v. Wade* were filled with young girls hidden away to give birth, only to have their babies stolen and given to "worthier" families.

While *Roe* and the cases that preceded it made birth control and abortion legal, they did nothing to curtail the coercive power our government wields over the bodies of those who can give birth. *Roe* limited abortion only to those who could afford it, while at the same time limiting the types of governmental assistance available to those who wanted to give birth and had larger families but didn't have the financial means. The same government that forbids abortion coverage in Medicaid insurance also allows states to put caps on how many children a mother can receive welfare benefits for. The same states closing abortion clinics and making it hard for the uninsured to access affordable birth control also periodically propose financial incentives for those who are poor to undergo sterilization procedures.[1]

This isn't a crisis the Trump administration caused. This is only a crisis that Trump has brought to the main stage, one that he has finally forced us all to acknowledge and motivated us all to fight— even those who until now thought abortion either a settled issue or one that didn't affect them directly.

Now, the question is how to organize, and how to do it without replicating efforts, without undermining the work that has gone on for generations, and without putting others in danger. This book is written primarily for those who are looking at ways to prepare for the worst-case scenarios in a post-*Roe* America—an America where pregnant people may need to travel across state lines, or obtain illegal abortion-inducing medications, or keep their abortions secret from partners, family, and the authorities. It is meant to provide an action plan that will allow you to do the type of activism that you are best suited for—whether it is providing financial support, offering yourself as someone who can protest or work outside the legal system because of the privilege that comes from your wealth, able-bodiedness, race, gender, or geographic location, or working within the political system to undo the oppressive laws that have restricted people's ability to control their own reproductive futures. And it is meant to provide a personal blueprint for dealing with an unplanned pregnancy when abortion may be difficult—if not impossible—to access.

These tactics aren't meant for everyone. They are meant for those who have the privilege to be able to put their time, skills, money, and even personal freedom into making abortion accessible for everyone. Now that we all recognize the threat and are ready to act, we can—and must—finally shoulder this burden together.

Where We Are Now and How We Got Here

How Did We Get Here?

On January 22, 1973, the United States Supreme Court ruled in a 7–2 decision known as *Roe v. Wade* that a pregnant person has the constitutional right to an abortion under that person's right to privacy. The ruling struck down all state abortion bans as unconstitutional, ending what was a growing patchwork of abortion legality that changed from state to state, ranging from legal in all circumstances to no abortion whatsoever.

The victory didn't last long. While the framework of *Roe* required that each state must make abortion legal until the point of fetal viability (then assumed to be at around twenty-eight weeks' gestation, or by the beginning of the third trimester), and after that if the pregnancy poses a threat to the pregnant person's health, state and federal legislators immediately jumped in to see how quickly they could limit that decision with restrictions to the procedure itself.

The biggest, earliest blow was the federal Hyde Amendment, introduced by Illinois Republican congressman Henry Hyde. Hyde, who was virulently opposed to abortion, proposed making it illegal for Medicaid to cover any abortions that were not medically indicated to save the life of a pregnant person. At the time, he said, "I certainly would like to prevent, if I could legally, anybody having an abortion, a rich woman, a middle-class woman, or a poor woman. Unfortunately, the only vehicle available is the . . . Medicaid bill."[2] That was 1976, and the amendment has been reaffirmed every year since, with a rape exception (the ability to obtain an abortion if a person becomes pregnant as a result of a sexual assault) being the only change to the ban.

This targeting of the poor has had the greatest impact on pregnant people of color. Because of deep-rooted and systemic racial inequality, they are far more likely to be using government insurance, and hence more likely to be blocked from obtaining abortion care without large out-of-pocket costs. As a result, approximately one in four pregnant Medicaid users seeking to terminate end up carrying to term simply because the financial burden is too great. Meanwhile, abortion opponents celebrate the "life-saving work" of the Hyde Amendment,[3] referring to the increase in the birthrate among those on Medicaid that occurred in the decades since the amendment passed, the clear sign that the amendment served its purpose in blocking the poor from obtaining wanted abortions because of the insurmountable costs.[4]

But passing the federal Hyde Amendment was just the first step. States also began restricting abortion access, creating barriers such as mandatory waiting periods, attempted gestational bans halfway through pregnancy, requirements on where abortions could be performed and who could perform them, parental notification requirements for minors seeking care, and even a rule requiring a wife to get permission from her husband to terminate a pregnancy.

It was this influx of rules that worked its way up to the Supreme Court in the 1992 case *Planned Parenthood v. Casey*, and led to the current trimester system and the idea of "undue burden." In the *Casey* decision, the Supreme Court ruled that states cannot ban abortion outright in the first trimester, although they can put laws in place if those laws are meant to protect the health and well-being of the person trying to end the pregnancy. In the second trimester, restrictions can be more involved and must balance the rights of the pregnant person with the growing interests of the fetus. By the third trimester—post-fetal viability—abortion should only be allowed in cases that protect the health of the person who is pregnant. And all of these rules should not place an "undue burden" on one's ability to obtain an abortion in the first place.

"Undue burden" became a term that abortion opponents decided to push to the limit. Beginning slowly, they proposed incremental state laws such as parental notification and consent requirements for minors seeking terminations, and "informed consent" bills with a mandatory waiting period between receiving information about the abortion from the clinic and the actual procedure—a process that was often allowed to be completed over the phone rather than face-to-face with clinic staff when first introduced. These incremental bills didn't cause immediate hardship for the majority of abortion seekers (although they did begin the process of creating ever higher hurdles for the young and the poor). Instead, they set the stage for drawing out how long it takes to schedule, travel, and obtain an actual abortion, and for introducing false or questionable "facts" as part of the medical process.

Then in 2011 everything shifted. Fresh off the Tea Party's sweep of the Congress and state legislatures, model legislation crafted by anti-abortion groups like Americans United for Life and National Right to Life spread across the country and passed—primarily in red states and areas already suffering from a lack of clinic access. These bills—twenty-week abortion bans, six-week heartbeat bans, bans on second-trimester dilation and evacuation (D&E) abortions, mandatory waiting periods (allegedly to offer that person a chance to potentially change their mind) that stretch seventy-two hours or longer and must be done in person, requiring multiple trips to a clinic, medication abortion bans, admitting privileges requirements mandating a clinic or a doctor providing abortions must have a relationship with a local hospital in case of a patient complication (a rule that often shuts down clinics because no hospital will work with them, either for legal reasons or for fear of protests), and even total abortion bans from the moment of conception—have proliferated year after year, cumulating in more than four hundred restrictions in the last eight years alone.[5]

The Right has two goals. First, they want to bring at least one of these model bills to the Supreme Court in order to overturn *Roe* and let states have the ability to make abortion illegal within their borders. Second, they want to try to get enough political power to control the House, Senate, White House, and two-thirds of the state legislatures all at the same time, so they can create and ratify an amendment to the US Constitution that declares "personhood" and the right to life begin at the moment of conception, banning all abortion (and possibly hormonal birth control) throughout the country.

This book primarily addresses the first scenario, although some chapters can serve as a resource for the second one, too. But if we do eventually end up in a country where people can no longer end or even prevent unwanted pregnancies, we will need more than a handbook—we will need an outright revolution.

What Will Happen Next?

For the immediate future, now that we have a new ultra-conservative majority on the Supreme Court due to the confirmation of Justice Brett Kavanaugh, there are four ways—three likely and one unlikely—that the reduction or even end of legal abortion access in the US may work out. Here are all of the scenarios.

Likely

1) A case makes it to the Supreme Court within the next few years that allows the bench to overturn *Roe*, and they do.

   ▪ There are already a number of cases in lower state courts and appeals circuits that could be reviewed at the SCOTUS level, allowing the court to rule on the issue in the very near future. Plus, if a federal twenty-week abortion ban were passed and signed into law, it would immediately be sent to the Supreme Court for review if anyone chose to challenge it.

   ▪ If the court rules that abortion legality should be left to the states to decide through any of these cases, that ends *Roe* and allows the trigger laws (laws on the books in certain states that immediately make abortion illegal if *Roe* is overturned) to go into effect, and opens the door for total bans in other states.

2) The Supreme Court rules that there is still a constitutional right to an abortion, but that the viability standard is outdated and "fetal pain" should be the new standard.

   ▪ If a state or federal twenty-week ban (twenty weeks into pregnancy being the point at which abortion opponents claim a fetus can "feel pain" in the womb, although the vast majority of medical experts disagrees with that statement) is heard by the court, the conservatives could rule that "fetal pain" makes a better point in the pregnancy at which a fetus's right to life outweighs the rights of the person carrying it to terminate, undoing the "viability" standard that has been in place since *Roe* but still technically leaving abortion legal.

   ▪ If this happens, anti-abortion policy makers and legislators are prepared to pass bills stating that fetal pain actually begins far earlier in the pregnancy, as early as six weeks' gestation. This will allow states to effectively ban abortion if they choose to, without actually violating the constitutional right to an abortion.

3) States pass any laws they want—but don't actually ban abortion completely—and the Supreme Court lets them.

- There's also the possibility that the court will simply refuse to hear any cases involving abortion whatsoever, going utterly silent on the issue. Because the state and federal judiciaries have been packed with conservative justices, especially since President Donald Trump was elected, states could very easily decide to pass the most restrictive laws they can short of an outright ban, and as long as a federal judge sides with them and the Supreme Court refuses to hear a challenge, they will stay in place.

- In many ways this could be a very appealing scenario for conservative politicians, allowing some states to ban abortion without the potential blowback from voters that would come from putting a full ban in place. If a restriction is so limiting that no clinics are left open, abortion is no longer available in that state even if it is technically legal. If a state bans abortion after a heartbeat can be heard, but clinics will not do a termination before that point because they need to be sure there is enough development visible to ensure it is not ectopic, that ends abortion. All SCOTUS needs to do is refuse to do anything at all.

Unlikely but Still Possible

4) The court could hear an abortion case and decide that the Fourteenth Amendment guarantees a right to life to all and that outweighs the right to privacy found in *Roe*. Abortion is now illegal everywhere.

- This one seems the least likely, as it would be too much of a change too fast and would guarantee the end of the GOP as a political power. It could happen eventually, but not unless the Republican Party gets to a point where it is so embedded in its majorities that it never needs to fear reelection again.

What Does This Mean for the Clinics Left Behind?

With the clinics that do remain, being able to book an appointment will be more difficult than ever. In Texas, when clinics closed because of the passage of the Texas Omnibus Abortion Bill (HB 2), which required all abortion providers to have local hospital admitting privileges, those few remaining clinics that could still operate were telling patients of wait times of up to a month before they could come in to end a pregnancy.[6] While some of those clinics reopened after the Supreme Court ruled HB 2 was an undue burden on the right to an abortion, that period is a stark foreshadowing of what America could look like post-*Roe*.

Plus, if abortion is only available in certain states, abortion opponents will increase their presence at those clinics that do remain, hoping to close them one by one. With fewer clinics to concentrate on, the "sidewalk counseling," protests, street preaching, and monitoring for alleged medical violations will increase in frequency, especially in states bordering those where abortion is illegal.

That also means that it will be far more difficult for those patients who need care to get inside. Besides the sea of bodies that encircles some abortion clinics currently—made up of both those who oppose abortion and those who are trying to help a patient access a clinic—an increased presence of protesters can often bring additional security or police, a situation that creates a far more volatile environment for those who are undocumented, who are of communities of color, or who have other reasons to mistrust officers. Escorts have reported experiences with patients who were afraid to enter clinics, worried that the law enforcement that was outside attempting to maintain order in more aggressive protests was actually there to search or arrest patients. For some patients, the presence of security can be just as intimidating as a screaming preacher or a gory abortion photo.

We will discuss the efforts of protesters at clinics later in the book.

What Happens When Abortion Is Illegal?

Abortion opponents frequently say it is overblown to claim that making abortion illegal puts those who can become pregnant in physical danger. You can expect them to consistently bring up Ireland having one of the lowest maternal mortality rates in the world despite decades under a total abortion ban (a ban that the general population overwhelmingly voted to toss out in a national referendum in 2018).

What the anti-abortion advocates ignore is that in Ireland, people frequently obtained abortions despite the ban, either by leaving to get a termination across the border in a country with less restrictive laws, or by obtaining medication through the mail to terminate in private. It was only those who could not do so—immigrants who couldn't leave the country, the poor, those trying to hide their pregnancies from partners or family members—who were forced to carry to term.

That same trend occurs throughout the world when it comes to abortion being illegal—it does not stop people from seeking it, it only divides them into those who have the resources to find a safe abortion where it is legal, and those who attempt illegal abortions with a variety of success.

According to the Guttmacher Institute, an international reproductive rights policy nonprofit, in Latin America and the Caribbean, where abortion is highly restricted or completely illegal in nearly every country, an estimated 6.5 million abortions still occur every year, at a rate of 44 per 1,000 women. Of those abortions, only one-fourth are considered "safe" abortions—i.e., abortions conducted using World Health Organization (WHO) protocols *and* carried out by trained providers. There are on average approximately 760,000 complications from unsafe abortions per year, and in 2014 approximately 10 percent of maternal deaths in that region (900 fatalities) were caused by unsafe abortions.[7]

Lack of access to safe, legal abortion *does* and *will continue* to kill those who have unwanted pregnancies—and it will be marginalized communities lacking the financial resources to find alternative methods that will suffer the most. Removing abortion restrictions and other barriers—especially financial ones—so people can terminate in trained medical settings if they choose to is always the best option, and the one we should be fighting for. But there are also ways to make obtaining abortions outside a medical setting safer, both physically and legally, and we will discuss these later in the book.

2

Roe Is Over—What Does That Look Like?

As the first chapter explains, it is highly unlikely that abortion is going to be made entirely illegal in the United States any time in the near future. What is likely is that a number of states are not going to have legal, accessible abortion anymore very soon—either because *Roe* is overturned and those states choose to make abortion illegal within their borders, or because *Roe* is left in place but is so decimated that those states can still close all of their clinics or place enough restrictions that an abortion is impossible to obtain (for example, if a state passes a seventy-two-hour waiting period requirement and has a six-week ban, it has made it virtually impossible to get an abortion while still technically allowing it to remain legal).

What Does Access Look Like Today, and What Could It Look Like Post-*Roe*?

In May 2018, researchers from Advancing New Standards in Reproductive Health (ANSIRH) at the University of California created a map they said showed the "abortion deserts" in the continental US. Using color coding to depict current clinic locations and populations based on how far away people lived from the nearest clinic, they showed that most of America is a spotted wasteland where pregnant people live over a hundred miles from care.

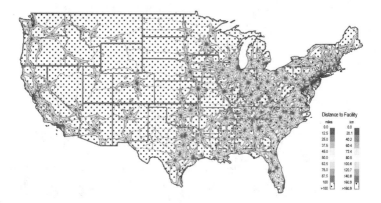

The map is alarming, but it is even more alarming if you remove those clinics that reside in states that are likely to make abortion illegal. Then you are left with this instead.

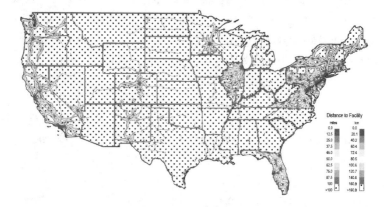

While most maps show which states likely will and won't have legal abortion, few show the real impact of how few clinics would remain in the states that may be left to provide abortions to patients. Using the most dire predictions, in the Midwest access would be limited almost exclusively to Minneapolis and Chicago. In the South there would be no care between the westernmost part of Texas and the eastern half of Florida.

This is likely the worst-case scenario we will be fighting when *Roe* is gone.

So what is the basis for predicting this sea of red taking over the United States? This is the most likely scenario based on a current study of existing laws, proposed laws, and the general hostility toward abortion rights from state legislatures. Information has been gathered from the Center for Reproductive Rights, the Guttmacher Institute, NARAL Pro-Choice America, Kaiser Health News, and the Safe Place Project, and was updated just after the 2018 midterms.

Alabama

In the 2018 midterms voters passed Amendment 2 "to recognize and support the sanctity of unborn life and the rights of unborn children, including the right to life." The new amendment to the state constitution will act as a trigger law and go into effect if *Roe* is overturned.

Alaska

Alaska does not have a trigger law and does say that there is a constitutional right to an abortion in the state constitution. At this point abortion cannot be restricted prior to viability. However, due to current restrictions in the state it is virtually impossible to get an abortion after the first trimester.

Arizona

Arizona has a ban on abortions that existed prior to *Roe* and would likely reappear if *Roe* is overturned. Arizona is unlikely to allow legal abortion in any case except if the pregnant person's life is in danger. There is no exception for sexual assault.

Arkansas

Arkansas also has a ban on abortions that existed prior to *Roe* and would likely be restored if *Roe* is overturned. The state also has "personhood" language in its constitution that allows it to promote laws that "protect the life of the unborn" from the point of conception. Arkansas's abortion ban and current language allow no exceptions of any kind when it comes to a termination.

California

Of all the states in the US, California is best prepared if *Roe* is overturned. The state protects abortion rights in its constitution and allows public insurance to pay for abortion procedures, and has approximately 150 clinics within its borders. California is also in the process of allowing medication abortion to be dispensed in on-campus health centers and expanding who is allowed to provide medication abortion to patients and perform some early first-trimester non-medication abortion procedures. On-campus medication abortion was vetoed in October 2018 by outgoing Democratic governor Jerry Brown, but Democratic governor-elect Gavin Newsom pledges to sign a bill when it is reintroduced.

Colorado

Colorado does not have any pre-*Roe* laws on the books, but it also does not enshrine the right to an abortion in its state constitution, leaving it vulnerable to legislative attacks when *Roe* is overturned. Although the state tends to elect pro–abortion rights legislators, there is always a risk of a shift in power in the state house. As of 2019 Colorado will have an entirely Democratic legislature and governor, giving it the opportunity to enshrine legal abortion access in the state constitution.

Connecticut

Connecticut has no pre-*Roe* bans and does protect abortion rights in its legislation, although there is no protection in the state constitution itself.

Delaware

Delaware will continue to have abortion access post-*Roe*, having removed its pre-*Roe* ban from the law books in 2017. The state has three abortion clinics, with first-trimester procedures available in Dover and Wilmington.

Florida

The state of Florida currently declares a right to an abortion in the state constitution—but a very conservative state legislature and a likely Republican governor may try to make inroads around that right if possible, so don't take the "safe" status for granted.

Georgia

Georgia's future is somewhat uncertain if *Roe* is overturned. While it doesn't have a trigger law or even a pre-*Roe* ban on the books, it has also shown a continuous hostility to abortion rights. Should *Roe* go down, expect that abortion will be made illegal or at least greatly limited in the state.

Hawaii

Hawaii was one of the first states to make abortion legal and will likely keep all rights intact regardless of what happens to *Roe*.

Idaho

Idaho does not have any official bans ready but between its state code language arguing a preference for "live childbirth over abortion" and the enthusiasm with which it tried Jennie Linn McCormack for illegal abortion for inducing her own termination in 2011, it would be highly unlikely for the state to not make abortion illegal completely.

Illinois

In September 2017 Illinois's pro-choice Republican governor signed Senate Bill 40, codifying the legal right to an abortion in the state if *Roe* is overturned.

Indiana

It's no surprise that the former home of Vice President Mike Pence will likely make abortion illegal if *Roe* is overturned. Although there isn't a trigger law, the number of abortion opponents in the state legislature (a veto-proof majority) makes creating a new ban a basic formality and one you should assume will happen.

Iowa

Iowa's state constitution says abortion is a right—but abortion opponents are fighting that in court with a recently passed six-week abortion ban, anyway. That ban—or something worse—could end up in effect after a new post-*Roe* precedent.

Kansas

The state supreme court is still in the process of deciding whether or not the Kansas Constitution includes a right to an abortion—a decision that was still pending as of August 2018. Kansas was one of the first states to allow abortion under very limited circumstances, but has since moved far to the right on abortion restrictions, including a near-total ban on all abortions after the second trimester. Even if the state supreme court does rule there is a right, that doesn't mean the legislature won't restrict the procedure in any way it can. However, Democratic governor-elect Laura Kelly pledges she will not allow new abortion restrictions in the state while she is in office.

Kentucky

Kentucky is very likely to ban all abortion if given the opportunity through the Supreme Court. The state is already in the process of trying to close the only clinic in operation, located in Louisville. That clinic is inundated by a mass of protesters nearly every single day it is open.

Louisiana

Louisiana still has a pre-*Roe* abortion ban on its books, and it also has a trigger law that will ban all abortion if *Roe* is overturned.

Maine

With some abortion protections already in place, abortion should remain accessible in Maine if *Roe* is overturned—as long as a slate of anti-abortion legislators isn't elected anytime soon.

Maryland

Maryland protects the right to an abortion in the state, and it currently has some of the least restrictive laws in the country. It is home to one of just three clinics in the country that provide third-trimester abortion procedures in cases of sexual assault, fetal anomalies, and other issues.

Massachusetts

Working proactively, the state just passed the NASTY Woman Act, which repealed all of Massachusetts's pre-*Roe* bans.

Michigan

Michigan has rapidly become a state with highly restricted abortion access, and it still has a pre-*Roe* ban on the books. But Democrats swept the state races in 2018, and Democratic governor-elect Gretchen Whitmer promises to reverse current abortion restrictions and codify the right to an abortion in the state once she is in office.

Minnesota

This state guarantees the right to an abortion in its state constitution.

Mississippi

If *Roe* is overturned, Mississippi's trigger law will go into effect, banning abortion completely. Even without *Roe* being knocked down, the state has passed a number of laws targeting the only clinic in the state: Jackson Women's Health Organization.

Missouri

Missouri literally wrote the law when it comes to ending abortion if the Supreme Court overturns *Roe*. The "Missouri Preamble" is the policy piece that, when added to a state constitution, declares that the state believes life starts at the moment of conception and must be protected from that point on.

Montana

Montana's state constitution provides a right to an abortion, so the state's five clinics are likely to stay open.

Nebraska

Nebraska has no laws in place or on the books to deal with *Roe* being overturned, but the state has only one legislative chamber and the Nebraska Right to Life chapter has quite a hold on most of the state senators (yes, including Democrats), so abortion isn't likely to stay around too long—at the very least it will be greatly restricted.

Nevada

The good news is that Nevada will likely be safe post-*Roe*. The bad news? You're probably going to have to go to Las Vegas to get an abortion—other than one clinic in Reno, the rest are all located in this city.

New Hampshire

Of all the states in the Northeast, New Hampshire is the most conservative when it comes to abortion. Neither the legislature nor the voters seem to see blocking access as a priority, though, which very well could mean that even if New Hampshire eventually puts more restrictions in place, the state is unlikely to ban the procedure altogether.

New Jersey

New Jersey's state constitution protects the right to an abortion, making it likely that the state will keep abortion legal regardless of what the Supreme Court does.

New Mexico

Despite having a pre-*Roe* ban still on the books, New Mexico has minimal abortion restrictions currently and is home to one of only three third-trimester clinics in the country. With a new Democratic governor in 2019, the legislature is likely to remove the old pre-*Roe* law. Should *Roe* be overturned there is a strong possibility that New Mexico will not only reject any possible bans, but it may well end up opening new clinics on its borders to accommodate those coming from other states.

New York

New York, unsurprisingly, is safe, although the legislature is working on providing more protections in the state law should *Roe* go down, such as expanding the types of medical professionals who can offer abortions—especially medication abortion—to include nurses or physicians' assistants, and being certain to codify that abortions after twenty-four weeks are allowed in cases of sexual assault or if there are fetal anomalies.

North Carolina

Considering the fact that the state was once so desperate to pass abortion restrictions that it actually grafted them inside a bill about motorcycle safety in order to get it through committee,[8] it's kind of a shock to learn there is no ban on abortion if *Roe* is overturned. That may or may not last—the state was already restricting access clinic by clinic in 2013; it probably will move aggressively to cut off even more access if it has the opportunity.

North Dakota

The state of North Dakota currently has a trigger law that will make abortion illegal if *Roe* is overturned just as soon as the legislature can act.

Ohio

Ohio's most recent attack on abortion rights was a heartbeat ban that only stayed off the books because it was vetoed by Republican governor John Kasich. Republican governor-elect Mike DeWine has promised to sign that ban into law if it is reintroduced. You can assume Ohio will restrict abortion as much as it possibly can as soon as it is allowed—and that its effort to close each clinic one by one through its licensing process will continue regardless.

Oklahoma

There is a pre-*Roe* ban on abortion still on the books in the state, and considering there are legislators who proposed a bill that explicitly states a pregnant person should be charged if caught obtaining an illegal abortion, you can bet the state will enforce that ban.

Oregon

Oregon is one of the most pro-choice states in the nation and does not have abortion restrictions. However, most clinics do not provide care after the first trimester and many of the clinics are located in the Portland area.

Pennsylvania

As in a number of states, what happens in Pennsylvania depends primarily on who is in the governor's office: a pro-choice governor is likely to veto new restrictions, and one who opposes abortion will probably sign them. Democrat Tom Wolf won the governor's race in 2018, making legal abortion in the state safe for now. Of course, abortion access is already limited, with most of the state's clinics located in the southeast corner.

Rhode Island

Rhode Island still has some existing laws that could punish those who receive abortions if *Roe* is undone, but Democrats in the state were working to have those stripped and to have the state codify *Roe*'s protections just before the legislature convened at the end of the 2018 session. It is probably safe to assume that the effort will begin again once the reality of a post-*Roe* America sets in.

South Carolina

South Carolina would be very likely to make abortion illegal, although there is no trigger law in place yet.

South Dakota

Like its neighbor to the north, South Dakota also has a trigger law for when *Roe* is overturned—but it goes into effect the very minute the Supreme Court acts.

Tennessee

Tennessee held a statewide vote in 2014 that allowed residents to decide if abortion rights protections should be stripped from the state constitution—and the voters said yes. That doesn't bode well for abortion staying legal post-*Roe*, especially since now there is nothing to stop legislators from banning abortion completely.

Texas

Considering the state of Texas was the "Wade" in *Roe v. Wade*, you can be sure it will immediately revert back to a total abortion ban. It even has its original ban still lurking, waiting for a reversal from the court.

Utah

Wondering where Utah will fall if *Roe* goes down? Check out some of its statutory language. According to the Center for Reproductive Rights, "[S]tate policy is that 'unborn children have inherent and inalienable rights' and Utah legislature intends to 'protect and guarantee to unborn children their inherent and inalienable right to life . . .' and that woman's liberty interest to abortion only applies in cases of rape, incest, fetal anomaly, or where woman's life or health are seriously threatened."[9] That's pretty explicit—as is Utah's pre-*Roe* ban, which it kept on the books.

Vermont

Vermont repealed its pre-*Roe* ban just a few years ago, leaving it very likely to keep abortion legal regardless of what the Supreme Court does. There are currently no state restrictions in place.

Virginia

In recent years the Virginia state legislature made a near-complete shift politically, starting with the election of a Democratic governor in 2013 and followed by a major blue wave in the state legislative seats in 2017. That puts Virginia in a much better position if *Roe* does get overturned than it was in six or seven years ago, when the legislature was passing mandatory ultrasound bills and regulations meant to shut clinics down. Reproductive rights groups in Virginia are now suing to get some of the remaining restrictions knocked down, which would be especially necessary if Virginia ends up being one of the few states to keep abortion legal post-*Roe*.

Washington

Like the rest of the West Coast, Washington will be keeping abortion legal to the fullest extent it is allowed under federal law.

Washington, DC

At this point DC has no restrictions, but it is important to remember that because it is not a state, it is subject to the whims of Congress (which is why whenever Democrats control Congress the city allows Medicaid to fund abortions, and whenever the GOP has control that rule is rescinded).

West Virginia

West Virginia still has a ban on abortion from before the *Roe* decision, so it is likely the state will make abortion illegal if *Roe* is reversed. Voters also narrowly passed an amendment in the 2018 midterms that states that "Nothing in this Constitution secures or protects a right to abortion or requires the funding of abortion," in preparation for a total post-*Roe* ban.

Wisconsin

The state government in Wisconsin took a hard right after the 2010 election, and as of 2018 it has yet to pivot back. The biggest threat to abortion rights has been Governor Scott Walker, who has signed every ban and restriction that came to his desk. Luckily, Walker was defeated in the 2018 midterms by Democrat Tony Evers, opening up the possibility of reversing current laws, creating new protections, and eliminating the state's pre-*Roe* ban.

Unfortunately, with a Republican-controlled state legislature, that may be difficult to do.

Wyoming

Wyoming has no major abortion restrictions other than a parental consent requirement, but it also has abortion opponents holding most of the power in the state legislature and governor's office. Those two facts together make a post-*Roe* scenario hard to predict, but with only one abortion clinic in the state—in Jackson Hole—any new bills could have an immediate and devastating impact even if they don't make abortion illegal altogether.

A list of all states, their open clinics, and their gestational limits can be found in the Resource Guide in the back of the book in the "State Resources" section.

3

Planning for Your Own Emergencies

Yes, abortion access is soon going to be even more limited than ever—maybe even illegal. But there are steps you can take now in order to be ready for anything in a post-*Roe* landscape. This chapter is about how to prevent pregnancy, help others prevent pregnancy, start a personal abortion fund, and talk to your doctor about abortion, birth control, and other reproductive needs now so you aren't blindsided later.

Emergency Contraception (EC)

If your first thought when Supreme Court justice Anthony Kennedy announced his retirement was "Abortion is going to be illegal! I'm going to make a Plan B stockpile!," well, you aren't alone. Just like after Donald Trump's Electoral College victory, social media exploded with tweets and posts about people purchasing Plan B to have on hand either for themselves, family and friends, or even strangers lacking access to a clinic.

Having a dose or two of emergency contraception available is always a good idea, regardless of the legality of abortion or birth control options. EC works prior to ovulation, preventing an egg from being released at a time when sperm may be present and stopping fertilization. Although some forms of EC can work for as long as a week after unprotected sex, most are at their most effective when taken within seventy-two hours of intercourse. Having a supply on hand allows more people to effectively take the medication at its optimal time to prevent pregnancy, and it eliminates issues like getting into a doctor or clinic for ella (ulipristal acetate, which is more effective than Plan B but also requires a prescription), finding a pharmacy that carries it, getting into a clinic that will offer it, or, in cases of sexual assault, going immediately to an emergency room for dosage, especially if that hospital ends up being religiously affiliated and refuses to provide the medication.

However, there is a vast difference between having a dose (or doses) for an emergency and "stockpiling" them for personal use or distribution. Here are some things to consider to ensure you are acquiring EC in the best way possible.

1) Are you buying locally, or online?
   ▪ If you are purchasing emergency contraception for future use, please consider only buying it from online sites. This ensures that for those who have an actual emergency and need medication immediately, there is still a supply on the shelf for them to buy and it isn't out of stock. Waiting two days or more for delivery because there is no place to purchase locally is the surest way for a person to end up with an unwanted pregnancy.
2) Do you really need that many doses?
   ▪ Yes, buying a bunch of EC feels like a really proactive way to stick it to Trump and the rest of the anti-abortion politicians. But remember, most EC has a shelf life of three to four years, and in some cases the clock may already be ticking. Twenty packs of EC do no one any good if they all expire because you really only needed four. Unless you have a real reason

to think that you might end up as a distribution channel for your friends or neighbors, limit how many you get at once. Odds are, you will be able to buy more later.

3) Is there a local organization that offers EC? Can you help them, instead?

▪ Let's be frank, getting emergency contraception from a stranger is a sort of freaky idea. Preventing a pregnancy—especially after intercourse—is a pretty private activity. No one really wants to reach out to someone they don't know in order to get medication, but they are more likely to contact reproductive rights and justice groups or feminist groups than private individuals. Don't recreate the wheel when there are already organizations distributing EC—offer those groups money or medication, or even offer to help distribute through their channels rather than try to do this alone.

Here is a list of places that currently provide emergency contraception distribution that you can contact and support:

Alabama Reproductive Rights Advocates (ARRA) (Alabama)
2824 Hunterwood Dr. SE, Decatur, AL 35603
865-465-9793
http://alabamareproductiverightsadvocates.com
lindadfoundation@gmail.com

Plan B NOLA (New Orleans Area)
504-264-3656
https://www.planbnola.com/

IndyFeminists (Indiana)
https://www.facebook.com/IndyFems/
(At this point IndyFeminists only communicates via Facebook Messenger.)

Mississippi Reproductive Freedom Fund (Mississippi)
2210 Hill Ave., Jackson, MS 39211
769-218-9413
https://msreprofreedomfund.org/
mississippireprofreedomfund@gmail.com

What You Need to Know About Emergency Contraception

First of all, just a friendly reminder that when we talk about EC, we tend to go straight to a discussion about medication. But when it comes to dealing with the aftermath of unprotected sex, the copper IUD is the most effective form of EC and can be placed by a practitioner up to five days after unprotected intercourse. Keep that in mind if you were already considering long-lasting contraception options—but obviously don't jump into an IUD just as a means of preventing a possible pregnancy after unprotected sex.

Of course, you can't keep an IUD lying around in case of emergencies like you can with pills. When it comes to medication EC, there are multiple brands, all with different price points and best practices. Plan B One Step, Next Choice One Dose, Take Action, My Way, and AfterPill all work up to five days post–unprotected sex but are most successful when taken within the first seventy-two hours. All are available without a prescription.[10]

ella is more effective than Plan B when used within three days of unprotected sex, and it is also more effective for people with a higher body mass index (BMI), generally people weighing over 165 pounds. However, it can only be obtained with a prescription, and if you are already on hormonal birth control it is less effective and makes your hormonal birth control less effective, too (so you might want to consider a different medication or even a copper IUD if you are worried about getting pregnant after forgetting to take your regular birth control pill).

Who Should Really Stockpile and Distribute EC

Of course, there are some cases where it does make sense to buy a lot of EC and act as a distributor. If you are in a community with no EC provider already—especially an area without much pharmacy access—and you are willing to be a public face for distribution (and especially if you have the ability to commit to it from both a financial and time perspective), this can be a good opportunity to provide concrete help. This may also be a valuable resource if you are on a college campus (especially at a religious college, which may not offer EC at the health center, and where students may not have transit options to get to a pharmacy). Resident advisors (RAs), floor leaders, or members of reproductive rights, human rights, civil rights, or LGBTQ rights campus groups would also be excellent public faces for EC distribution in your college or university.

To prepare and lay the groundwork for your new group, go to the "Finding Your Personal Cause" and "Avoiding Surveillance" chapters and follow the tips for creating your own support network.

What to Do Instead to Ensure More Access to EC

Distributing EC is helpful, but the biggest way an individual can help those who need emergency contraception is to be sure that stores are stocking it regularly and are allowing people to purchase the medication without restrictions. EC is available for purchase regardless of gender or age and without ID. Check with all of your local retailers to ensure it is in stock, and, if not, ask them to carry it. Contact the corporate offices of those stores that do have it available and thank them for keeping it on the shelves. Make sure to report any issues with purchasing (such as a pharmacist saying they have a religious objection and not finding another person to complete the transaction, a demand for ID, a refusal to sell to someone presenting as male) to the National Women's Law Center at 866-745-5487 or coverher@nwlc.org. Also contact your state pharmacy board, the corporate office of the pharmacy, and local media outlets.

Birth Control Pills

Even with abortion banned in some states, it's unlikely that birth control will be banned, too. However, it very well may get harder to access from a logistical or financial standpoint, especially if the government continues to defund family planning clinics and reallocates those funds to entities that don't offer hormonal birth control.

According to the Guttmacher Institute, the rate of unintended pregnancy among the poor is five times the rate of unintended pregnancy among those of higher income levels, and the rate among the black community is more than double that of the white community.[11] One of the biggest barriers to pregnancy prevention is the ability to access birth control, either because of cost, no access to doctors for a prescription, or transportation issues that make obtaining pills at a pharmacy too difficult.

As of June 2018, Washington, DC, and fifteen states allow those who use the birth control pill to obtain a full year's supply at once (although some of them require you obtain a shorter supply of just a few months first, then they allow twelve months' worth). Those states are California, Colorado, Connecticut, Hawaii, Illinois, Maine, Maryland, Massachusetts, Nevada, New Jersey, New York, Oregon, Vermont, Virginia, and Washington.[12] Other states have legislation still pending. These increased birth control supplies may be able to cut down on the logistical barriers that prevent reliable birth control pill usage, especially if family planning clinics continue to close.

If you are in a twelve-month state, take advantage of the access if possible. If your state claims to offer this service but no doctors seem able to put it into practice, contact the local legislators initiating the legislation and let them know. If you are in a pending state, or your state has not brought up a bill, reach out to your legislators to see what can be done to speed the process up. Remind politicians— especially Republican ones—that if abortion is being restricted it is imperative that they do all they can to support preventing unwanted pregnancies in the first place.

Can You Use Birth Control Pills as EC?

Before emergency contraception was so readily available, health clinics would sometimes give out birth control pills with special instructions on how to take them in order for them to work as emergency contraception.

Using birth control packs this way isn't nearly as necessary anymore, but it could still work in a pinch if you happen to have some around. This information on how to create an EC dose was found at the blog *A Womb of One's Own* (https://wombofonesown.wordpress.com).[13]

Not every birth control pill contains the active ingredient in Plan B. If your birth control pill does, you'll see that after the brand name, in parentheses, the word "levonorgestrel" will appear. Contraceptive pills combine levonorgestrel with other hormonal ingredients, and the dose of each ingredient will be listed on your medication packaging.

In order to use a levonorgestrel birth control pill as emergency contraception, you'll want to first compute how many pills you will need to take. First, look at how many milligrams of levonorgestrel are in each pill. For most birth control pill formulations containing levonorgestrel, this will be .5–.6 mg. This means that in order to bring the total amount of levonorgestrel to 1.5 mg, you will typically need three pills, taken in a single dose as soon as possible after having unprotected sex. 1.5 divided by the number of milligrams per pill (or 1,500 divided by the number of micrograms per pill) will give you the number of pills required.

Round UP, not down: slightly too much medication is better than slightly too little. However, it is unnecessary to use extra pills significantly beyond the 1.5 mg dosage. Many websites containing information on how to use levonorgestrel-containing birth control as emergency contraception say that women should take, depending on the brand of birth control being used, up to twelve total tablets containing .5 mg of levonorgestrel each (divided into two doses). This is unnecessary and may even be harmful. The amount of total levonorgestrel in such a dosage is substantially more likely to cause side effects—mostly of the gastrointestinal variety—without significantly enhancing the ability of the pills to prevent unwanted pregnancy.

It is absolutely essential to make sure you *only use active pills* when using contraceptive pills as Plan B. Most forms of contraceptive pills come in monthly packs that include twenty-one days of active pills and seven days of placeholder sugar pills. The three weeks of active pills are generally colored differently from the week of inactive (sugar) pills in the pill packet. Inactive pills have no medication at all, so using them won't help you to prevent a pregnancy.

Users of emergency contraception should know that EC involves the risks of taking any hormonal birth control pill (though the fact that it is taken infrequently and only for a day at a time makes long-term side effects unlikely). Many users report minor gastrointestinal distress or being nauseated. Much less frequently, blood clots have been known to form as a result of the active ingredient in these pills. Blood clots are a serious side effect (possibly even lethal if one dislodges and causes a pulmonary embolism, stroke, or heart attack) but are rare. If you notice severe leg pain, shortness of breath, or any symptoms of a stroke or heart attack after taking emergency contraception, go to the emergency room immediately—these could indicate the formation of a blood clot.

Condoms

Whether or not abortion or even birth control is legal, it's always good to have condoms on hand for pregnancy prevention and avoiding sexually transmitted infections. Buying them in bulk is cheapest, and they last four to five years. Buying condoms online is the best way to get the cheapest rate, and stick to known brands (Trojan, Durex, etc.) to ensure high quality.

Also be aware, however, that in some jurisdictions, having multiple condoms on your person can be considered "evidence" of potential sex crimes. While most states—most notably New York and California—have banned police from considering condoms as an "instrument of a crime" when arresting sex workers, prosecutors in Allegheny County, Pennsylvania, still use that as an arresting charge. Critics worry that the continued practice is leading to less-safe sex acts and the spread of STIs. Be sure to pay attention to any local laws, but also continue to practice the safest sex possible if you want to avoid pregnancy or disease.

Long-Acting Reversible Contraception (LARC)

When it comes to preventing unwanted pregnancy, there is almost nothing more effective than LARC. Implants and intrauterine devices (IUDs) have no potential for user error like birth control pills or condoms, making them the most reliable way of preventing pregnancy that's out there.

They are also far more expensive than any other method—at least out of pocket. If your insurance covers them currently, do consider taking advantage of this, as once they have been inserted they can prevent pregnancy anywhere from three (implant) to ten (Copper IUD) years.

But also be aware of potential concerns before jumping into a LARC. Implants and IUDs are often difficult if not impossible to have safely removed without a health care provider's assistance. While it may not be difficult to find a doctor or clinic willing to provide one now, there could be a far larger barrier when it comes to a removal—especially an early one. This can be especially true for people of color, who have historically been subject to racial bias in the medical community and stripped of their reproductive autonomy, coerced and outright forced into birthing, birth control, and sterilization procedures without consent. A "reversible" contraceptive method is only as reliable as your access to a medical professional willing to participate. If you switch doctors over the years, or if your family planning center closes, it may be much harder to get off birth control than it was to get on it.

Another issue to weigh with LARC is which type to choose and the possible complications that might arise. Implants release etonogestrel, a form of progesterone, whereas IUDs like Mirena, Skyla, Kyleena, and Liletta release levonorgestrel, another progesterone. As with all hormonal contraceptives, you may experience some side effects like irregular spotting. Copper IUDs (ParaGard) do not have a hormonal aspect, but some people do get heavier, more painful periods. Be prepared to adjust if it turns out the LARC you begin with isn't the one that is right for you.[14]

For more information on which type of birth control might be your best fit, try the "Method Explorer" and other guides at Bedsider (www.bedsider.org).

Sterilization

Obviously if you want to completely avoid pregnancy for good in a post-*Roe* era you could seek out permanent birth control (sterilization). This procedure can be obtained by either gender, and in some states or through some insurers the costs will be covered. However, it is not meant to be reversible and will render a person permanently infertile. Be positive that this is a decision you are completely certain about before contacting a doctor.

Also, be cognizant of the historical legacy of sterilization, which has long been used by the government as a means of permanently limiting the reproductive rights of populations like poor people of color, the mentally and physically disabled, and others, either through financial coercion or without proper informed consent.

Setting Up a Personal Emergency Abortion Fund

No one ever plans to need an abortion, but maybe everyone should, just in case. Not having the money to pay for an abortion—and the expenses surrounding it, such as time off work, travel, lodging, childcare, and more—is what causes many people to delay the procedure, which, ironically, can then drive up the costs. A look at one Las Vegas area abortion clinic's weekly price sheet shows how dramatic the increase can be. At that clinic, an abortion at fourteen weeks' gestation can be obtained for $550 or less (a price that is actually quite low compared to what many clinics in the country charge). From that point onward, it increases $100 per week for each week between weeks fourteen and seventeen, $300 a week from weeks eighteen to twenty-one, then $200 each week until twenty-three weeks' gestation, by which time the price is $2,500.[15]

For some lower-income patients it becomes a cycle they cannot break, eventually becoming too expensive for them to terminate before the gestational limit is reached. According to Advancing New Standards in Reproductive Health (ANSIRH), a research group at the University of California, San Francisco, those who cannot access services because of cost are four times as likely to be in poverty four years later than low-income people who were able to obtain their abortions.[16]

Abortion funds and practical support groups can help with all that, but as need grows and expenses increase—especially as clinics close and states cut off all legal access, forcing patients to travel farther to the fewer available clinics—these groups will only be able to do so much. If you are privileged enough to have the ability, it wouldn't hurt to save up for your own potential emergency. If you don't need it, that money can always be used somewhere else, or even eventually given to an abortion fund to assist others in need.

In the first step for setting up a personal abortion fund, consider actually investing in pregnancy tests themselves. After all, ruling a pregnancy in or out is imperative before deciding what you need to do. Consider purchasing some cheap pregnancy tests to have around so they are available if you think you might be pregnant.

This is especially helpful if you happen to have irregular periods and aren't as sure of when your next cycle may be coming.

Pregnancy tests at the Dollar Store or another discount retailer are just as effective as the twenty-dollar tests you can purchase at your pharmacy, so pick up a few to have on hand. You can also purchase cheap bulk testing strips at online retailers like Amazon by searching for Wondfo, where you can get them for as little as twenty cents a strip.

But what if you do find that second line on your test? How much should you set aside to be prepared? In the wake of the Texas clinic closures following the implementation of HB 2 in 2016, *Cosmopolitan* magazine's Hannah Smothers asked Natalie St. Claire of Fund Texas Choice that very question. St. Claire's advice? Set aside enough for the procedure ($300–$1,000 for a first-trimester abortion, depending on gestational age, procedure type, anesthesia, and additional medical needs like being Rh positive), add in whatever travel you may need (gas, plane tickets, lodging, etc.), food costs for a few days, child care costs if you have young children, and two or three days' lost wages in case you need to go to a state with a waiting period or you need some recovery time and you are unable to take paid time off.[17]

Bundled together, yes, that's a lot of money. Start small as you develop your fund, working with what you know can't be covered elsewhere. First check to see if your state or private insurance covers abortion, whether you have a clinic in your state currently, and if your state is one of the ones that will ban abortion post-*Roe*, and if so where the best available clinic might be. The sooner you can terminate the pregnancy, the less it will cost, so consider things like irregular periods that make it difficult to date a pregnancy, face-to-face meetings with one or more days in between at your local provider, or how booked the clinic might be (clinics in low-access states like Montana, Mississippi, Alabama, and Louisiana often have longer waits for scheduling than in states with easy access and multiple clinics). Also think through potential decisions like waiting for vacation time to accumulate or scheduling work so you can take time off without losing a paycheck, and remember that delaying an abortion until later in gestation is likely to increase the cost.

The scenarios can be overwhelming, which is why it is good to plan ahead before this becomes an emergency.

Need a step-by-step breakdown? Here's a good "average" budget that takes into account a number of variables:

- Procedure: $500
- Gas: $50
- Airline ticket: $250
- Hotel for two nights (forty-eight-hour waiting period): $100 a night/$200
- Food: $30 a day/$90
- Childcare: $100 a day/$300
- Lost wages: $15 an hour (eight-hour days)/$360

Total fund = $550 to $1,700, depending on your location and personal situation

The bill is a big one, which is why people struggle so much to pay for an abortion when the need arises. Try to set aside a little now if you can. Open a separate account just for this and set an automatic transfer for ten dollars a month, or some other small amount you aren't likely to notice. If you get a bonus or some money as a gift, toss it in there too. None of it may seem like much, but every bit helps if you do find yourself in a real emergency.

Of course, there are groups that will help with all of this (funding, travel, meals, lodging) if you do get in a bind. Practical support groups and NNAF abortion funds are all listed in the "Finding Your Personal Cause" chapter and are also broken down by state in the "State Resources" section of the Resource Guide. If you need help, you will not be alone.

Having "The Talk" with Your Doctor

If you have a regular physician or clinic because of a private health insurance plan, now is the best time to have a frank discussion about where they stand on medical issues surrounding reproductive autonomy. Questions you should be asking include the following.

- Do you treat LGBTQ patients? Do you feel uncomfortable treating survivors of sexual assault?
- Do you support all forms of birth control—and will you provide nonjudgmental prenatal care—regardless of the age, gender, race, marital status, or number of children of the person asking for it?
- Would you support me and help facilitate things if I decided that I wanted to be sterilized, either now or down the road? (Some physicians have concerns about permanent birth control for those who are young, who have never had children, or who have never been married. While those may all be valid concerns, ultimately your physician should recognize that you should have the final say about your body.)
- If I became pregnant and there was a medical concern that could require an abortion, would you object to the abortion? Would you have the knowledge to perform a procedure or know who to connect me to who could perform it in the safest way possible inside a medical setting? (Especially find

out if your doctor can perform or can refer you to someone who can perform a D&E in a medical emergency, rather than simply inducing labor.)

- Would you provide me with information if I became pregnant and did not want to give birth? Would you be willing to offer medication to end the pregnancy if it was still early, or refer me to someone who would? Would it change how you treated me, medically? Would you even still want me as a patient?

- Would you report illegal activities that affect my medical care to the police if I told you about them?

All of these questions can be awkward and uncomfortable, but they are also questions you need to ask now in order to determine if your doctor will always consider your physical and mental needs first. You are the patient, and their duty should always be to support your best medical outcomes.

Want to report a doctor who doesn't put your reproductive rights first, or recommend health care professionals who support full-spectrum care? Use the database at www.obgyNOPE.com to share info on your providers.

4

How to Get Started Organizing Now for a Post-Roe America

How Can You Protect Access in a State Where Abortion Is Still Legal?

Just because it looks as if your state is still going to have legal access to abortion, that doesn't mean it will remain that way. All it takes is one election to change the entire makeup of your state legislature and open up an opportunity for more restrictions to pass down the road.

Get Involved Politically

We all know the most powerful thing we can do as citizens is to vote, and to support candidates who will uphold access to reproductive health care. But after that, the best way to protect against future abortion restrictions is to push your current lawmakers to pass a bill that establishes abortion as a constitutional right in your state.

First, be absolutely positive that your state does not have any trigger laws, total abortion bans, or other archaic restrictions that may have been on the books prior to *Roe* and were never removed once abortion became legal. If you do, press your local state legislator to introduce a bill to strike them down.

Second, encourage your legislators to propose a bill to codify abortion rights in the legislature and even the state constitution.

There are many different ways to approach it based on the political layout of your state, such as passing a reproductive parity act that requires insurers who cover prenatal care to cover abortion services as well, legislating a requirement that state-based insurance plans and state Medicaid cover abortion services, or even pushing a full bill to demand equality for women both medically and economically.

In 2016, the Public Leadership Institute released a number of proactive model reproductive rights and health bills for state use, all of which can be found at http://publicleadershipinstitute.org/ model-bills/reproductive-rights/29-model-bills-playbook-abortion-rights/.

A sample of a strong bill to champion is the "Women's Equality Dignity and Fairness Act," which legislates for abortion coverage in insurance, repeals all state abortion restrictions, rejects any legislative bill that puts medically unnecessary requirements on abortion clinics in an effort to close them down, expands which medical providers are allowed to offer abortions, and more. The sample bill can be found in the Resource Guide at the back of the book.

Also don't forget to look for new ways to improve access in your state, especially since more people will now be depending on it. Even with abortion legal, access can remain limited for populations who find it difficult to travel for financial or logistical reasons. Opening more clinics—or adding abortion services to existing health centers— creates an easier path to abortion expansion than starting fresh.

California has been leading the way in this respect, allowing more medical professionals like nurses and physicians assistants to offer birth control, medication abortion, and early first-trimester abortions, and requiring that public college and university campuses offer medication-abortion options in their local health clinics (a policy change that was vetoed in September 2018 by Democratic governor Jerry Brown but is expected to be reintroduced and signed into law by governor-elect Gavin Newsom). For students unable to leave campus due to transportation issues and for rural area patients far from large urban clinics, these two tactics mean more nearby options, lowering costs and wait times for abortion care.

Take Your Battle Hyper-Local

Once abortion is illegal or inaccessible in some states, abortion opponents will then turn their attention to closing the clinics that still remain in the states that have access. As we've seen in the past, that could come in a variety of ways. They may purchase nearby buildings in order to directly interact with patients entering clinics, or use professional sound systems outside clinic doors to loudly implore, preach at, frighten, or guilt patients waiting for any appointment. They might leaflet neighborhoods with personal information about abortion clinic staff, or harass waste management companies or other businesses that have the clinic as a client. They may even file health department complaints and demand city records to find information about potential complications from abortion or other private patient information.

If you have an abortion clinic in your city, there are a number of ways that you can fight to protect abortion access at the local level, both as a resident and as an activist.

Run/Vote in City Council Elections

In some ways your city-level government may well be the most important governing body when it comes to keeping abortion accessible. If a state allows abortion to remain legal but the city somehow makes it impossible to operate a clinic it doesn't matter if the procedure is legal or not.

City councils have already become abortion clinic gatekeepers by changing zoning requirements for existing clinics or conversely by changing zoning laws to allow in those who want the clinic to shut down.

Some examples of how this works are:

1) In 2013 the city council of Fairfax City, Virginia, voted to change their zoning laws, creating a new category called "medical care facility," which would require the current abortion clinic to obtain a $4,800 special use permit as well as approval by the council itself to continue operating. As a result of the new ordinance NOVA Women's Healthcare shut down. In 2015 another city council, this time in Manassas, Virginia, followed suit, resulting in the closure of Amethyst Health Center for Women. In both cases no new clinics opened in either city because the process was too burdensome.[18]

2) In 2014, when Dalton Johnson attempted to move his abortion clinic into a new building in order to meet the new standards for clinics passed by the state of Alabama, the city council refused to offer him a zoning variance for a medical business, despite the fact that his building had previously housed a doctor's office and was also home to a dentist. While the medical variances had previously been rubber-stamped, the council forced Johnson to wait for months for approval before finally agreeing. During that period of time, there was no abortion access at all in northern Alabama.[19]

3) In October 2017 Whole Women's Health announced plans to open a new clinic in South Bend, Indiana, that would offer only medication abortions.[20] They applied for a license from the state only to be rejected, beginning a long court process that as of September 2018 is still unresolved, with the clinic yet to actually see

patients. However, during this time a crisis pregnancy center (an anti-abortion and often religious nonprofit whose goal is to convince pregnant people not to end their pregnancies) was able to purchase a building next door to the proposed clinic and seek out a rezoning action from the city council. The rezoning process took less than two months to get official approval. Luckily, a veto of the rezoning decision by South Bend's mayor forced the crisis pregnancy center to discard their new location next door and move in across the street instead.[21]

What You Can Do—Direct Action

You don't need to be on the city council to help your local clinic. Here's what you can do to directly impact your city's clinic(s).

1) Go to city council meetings.
   - Check their agendas and see if they are doing anything involving zoning around your clinic.
   - Ask the council about noise ordinance enforcements or if there are any buffer zones that could be put in place to protect patients. (Contrary to popular belief, buffer zones are still legal even after the *McCullen v. Coakley* Supreme Court ruling of 2014, just not thirty-five-foot buffers.)
2) Frequent businesses that are near clinics.
   - Among the biggest problems facing clinics are landlords who do not want to continue renting to them or neighbors who are hostile to them because they believe the chaos drives away customers. When businesses aren't being harmed by— or are even benefitting from—being next to a clinic, they are far more likely to work with the clinic and support them when they are attacked by protesters or city government.

3) Support and utilize services that do business with clinics.

- One of the ways abortion opponents try to close clinics is by intimidating their vendors. They will target the person who delivers their packages; they will harass those who repair their roof. They will call out the restaurant that drops off their lunches in the hope of completely isolating the clinic and its staff. Local clinics often ask for community support when that happens. Be there for them.

4) Offer emotional support.

- Clinics like cards, flowers, anything that makes them feel like they are appreciated, especially when they are being inundated with harassment. These signs of support help prevent staff burnout, and that keeps clinics open, too.

Use Your Tools to Ensure Diversity of Participants. It isn't necessary to be able-bodied or financially secure to do direct action to support clinics. Thanks to online tools and social media organizing, any person with access to a computer or phone and Internet can take part in efforts like petition creating, e-mail and text campaigns, awareness raising, and more. Newer online apps like ResistBot can help people contact government entities more easily, and allow more participation from those who are unable to organize in a physical, face-to-face setting due to work schedules, childcare, transportation issues, or disability. Be sure that if you are starting a campaign, you are working in a way that includes all supporters, such as by holding virtual, recorded meetings that are captioned and can be played when an activist is most able to tune in, making childcare available during meetings so more parenting attendees can participate, and meeting at locations that are directly accessible to those with mobility issues and those who use mass transit.

Do You Want to Get Even More Directly Involved?

Many clinics use volunteers. Some have clinic escorts to help patients navigate their way past protesters and into the clinic itself; others have volunteers who talk to patients during their procedures to help them feel relaxed and supported (abortion doulas). Others call volunteers in on days when they expect larger, specialized, one-off protests, such as on Good Friday.

Always contact your local clinic before arriving to help. Expect to be vetted in some way by the clinic, which will want to ensure its patients and staff stay safe. Then assume that you will go through a training (perhaps more than one) before you actually interact with patients.

ALWAYS follow the clinic's lead. Do not show up at the clinic until you are invited and especially do NOT take it upon yourself to "counterprotest" or hold any other activity outside a clinic without explicit consent. To patients seeking a termination, there is no difference between anti-abortion protesters and pro-choice protesters: both are there, interfering with their attempt to easily and privately access the clinic.

We will discuss how to get involved with organizations supporting abortion and clinic access in more detail in the "Finding Your Personal Cause" chapter.

How Can You Protect Access if Your State Makes Abortion Mostly or Totally Illegal?

Then, of course, there is what to do if your state makes abortion nearly or completely illegal in all cases. The good news is, things aren't as hopeless as they seem. As long as abortion is legal in the

United States as a whole, there is always the possibility that abortion bans can be struck down with subsequent laws if there is enough turnover in the state legislature. Once residents of a state see the actual impact of no longer having legal abortion available, there is a strong possibility that voters and legislators will realize that total bans do far more harm than good.

Until that happens, there are some places where you can make the most impact legislatively even without legal abortion in your state.

Protect the Access That Does Still Exist

While it may not seem like it, a total or near-total state abortion ban still isn't the worst thing that could happen. The worst thing that could happen would be if there was a total ban and a person who wanted to end a pregnancy couldn't leave the state to do it.

This sort of *Handmaid's Tale* scenario doesn't seem likely for the general population, but it could easily become a reality for minors wanting to end a pregnancy. For over a decade Congress has introduced in some form a federal Child Interstate Abortion Notification Act (CIANA)—a bill that would make it illegal for anyone other than a minor's legal guardian to take that child to another state to obtain an abortion, with the adult who crosses state lines subject to criminal prosecution.

While CIANA would impact all minors seeking care, it is those who are poor and especially those who come from immigrant families who would be most affected. Many southern states have parental notification laws that require notarized birth certificates or other costly documentation to prove a familial relationship. Those who are in the country without papers may be unable to officially approve an abortion for their child even though they are legal guardians— especially now that the Trump administration is more aggressively deporting immigrants. Others may be incarcerated, too ill to travel, or unable to get off work, or they may have too many children to care for at home or other obligations. There are a myriad of reasons why another adult could need to take a minor across a state line for an abortion rather than the pregnant teen's legal guardian, but CIANA rejects all of these factors.

It would not be surprising to see some form of CIANA reintroduced now and for the bill to finally pass—especially if some states had no legal abortion at all. However, we also need to be vigilant about individual states passing their own similar laws that may equate helping a person leave the state with "procuring" an illegal abortion, especially for minors who have little ability to travel on their own.

Also be prepared for any "cleanup" of exceptions that are left in current total bans. Check to see if your state allows an exception to its abortion bans if the pregnant person's health is at risk, or if they were impregnated as a result of sexual assault. While most people—including many who identify as pro-life—believe that a person should be allowed to terminate if that person was impregnated through sexual assault, many anti-abortion groups reject that exception, primarily because they believe that people may make up rape claims in order to obtain an abortion.

Pressuring your legislators to ensure that at a minimum victims of sexual assault still have access to abortion care—and aren't forced to carry to term just because of the state they live in—is not just a reasonable action that reflects the majority's beliefs on abortion. It also offers a clear incremental step toward repealing abortion bans as a whole down the road, and it exposes just how radical the Right's position has become.

Work to Pass a Bill to Protect Those Who Experience Poor Pregnancy Outcomes

Maternal mortality and poor pregnancy outcomes are rising all across the US already, and that increase is especially concentrated among pregnant people of color. Due to poverty, lack of affordable, consistent preventive health care services including and beyond contraception, and longstanding systemic racial bias in medical care and treatment, black and brown people are far more likely to be less healthy when they get pregnant, receive less prenatal care, and face greater risk of miscarriage, stillbirth, and premature labor.

And if *Roe* is overturned, every single instance of these poor birth outcomes could be investigated as a potential illegal abortion.

If there is just one bill to be championed in states where abortion is greatly or completely restricted, it would be the Public Leadership Institute's "Pregnant Women's Dignity Act." The model, which would be highly beneficial in both blue and red states alike, demands that law enforcement not be called in to investigate when a person miscarries or delivers a stillbirth. Even with abortion technically legal, numerous people have been arrested and prosecuted, either for allegedly inducing their own abortions, for miscarrying fetuses on the cusp of viability and not seeking medical attention in time, for miscarrying and disposing of fetal remains without alerting medical practitioners or authorities, for unfavorable birth outcomes after illicit drug use, and even for premature labor after a suicide attempt.

Once abortion is illegal ALL miscarriages will potentially be subject to questioning by the authorities, with doctors, police, and district attorneys able to decide at their own discretion what constitutes a "suspicious" circumstance that might lead to a more in-depth investigation. The Pregnant Women's Dignity Act protects all people from having their unsuccessful pregnancies scrutinized, allowing every pregnant person the same freedom in their birth outcomes.

The model bill can be found at http://publicleadershipinstitute. org/abortion-rights/pregnant-womens-dignity-act/. It is also included in the Resource Guide at the end of the book.

Direct Action in States Where Abortion Is Illegal

It's a daunting prospect. With abortion illegal in particular states, there will be three options: getting pregnant people who want to end their pregnancies to states where they can do that, getting them the tools to end their pregnancies in their home states (as well as their literal homes), even if that means defying local laws, and supporting those who are arrested should any illegal actions be discovered and prosecuted.

Each of these options will be explored in detail in the next few chapters.

5

Finding Your Personal Cause

It's completely understandable if your first reaction to the unraveling of abortion rights is to want to give all of your money to pro-choice organizations, convert your spare bedroom into an abortion Airbnb, buy out your local pharmacy's stock of Plan B, or even start researching how to make a manual vacuum aspirator.

Take a minute and pause. You don't have to do everything yourself, and a lot of activists have been planning for this moment for decades. The bad news is that abortion is now going to be mostly or completely illegal. The good news is that national and local organizations—especially reproductive justice groups—have been on the ground for decades preparing for this possibility. They were doing the heavy lifting on reproductive rights and access issues while most of the privileged population of America was content to believe that abortion was a "settled issue" and *Roe* would never be overturned.

Rather than replicate efforts, look first to these groups and find out how you can best support those who already have their networks in place.

National Network of Abortion Funds

The National Network of Abortion Funds (NNAF) is an organization that spreads across nearly every state in the nation, helping to fund-raise for those who need abortions but cannot afford them. Because of their locations and reach, as well as their work with individual abortion clinics and funds in states, NNAF has become not just a fund-raising organization but also a political action network, fighting against abortion-funding bans and other restrictions that make it more difficult for pregnant people to access legal abortion care. They also work to center the needs of people of color and other marginalized communities in their advocacy, since those are the groups in the most need and who face the greatest risks if they cannot access care.

NNAF has endorsed a number of regional funds and affiliates, and that information will be available later in this chapter, but unlike other organizations in the book, NNAF also offers a personal membership option as well. By becoming an individual member, you are not just providing financial support to the network but you will also receive monthly news updates about abortion access, including actions that you may be able to participate in and networking opportunities with your regional fund. NNAF is joining together funders, providers, those who have had abortions, and their allies to create a strong advocacy circle that will promote racial, economic, and reproductive justice, and by becoming an individual member you will be an integral part of that network.

You can join NNAF as an individual member at https://nnaf. formstack.com/forms/membership, or call 617-267-7161.

National and State Reproductive Rights Organizations

NARAL Pro-Choice America and State Affiliates

NARAL Pro-Choice America existed before *Roe*, and it will probably be there long after *Roe* is gone. As one of the first organizations to publicly lobby for abortion law reform and repeal, NARAL networks across the country to keep abortion legal. The national NARAL group can be reached at:

NARAL Pro-Choice America
1156 15th St. NW, Suite 700. Washington, DC 20005
202-973-3000
https://www.prochoiceamerica.org/

The following states have local branches where you can assist in on-the-ground work like funding, canvassing, lobbying, and more.

ARIZONA

Pro-Choice Arizona
4141 N. 32nd St., Suite 105, Phoenix, AZ 85018
602-258-4091
http://www.prochoicearizona.org/
info@prochoicearizona.org

CALIFORNIA

NARAL Pro-Choice California
335 S. Van Ness Ave., San Francisco, CA 94103
415-890-1020
https://prochoicecalifornia.org/
info@prochoicecalifornia.org

COLORADO

NARAL Pro-Choice Colorado
PO Box 22485, Denver, CO 80222
303-394-1973
https://prochoicecolorado.org
choice@prochoicecolorado.org

CONNECTICUT

NARAL Pro-Choice Connecticut
1 Main St., Suite T4, Hartford, CT 06106
203-787-8763
https://www.prochoicect.org
info@prochoicect.org

GEORGIA

NARAL Pro-Choice Georgia
202-973-3000
https://prochoicegeorgia.org/
georgia@prochoiceamerica.org

ILLINOIS

Illinois Choice Action Team
1333 W. Devon Ave. #253, Chicago, IL 60660
312-458-9169
https://www.ilchoiceactionteam.org/
info@ilchoiceactionteam.org

IOWA

NARAL Pro-Choice Iowa
https://prochoiceiowa.org/
iowa@prochoiceamerica.org

MARYLAND

NARAL Pro-Choice Maryland
8905 Fairview Rd., Suite 401, Silver Spring, MD 20910
301-565-4154
https://prochoicemd.org/
info@prochoicemd.org

MASSACHUSETTS

NARAL Pro-Choice Massachusetts
15 Court Sq., Suite 900, Boston, MA 02108-2524
617-556-8800
https://prochoicemass.org/
choice@prochoicemass.org

MINNESOTA

NARAL Pro-Choice Minnesota
2300 Myrtle Ave., Suite 120, Saint Paul, MN 55114
651-602-765
https://prochoiceminnesota.org/
info@prochoiceminnesota.org

MISSOURI

NARAL Pro-Choice Missouri
1210 S. Vandeventer Ave., St. Louis, MO 63110
314-531-8616
https://prochoicemissouri.org/
naral@prochoicemissouri.org

MONTANA

NARAL Pro-Choice Montana
PO Box 279, Helena, MT 59624
406-813-1680
https://www.prochoicemontana.org/
npmtinterim@gmail.com

NEVADA

NARAL Pro-Choice Nevada
702-751-4219
https://prochoicenevada.org/
nevada@prochoiceamerica.org

NORTH CAROLINA

NARAL Pro-Choice North Carolina
4711 Hope Valley Rd., Suite 4F-509, Durham, NC 27702
919-908-9321
https://prochoicenc.org/
info@prochoicenc.org

OHIO

NARAL Pro-Choice Ohio
12000 Shaker Blvd., Cleveland, OH 44120
216-283-2180
https://prochoiceohio.org/

OREGON

NARAL Pro-Choice Oregon
PO Box 40472, Portland, OR 97240
503-223-4510
https://prochoiceoregon.org/
info@prochoiceoregon.org

SOUTH DAKOTA

NARAL Pro-Choice South Dakota
605-334-5065
https://www.prochoicesd.org/
info@prochoicesd.org

TEXAS

NARAL Pro-Choice Texas
PO Box 684602, Austin, TX 78768
512-462-1661
http://prochoicetexas.org/
info@prochoicetexas.org

VIRGINIA

NARAL Pro-Choice Virginia
PO Box 1204, Alexandria, VA 22313-1204
571-970-2536
https://naralva.org/
info@naralva.org

WASHINGTON

NARAL Pro-Choice Washington
811 First Ave., Suite 675, Seattle, WA 98104
206-624-1990
https://prochoicewashington.org/
info@prochoicewashington.org

WISCONSIN

NARAL Pro-Choice Wisconsin
612 W. Main St. #200, Madison, WI 53703
608-287-0016
info@prochoicewisconsin.org

WYOMING

NARAL Pro-Choice Wyoming
PO Box 271, Laramie, WY 82073
307-742-9189
https://prochoicewyoming.org/
naralprochoicewy@netscape.net

Planned Parenthood Action Fund

As the state and federal governments increase their attacks not just on abortion but on birth control access, too, Planned Parenthood Federation of America has increased its own action fund to organize against political attacks. In some states, like Missouri or South Dakota, Planned Parenthood is the only remaining abortion clinic left, and a number of states have Planned Parenthood health care centers as their primary source of contraception and STI testing and treatment for those who are uninsured or underinsured. If you are looking for a direct way to politically support Planned Parenthood by lobbying or otherwise doing advocacy in your state, contact the national Planned Parenthood Action Fund (PPFA), and they will get you connected to your local affiliate. The individual state action funds are also listed in the "State Resources" section of the Resource Guide.

PPAF's national offices are located in DC and New York City:

1110 Vermont Ave. NW, Washington, DC 20005
Phone: 202-973-4800

123 William St., 10th Floor, New York, NY 10038
Phone: 212-541-7800

actionfund@ppfa.org

Lady Parts Justice (LPJ)

Founded by comedienne Lizz Winstead, LPJ battles the right wing with humor. LPJ undertakes state and local campaigns to increase voter outreach, support local independent clinics with practical and financial support for special projects, and perform awareness-raising activities across the nation.

https://ladypartsjusticeleague.com/
https://ladypartsjustice.com/contact-us/
Donations: https://ladypartsjusticeleague.com/donate/
info@ladypartsjusticeleague.com

Storytelling Projects and Art

One in four people who can get pregnant will have an abortion at some point in their lives, and yet our society remains solidly afraid of talking candidly and explicitly about real abortion experiences. For decades anti-abortion activists speaking out about their regrets have been the only ones to publicly talk about abortion.

Storytelling projects are breaking down the stigma surrounding abortion, helping people better understand that there aren't "good" abortions or "bad" abortions, that every abortion is an individual experience and just as valid as anyone else's.

National Network of Abortion Funds's "We Testify," the "Shout Your Abortion" campaign, and Abortion Conversation Project all use different tactics to break down the silence and stigma around abortion, from empowering storytellers to talk to lawmakers, to engaging social media users to talk about their own experiences in more public ways, to funding projects meant to end the silence and shame society wraps around the procedure and the people who obtain it.

We Testify

https://wetestify.org/
https://wetestify.org/testify/

Shout Your Abortion

https://shoutyourabortion.com/
ShoutYourAbortion@gmail.com

Abortion Conversation Project

http://www.abortionconversationproject.org/
abortionconversation@gmail.com

Art, too, has become a means of breaking down abortion stigma and is especially important in a landscape where there isn't one clear symbol that is universally recognized as an icon of the pro-choice movement. Artists like Heather Ault of 4000 Years for Choice and Megan Smith of Repeal Hyde Art Project are working to change that by introducing new visual images that better represent the history, diversity, complexity, and strength that comes with embracing bodily autonomy.

4000 Years for Choice

https://www.4000yearsforchoice.com/
https://www.4000yearsforchoice.com/pages/contact

Repeal Hyde Art Project

http://www.repealhydeartproject.org/
megan@repealhydeartproject.org

All-Options Pregnancy Centers

The Right may love to call us "pro-abortion," but let's be clear, we are "pro-abortion" only in the fact that we believe anyone who wants an abortion to be able to access one safely and easily without hurdles, roadblocks, or waits. But the last thing we want is for a person who really wants to stay pregnant and give birth to find themselves seeking out an abortion because they don't feel they have the resources they need to make it through the pregnancy.

Pregnancy centers do serve an important role in our society, offering financial, material, and governmental support to people who want to give birth and don't have everything they need. Unfortunately, pregnancy centers are almost exclusively a tool of abortion opponents seeking to convince someone not to end a pregnancy, and as such offer medically biased and sometimes outright false information. Anti-abortion pregnancy centers will try to trick or coerce people into giving birth when they do decide they want an abortion, imposing their choice on the person who is pregnant. And then, in many cases, they rip that assistance away shortly after the birth, or within a few months, claiming they are trying to help that person not develop a "cycle of dependency" on outside help.[22]

But pregnancy centers don't have to be coercive, or political. In Indiana, All-Options Pregnancy Center offers counseling to those who are truly conflicted about their unplanned pregnancy. They advise on the pros and cons of abortion, birth, parenting, and adoption, holding no choice as more valid than another and offering resources and support for each option if the person wants it. They recognize that the person who is pregnant and considering an abortion today may be a person who already gave birth, or who will give birth in the future under different circumstances, or someone who had an abortion in the past and wants to consider different options this time. They believe people who give birth and people who have abortions are all the same people, just at different stages of their lives.

To learn more about All Options Pregnancy Resource Center, go to https://alloptionsprc.org/, or call 812-558-0089.

They also have a wish list of items that can be easily sent to their location:

- Diapers (sizes 4, 5, 6)
- Pull-ups/training pants 4T/5T
- Wipes (fragrance-free)
- Hot/cold packs
- Baby blankets
- Feminine hygiene products
- Diaper rash ointment
- Baby powder
- Baby lotion
- Condoms
- Wet bags for cloth diapers
- Hats and gloves for babies/children
- Individually wrapped chocolates (for care kits)
- Baby boxes

Gifts and donations can be sent to their physical address at 1014 Walnut St., Bloomington, IN 47401.

We need more of these nonjudgmental, secular resources outside the bounds and rules of the religious Right. Supporting All Options is just the first step in getting there.

Abortion Funding

Pre- or post-*Roe*, with legal abortion in every state or without it, funding abortions is going to be the absolute most important thing you can do to keep the procedure accessible. Luckily, it's also one of the easiest things you can do.

According to the Guttmacher Institute, as of 2014 about 75 percent of those who seek abortions are low-income, making abortion costs a major hardship financially—one that many are unable to cover without outside assistance.[23] Because such a large proportion of those who are low-income are also people of color, the inability to obtain an abortion because of financial needs isn't just an economics issue but a racial justice issue, too.

When it comes to making sure that people can afford the procedure, a good first stop is the NNAF. NNAF funding can be used in every state in the nation, and donating to NNAF offers the most flexibility when it comes to supporting a variety of patients across the country.

You can donate straight to NNAF on their website at https://nnaf. formstack.com/forms/donate.

If you prefer to do it by check, you can fill out a form that can be found at https://abortionfunds.org/cms/assets/uploads/2017/03/ NNAF-Donation-Form_fillable_041117.pdf.

And send your check to:

National Network of Abortion Funds, PO Box 22457, Philadelphia, PA 19110

If you want to speak directly to someone about other means of donating, such as monthly donations, matching gifts, or stock designations, call 617-267-7161, ext. 2.

Specialty Funds

But maybe you want to fund something more local? Or you want to make sure that the people in areas where legal abortion is likely to disappear can get to whatever clinics remain for help? There are also regional abortion funds, state-based funds, and even funds for those who need to travel for late-second- or third-trimester abortions.

When *Roe* is overturned, there is a very strong possibility that

Florida will be the only state in the Southeast with legal abortion care. For many people seeking abortions, that will likely mean a plane ticket to a city that offers care somewhere in the northern part of the country, an additional expense on top of the abortion itself.

To specifically help those in the South, consider donating to NNAF's "Parker Fund," named after Dr. Willie Parker, who provides abortions primarily in Mississippi and Alabama, where restrictions have already made it extremely difficult to terminate a pregnancy. "I have made providing abortions in the South my life's work because I believe that all women deserve access to safe, legal abortion care," Dr. Parker told *Glamour* magazine in 2018. "That includes women living in the South, women of color, and women with low incomes. When laws like [abortion restrictions] go into effect, these women are at the greatest risk of going without the care they need and facing the harmful consequences that accompany such a void."[24]

If you want to provide more support for those with late second- and third-trimester pregnancies, those who are terminating with medical complications, or those who have extreme circumstances to overcome like incarceration or trying to obtain a termination without notifying a partner or parents, you should consider donating to the Tiller Fund, started in memory of the late Dr. George Tiller, assassinated in his own church for his work in providing abortions.

Both funds can be reached at this URL, and you can designate the fund recipient there: https://nnaf.formstack.com/forms/fundabortion.

State and Regional Funds

Funding abortions can also start literally at your front door. There are funds in nearly every state that help provide either for those having an abortion at a clinic in the state, or for those from that state who need to travel elsewhere for care.

Not all funds function in the same way. Some funds are places patients should contact directly to get assistance, and the fund will work with the clinic. Other funds are ones where the patient contacts the clinic, and the clinic will then contact the fund. Some funds will also provide financial support for costs related to obtaining the abortion, or arrange for additional needs like lodging or travel, providing practical support aspects, too, but not all funds do both. Patients should be sure to understand what the fund can and can't provide and who will initiate the contact with the fund—the patient or the clinic. All funds are in desperate need of more financial support from donors and more volunteers to work their hotlines.

Check the state-based resources section in the back of the book to find state abortion funds to support.

How Should You Donate?

If you have a chunk of change you want to donate, go right ahead and do it—every fund would be more than grateful for the support. But while one donation is a huge help, recurring donations are even better since they help these organizations plan for expenses coming down the road, too, and let them know that even if the fund goes dry in August, September means a fresh start.

If you have the financial ability, consider becoming a monthly donor. A five- or ten-dollar-a-month donation may hardly be noticeable in your account, but being able to rely on it doesn't just help organizers plan ahead, it saves them the resources needed to fund-raise if they run out of money down the road. As one activist on Twitter suggested just after Justice Kennedy announced his retirement, if churches can rely on people to give 10 percent of their income in tithes, shouldn't those who support reproductive rights and have the financial means consider doing something similar for abortion funds?

Donating Things Other Than Money (Gas Cards, Restaurant Cards, and Other Gifts)

Gas cards are one of the best items to donate to any group that assists abortion patients. While abortion funds tend to help primarily with payment for the procedure itself (often working directly with a clinic to ensure the procedure is paid for), there are a large number of incidentals that may not end up in the initial cost that can still create barriers to getting the abortion itself.

Cards to gas stations can be especially useful, as they not only can be used to close the gap in travel expenses (especially for patients who are forced to drive to a clinic twice due to mandatory in-person waiting periods of twenty-four to seventy-two hours, or those who need to leave the state in order to get an appointment at all), but they can also be used to purchase food, drink, painkillers, sanitary pads, and other necessities while a patient is away from home.

"We like to do gas card drives," explained Meg Stern, a reproductive justice activist and support fund director at Kentucky Health Justice Network. "We ask donors to buy Kroger cards, or prepaid credit cards when they shop. It's an easy way for them to make an impact, especially if they accumulate points for buying cards."

If you want to put more effort just into being sure that the person getting an abortion and any support people they bring with them are actually eating, you can also purchase restaurant gift cards to give to local groups for the patients they are assisting. Ask whichever organization you are supporting which restaurants are closest to the clinics or the hotels where patients may be staying, and especially focus on places that offer delivery so an abortion patient doesn't need to put any more effort into traveling than necessary.

Cards for gas, restaurants, even hotels can all be obtained at discounts if you use customer loyalty programs, and also if you transfer credit card points to purchase them. If you are looking for the best way to use these loyalty or rewards programs to benefit someone trying to access abortion, contact a fund or your local reproductive rights or reproductive justice organization and ask them exactly what they need (food cards, gas cards, hotel rooms), then address those specific requests.

Of course, some people will be traveling from other states, or from rural areas, and in their cases a Holiday gas card or a certificate to Domino's for a delivery doesn't do much good because those vendors aren't out there. In those cases, Stern says, her group offers Visa cards instead.

Some advocates may feel somewhat uncomfortable with the idea of essentially offering straight cash to a patient, but Stern feels such concerns are unjustified. She says these cards provide the biggest flexibility for a patient, allowing them to pay a sitter or family member who is watching their children or maybe pay a bill they had to put off for a month to have enough money to pay for the procedure, among other things. "We aren't trying to be gatekeepers," Stern said. "The more power we can put into the patients' hands, the better."

Stern notes, however, that because Visa cards have a surcharge attached, their group is more likely to purchase other cards.

Donating Miles and Hotel Points

At this point, there isn't really an easy way to donate airline miles in order to help a person fly to a clinic for an abortion. Every airline has its own specific frequent flier program, and while some do offer ways to pool miles (either various people into one pool, or various airlines into one pool for one individual), the actual transfer of miles tends to be an expensive process. If you want to dedicate miles, consider contacting your local abortion fund or practical support group for suggestions.

Hotel points and loyalty programs for lodging also come with the same roadblocks when it comes to donations. If you are still invested in finding a way to give hotel points to people who may need to stay overnight near a clinic, again, talk to a local fund, a practical support group, or a local reproductive justice or rights group about which hotels are most likely to be used and how you can directly assist.

Practical Support Groups

There is a distinct difference between an abortion fund and a practical support group, although there are a number of funding groups that provide practical support as well as part of their case management.

For the most part, abortion funds exist to help those who need an abortion find the financial resources to cover the expenses (the procedure, gas, hotel if necessary, and so on). Some work directly with the clinics to find funding, others directly with the patients to meet their needs.

A practical support group, on the other hand, may do abortion funding, but much of their mission is to handle the nonprocedural needs of patients, such as providing transportation to a clinic or a place to stay if the patient needs to remain in town overnight, or making sure meals are delivered to the patient's hotel or home so the patient can rest, or even finding childcare so the patient can make it to a multihour appointment. Practical support groups are also a lifeline for patients with language barriers or disabilities, providing translation services and additional physical support, and ensuring that those who need accessible clinic entrances or transportation can get them. Practical support is also a necessary part of aiding minors navigating the abortion process, from helping them get to clinics to handling judicial bypass in parental-notification-and-consent states.

While abortion funding already exists in many states, the practical support networks needed to help patients overcome the additional roadblocks besides just paying for an abortion aren't nearly as prevalent. Practical support networks were thrust into the media more prominently starting in 2014 as the Texas Omnibus Abortion Bill was put into effect, at one point closing more than half the clinics in the state and leaving the remainder located in just five large urban areas. The Cicada Collective, which had formed in April 2013, began the very public work of arranging travel for Texas patients trying to get to the closest clinic for care, a job that conservative media derisively called "abortion vacations," as if Texans were jaunting off for a weekend on the beach.

Since then, practical support groups have spread across the country, arranging travel, meals, and places for patients to stay when they need to cross long distances for care. Some of the most public abortion practical support groups are below, organized geographically, and all of them need donations and volunteers.

(If you are calling one in order to obtain support for your own abortion, always leave your name, a phone number to be reached at, where you live, what clinic you will be using, and the date of your appointment.)

Southeast

P.O.W.E.R. HOUSE (MONTGOMERY, ALABAMA)

Run by the Montgomery Area Reproductive Justice Coalition, the P.O.W.E.R. House can be used by the patients of Reproductive Health Services of Montgomery and their companions. It offers shelter, a night's stay with enough notice, and a place for a patient's support person to wait with children if they have been brought to town for the appointment.

https://montgomeryareareproductivejusticecoalition.wordpress.com/
montgomeryareareprojustice@gmail.com

ACCESS REPRODUCTIVE CARE SOUTHEAST (ARC SOUTHEAST)

Serving patients in Alabama, Florida, Georgia, Mississippi, South Carolina, and Tennessee, ARC can help arrange rides to clinics, escorts to an appointment, or lodging near abortion clinics throughout the Southeast.

855-227-2475
https://www.arc-southeast.org/
Or contact them via their support request page at https://www.arc-southeast.org/
  assistance-form.

ARKANSAS ABORTION SUPPORT NETWORK (AASN) (LITTLE ROCK)

AASN is able to provide limited rides to the state's abortion providers in Little Rock and Fayetteville.

501-712-0671
https://www.arabortionsupport.org

Texas

FUND TEXAS CHOICE

This organization helps cover transportation and lodging expenses for those who need to travel to access an abortion in Texas or for Texans accessing care outside the state. This includes bus and airplane tickets as well as hotel rooms and other necessities. This group serves all of Texas.

844-900-8908
https://fundtexaschoice.org/

BRIDGE COLLECTIVE (AUSTIN)

Bridge provides transportation and lodging specifically for patients using Austin-area clinics. Lodging is often provided in the homes of their volunteers. Volunteers have all been trained and vetted by the group to ensure safety.

512-524-9822
https://thebridgecollective.org/STANDinfo

CICADA COLLECTIVE (DALLAS/FORT WORTH)

This group provides practical support such as lodging, transportation, and abortion doulas to North Texas abortion clinics.

940-441-3337
http://www.cicadacollective.org/ntx-abortion-support-network-ntx-asn.html
ntx.asn@gmail.com

CLINIC ACCESS SUPPORT NETWORK (CASN) (HOUSTON)

Like the others, CASN provides practical support like rides and overnight lodging for patients coming to Houston-area abortion clinics.

281-947-2276
http://clinicaccess.org/index.html

FRONTERA FUND (RIO GRANDE VALLEY)

The Frontera Fund specifically assists those in the Rio Grande Valley, either those seeking an abortion in the valley or those trying to travel from the valley to other clinics. The group primarily provides financial support to cover hotel costs for these patients.

956-307-9330
https://lafronterafund.org/

Southwest

NEW MEXICO RELIGIOUS COALITION FOR REPRODUCTIVE CHOICE (ALBUQUERQUE)

Home to one of only a few third-trimester providers in the country, the city of Albuquerque often sees many out-of-state patients. The New Mexico Religious Coalition for Reproductive Choice provides food, lodging, and transportation to those in need of services to make that trip a little easier.

http://nmrcrc.org/if-you-are-pregnant/financial-assistance/
officeassistant@nmrcrc.org
(Note: please attempt to use the secure request form found on the financial assistance
   page before trying to contact the group via e-mail.)

West Coast

NORTHWEST ABORTION ACCESS FUND (NWAAF) (NORTHWEST AND HAWAII)

Set up specifically for those in the Pacific Northwest, NWAAF's travel support program will help arrange transportation and patient stays in local homes to help make an abortion more accessible. NWAAF funds those in Washington, Oregon, Idaho, and Alaska.

866-692-2310, ext. 3
https://nwaafund.org/travelhelp/

CASCADES ABORTION SUPPORT COLLECTIVE (OREGON)

Located in Oregon, this group provides abortion doulas for support during procedures, as well as transportation to clinics in Portland, Oregon, and Vancouver, Washington.

503-610-0692
http://www.cascadesabortionsupport.org/
cascadesabortiondoulas@gmail.com

ACCESS WOMEN'S HEALTH JUSTICE (CALIFORNIA)
Access will provide transportation and lodging for those who may need to travel within California in order to access an abortion clinic.

800-376-4636 (English); 888-442-2237 (Spanish)
https://accesswhj.org/how-access-can-help

Midwest/Rust Belt

KENTUCKY HEALTH JUSTICE NETWORK
This Louisville organization coordinates support needs for those heading into Kentucky from neighboring states or those who may need to leave the state in order to access care.

855-576-4576
http://www.kentuckyhealthjusticenetwork.org/
info@khjn.org

MIDWEST ACCESS COALITION (MAC) (CHICAGO)
Located in Chicago, MAC offers travel coordination and funding, lodging, food, medicine, and emotional support for those seeking a termination in the Midwest, or Midwesterners who need to leave the region to get an abortion.

847-750-6224
https://midwestaccesscoalition.org/
info@midwestaccesscoalition.org

East Coast

HAVEN COALITION (NEW YORK)
Haven Coalition offers lodging and personal escorts to and from abortion clinics in all five boroughs of New York City.

http://www.havencoalition.org/
havencoalition@gmail.com

BRIGID ALLIANCE (NEW YORK)

Brigid is an abortion travel support group that is in the process of expanding services. They provide practical support like travel, meals, and childcare for those seeking later-second-trimester care at Choices Women's Medical Center, ParkMed NYC, and Planned Parenthood NYC. These providers all provide pregnancy terminations up to twenty-six weeks in. They are also working to expand their network beyond the New York area, and they connect patients seeking third-trimester care with providers that offer it.

https://brigidalliance.org/
info@brigidalliance.org

Support for Those Attempting Self-Managed Abortion Care

Self-managed abortion at this point isn't legal in the United States, but that hasn't stopped those who either cannot or choose not to access a clinic from inducing their own abortions. To help address those who are already determined to self-induce, Women Help Women launched Self-Managed Abortion: Safe and Supported, an informational website on World Health Organization protocols for self-induction and a help line for those who may be considering self-managed care, staffed by English- and Spanish-speaking advocates from overseas.

SASS

https://abortionpillinfo.org/en/sass
Donations: https://womenswallet.nl/donate/sass?z_language=en

Legal Support Groups

One of the biggest battles in abortion rights has been fought in the courts over the last five decades, and whether or not *Roe* is overturned, that will continue to be the case. We need lawyers to stop future restrictions, we need lawyers to protect the access that remains, and we need lawyers to defend the new bills we will be passing strip bad laws off the books when we eventually expand access again.

Also, unfortunately, we are going to need a lot of lawyers to defend those who are arrested for managing their own abortions in states where abortion is made illegal, or who assist those people in determining their own reproductive future.

There are already a number of groups that are training lawyers, or that have legal staff who are assisting those already attempting to access abortion care in an age where abortion is often legal in name only. You can support them financially or with your volunteer hours. Here is where to reach out.

Jane's Due Process

Established in Texas in 2001, JDP connects pregnant minors with legal representation to help them navigate the parental consent process or seek judicial bypass or emancipation if they wish to abort, or address pregnancy discrimination issues in school or work if they choose to remain pregnant.

24-7 hotline: 866-999-5263; Administrative line: 512-444-7891
8 a.m.–11 p.m. text: 866-999-5263
https://janesdueprocess.org/
https://janesdueprocess.org/donate/

SIA (Self-Induced Abortion) Legal Team

SIA offers information on rights a person has if they choose to manage their own abortion outside a clinical setting. The team can be contacted on its legal help line if a person is being questioned by police over a miscarriage.

Legal helpline: 844-868-2812; Signal secure phone or message: 707-827-9528
https://www.sialegalteam.org/
Send an encrypted message from ProtonMail Account to sialegalteam@protonmail.com

If/When/How

Formerly Law Students for Reproductive Justice, If/When/How is a national nonprofit that trains, networks, and mobilizes law students and legal professionals to "work within and beyond the legal system to champion reproductive justice." The group also has a Supporting and Centering People of Color Initiative to ensure more marginalized communities have their voices uplifted and brought to the forefront of the legal movement.

1730 Franklin St., Suite 212, Oakland, CA 94612
510-622-8134
https://www.ifwhenhow.org/
info@ifwhenhow.org

Donations online: https://www.ifwhenhow.org/give/

Donations by mail:
ATTN: Development
1730 Franklin St., Suite 212, Oakland, CA 94612

Center for Reproductive Rights

The Center for Reproductive Rights has been the legal representation for many people in the state and federal reproductive rights cases in the country, and will continue to be even if *Roe* is overturned.

Center for Reproductive Rights
New York Headquarters. 199 Water St., New York, NY 10038
Main phone: 917-637-3600
Main fax: 917-637-3666
https://www.reproductiverights.org/
Donations online: https://www.reproductiverights.org/about-us/donate
Donations by phone: 917-637-3619
Donations by mail or fax: https://www.reproductiverights.org/sites/crr.civicactions.
    net/files/page_uploads/crr_donate-mail_fax_form.pdf

ACLU Reproductive Freedom Project

The ACLU Reproductive Freedom Project is the reproductive rights arm of the American Civil Liberties Union, and supports legal challenges against state-based legal restrictions.

125 Broad St., 18th Floor, New York NY 10004
212-549-2500
https://www.aclu.org/issues/reproductive-freedom
Donate online: https://www.aclu.org/donate-aclu?ms=web_horiz_nav_hp

Advocate for New Abortion Providers

Of course, it doesn't do any good to fight to keep abortion legal if there is no one to actually provide the care. Training new abortion providers is imperative to maintaining abortion access, but more medical schools are either allowing students to opt out, moving abortion training programs off-site to make them more difficult to access, or just eliminating them altogether.

"More than a third of ob-gyn residency programs don't offer routine abortion training," writes Dr. Jody Steinhauer, the founder of

Medical Students for Choice, in the *New York Times.* "Some programs offer training only on treating someone who is managing a miscarriage, so those residents do not gain skills in counseling and caring for women who want to end their pregnancies. Most family medicine residency programs still have no abortion training at all, even though family physicians are critical for providing high-quality family planning within primary care services."[25]

The lack of abortion training in ob-gyn practices endangers all people who can get pregnant. After all, despite the claims from abortion opponents, there really is such a thing as a medically necessary abortion, and simply waiting on an induced labor rather than actively providing medical care is the surest way to put a patient's life at risk.

To encourage more medical schools to provide full-spectrum training, contact your local colleges and universities and ask them if they currently offer abortion training on site. If not, demand to know why they choose to limit their students' medical training. Consider directly contacting the college or school board to advocate for abortion training, especially if you are an alumnus or donor. Also ask if they support any of the programs listed below, and consider gathering other alumni to petition them if they say they do not. The more noise we make, the more likely they are to listen.

Medical Students for Choice

PO Box 40935, Philadelphia, PA 19107
215-625-0800
Fax: 215-625-4848
students@msfc.org
https://www.msfc.org/
Donate: https://www.msfc.org/about-us/giving-to-msfc/

Ryan Program

https://ryanprogram.org
https://ryanprogram.org/contact/
info@ryanprogram.org

Provide

PO Box 410164
Cambridge, MA 02141
617-661-1161
https://www.providecare.org
https://www.providecare.org/contact/
Donations: https://www.providecare.org/donate/

Clinic Escorts

For almost as long as there have been clinic protesters, there have been clinic escorts. Escorts serve as a safe contact for patients outside a clinic, assisting them in navigating past those who may be trying to block their path or who continue to interact physically or verbally with them or their companions even after being told to stop.

While the escorts may not be directly associated with or connected to the clinic they are escorting at, clinic escorts are always there with the acknowledgment and consent of the clinic. Note: coming to a clinic without the permission or knowledge of that clinic is *not* helping patients—it is no different from what abortion opponents do.

The biggest issues to remember as an escort is that you are there for a patient, and your presence must balance out any harm that comes from you being on the sidewalk. To a patient trying to access care, all people in front of the building add to the already often stressful experience of trying to enter an abortion clinic. Escorts are there to de-escalate that stress as much they can.

Things to Know About Escorts

An escort is not a counterprotester. They should never have signs or make political statements. They are there to tell the patient that they don't have to speak to protesters or "counselors" if they choose not to, and to move them quickly and safely into the clinic. They should never interact with those who oppose abortion when they are in front of the clinic, whether there is a patient present or not. That can cause confusion for a potential patient who may be coming in or leaving, and it can also escalate tensions in front of the clinic.

An escort reflects on the clinic. Regardless of whether your group is directly organized by the clinic or is an independent venture, your actions will reflect on the clinic itself and how the community views it.

Escorting is not just a physical commitment but also an intense emotional one. You must be caring, empathetic, and also able to control your temper when abortion opponents not only attack you with violent and incendiary rhetoric—even in some cases physically engage—but also attack the patients and their companions. In some cases protesters are at the clinics specifically to try to provoke a reaction from patients, escorts, and staff that they can then use to sue the clinics, the volunteers, or even the local police force if it gets involved. They will often use sexist and racist attacks, telling people of color they are participating in their own genocide or telling male-presenting companions to "be a man and rescue your baby," and the escort must not only not respond but attempt to deescalate the situation if the patient or companion interacts. You must assume that there is a camera on you at every moment and you must be able to remain completely composed at all times.

It is far more difficult than it sounds, and not something everyone is capable of doing. If you know this doesn't suit your temperament but you still want to directly support clinic escorts, consider donating to the Clinic Vest Project, which provides escort vests for free to groups across the country. Because abortion opponents often try to purchase vests in the same colors as the escorts', many escort groups find themselves forced to rotate vests frequently to prevent confusion for the patients.

You can contact the Clinic Vest Project at http://www.clinicvestproject.org/ and donate at https://www.mightycause.com/organization/Clinic-Vest-Project. Or you can send a check to:
2735 N. Clark St. #181, Chicago, IL 60614

How to Get Involved with an Escorting Group

So you've thought it through, and you really do believe you are ready to help directly assist pregnant people at the clinics and do so in a way that is safe for the patient, the clinic, and yourself. How exactly do you get involved?

1) *Contact your local clinic.* Want to escort at a nearby clinic? Just contact them directly and ask them if there is an escort group. They'll likely be more than happy to tell you who to contact to get involved. Remember, though, many clinics do not use escorts—to minimize activity in front of a clinic, because they feel escorts aren't needed there, or for other reasons. If you ask them and they say they do not use escorts, absolutely do not under any circumstances go to the clinic and attempt to escort anyway.

2) *Contact your local abortion fund.* Your fund is likely to know the clinics better than anyone and can probably tell you what sort of opportunities there are to volunteer—either at the clinic or with the fund itself. There are many face-to-face volunteer opportunities

beyond escorting, and a fund can redirect you if your skills are a better fit somewhere else, or make the introduction if escorting is your calling.

3) *Check social media.* Try googling "clinic escorting" or "clinic defense" and your target city name, or searching on Twitter. Both should provide you with nearby groups to contact.

Some clinic groups that are open to more volunteers are listed in the "State Resources" section of the Resource Guide.

Offering a Place to Stay

As patients are forced to travel longer distances to get to legal clinics, it will be imperative that they have places to stay in order to make it to their appointments. If all of the South bans abortion, as some expect, pregnant people could be traveling as many as eight hours in one direction just to receive care. That will mean a minimum of one night's stay, maybe more, adding at least a hundred dollars onto a basic first-trimester abortion cost.

There are already programs out there looking at a way to lodge patients with people near the clinic on a case-by-case basis. In Madison, Wisconsin, NARAL Pro-Choice Wisconsin launched a sleepover program to offer rooms hosted by vetted supporters, allowing patients to spend a night in town at no cost if necessary.

As abortion access disappears, there is no doubt that these sorts of programs will become even more necessary, but the reality is that they are also extremely resource-heavy from a nonprofit or volunteer point of view. Not only does the practical support group sponsoring the program have to vet sponsors, but it also has to coordinate calendars, openings, and other moving parts, making such programs rather labor intensive.

Some reproductive rights activists suggest that the effort and financial backing needed for vetted overnight stays would be better spent on simply providing volunteers and money to the support groups themselves in order to allow them to more easily streamline the work and keep it all under one roof, as well as to better ensure the comfort and privacy of the patient through a hotel or other arrangement. But there are practical support groups who do this sort of work and find it extremely helpful for patients in need.

If you are interested in offering your room or home to a person needing an overnight stay in order to get an abortion, contact your state NARAL affiliate or abortion funds affiliate to discuss the possibility. But before doing so, here are a few things to consider:

1) *Will you be providing privacy or support?* Some patients—especially those who may be staying for longer procedures—may need a host who can also bring them food, drive them to the appointment and back, or pick up medications or other items. Others may want to be left completely alone and not have any interaction with another human. Can you meet both of those needs, depending on what the guest wants? If the person wants privacy, are you able to provide a completely private space, or are there shared spaces you can't avoid?

2) *How available will your space be?* Are you going to always have an empty room, or is it just a few times a month or year? Is this a set schedule, or does it change randomly? The more work a support group needs to put into using your space for patients, the fewer resources they have for other support work.

3) *Is the space accessible?* Can it be easily accessed by wheelchair or walker? Is the bathroom wide and easy to use? Are there stairs? Is the bed high? Is there parking? If you are going to offer your home or property, you need to be sure it will meet the needs of anyone who may use it.

4) *Are you concerned about damage?* Offering a space to stay isn't like operating an Airbnb. Patients who have had abortions will have some bleeding, and there may be other health or medical needs to address too. Also, some may need to bring family, especially young children. Be prepared to childproof, and know that breakage may very well happen regardless.

If you have concerns about any of the above, consider a different way to help, including renting out the space now and giving the proceeds to a local support group to allow them to rent hotel rooms more easily.

Thinking Big. Really Big.

Of course, in an ideal world, we could put the infrastructure in place to offer all sorts of assistance to people who need to travel for abortion care. Much as abortion opponents have purchased properties adjacent to abortion clinics in order to set up their crisis pregnancy centers, with enough financial backing practical support groups could purchase buildings that are strategically placed for maximum impact—perhaps even former abortion clinics themselves.

These "abortion hostels" would offer office space for the organization to work out of, as well as a few bedrooms to be used by patients in need. Patients could leave their children in an open common area to be watched by volunteers while they are at the clinics. Finally, a kitchen area would offer a centralized place to prepare meals for patients either staying in the hostel or nearby to help them reduce extraneous costs associated with the procedure.

"Abortion hostels" could also exist in cities where there is no clinic to serve as a gathering point for patients out in the vast landscape of states that will no longer have legal abortion. A hostel in Little Rock, for example, could act as a place for those in surrounding areas to join up and commute together to a clinic in Illinois, with the hostel hosting a passenger van or bus for patients, reducing travel costs like gas or bus tickets and providing the opportunity for patients to travel through the night in order to be at the clinic early for a procedure.

Even faster, obviously, would be airlifts for those who need to cross a large number of states to access care—especially those reaching later gestations or with medical complications. The idea of privately flying patients may seem extreme, but it's not completely without precedent. Already there are groups like Air Care Alliance (http://www.aircarealliance.org/directory-groups) that organize volunteer pilots who have their own personal aircrafts and are willing to donate their time to transport people who require medical care. There is no reason not to believe there are pilots who would be happy to help abortion patients in need if someone just reached out to them.

Obviously vans, charter buses, hostels, airlifts, and the like are major expenses (and in some cases probably outright pipe dreams) and would require massive fund-raising and a large amount of coordination between local and national volunteers. But it is a network that has to exist in a post-*Roe* era, and it is our job to do everything we can to be sure that those already building this network have the resources they need to complete it.

Giving without Giving Yourself Away

Of course, there may be some people who want to give their support to these causes but are concerned about privacy. Maybe they are worried that a partner or family member will see a donation on a credit card statement or a canceled check, or they may have other reasons to try to keep their support as anonymous as possible, especially in hostile red states. For that reason I have tried to include physical addresses whenever possible so financial donations, gift cards, and other assistance can be sent directly to organizations. I have also included phone numbers for those without mailing addresses, with the hopes that potential donors who don't want to donate online can call directly to get an address if it is unlisted.

6

Let's Talk About Reproductive Justice

There is a common misconception that "reproductive rights" and "reproductive justice" are two synonyms that can be used interchangeably. They most definitely are not. The reproductive rights framework advocates and organizes on behalf of abortion and contraception rights. Reproductive justice, on the other hand, focuses on other equally important issues including reproductive health care access, pregnancy and childbirth, maternal mortality, reproductive technology and assistance, and so on. The framework intentionally includes these issues but also goes far beyond just reproductive health and rights to highlight the intersections of race, class, gender, socioeconomic status, immigration status, religion, and the other intersections of women and people's lives. Birthed by black feminists and led by women and queer people of color, reproductive justice organizations center the voices of the marginalized, dismantling the racial and economic power structures that have kept middle- and upper-class white women in leadership roles and at the helm of activism campaigns. Reproductive justice focuses on an intersection of all human rights, while other frameworks offer a siloed, less effective strategy that does not center those most vulnerable. According to SisterSong, one of the leading reproductive justice organizations in the nation, "Abortion access is critical, and women of color and other marginalized women also often have difficulty accessing: contraception, comprehensive sex education, STI prevention and care, alternative birth options, adequate prenatal and pregnancy care, domestic violence assistance, adequate wages to support our families, safe homes, and so much more."[26]

While a lot of organizations may claim to support reproductive justice, there is little to show that they are living the tenets. Now, we not only have the opportunity to change that, but we have the obligation too. Less than 25 percent of Hispanic women and less than 4 percent of black women voted for President Trump in the 2016 election, yet an astounding 52 percent of white women supported him—and pushed him into the White House.[27] Our current reproductive rights national leadership remains nearly as monolithic in race, age, and geography as they have been since *Roe* was decided nearly fifty years ago. Losing *Roe* gives us the perfect foundation to start again from scratch, rebuilding the movement as local, grassroots, intersectional, and focused on decentralizing power and resources and instead investing it with those who have been and will be the most affected by the policies.

Most of this handbook is filled with actions on how to give. This is the one chapter where instead we will discuss how to take. If we are ever going to build a truly intersectional movement concentrated on true social justice, we have to support and build up the groups that are already doing that work, but just as importantly we have to send a message to organizations and advocates that aren't willing to apply a reproductive justice lens to the work they do.

Before you consider donating, volunteering, or otherwise working with a national organization doing work around reproductive health or rights, ask yourself these questions.

Are there any people of color in leadership in this organization?

Have I looked at their board? Do they have diverse members from different communities on it?

Is there a reproductive justice group already working in this same area? Have I reached out to them first?

Has this organization formed a coalition with other groups that center marginalized communities in their activism and leadership? If so, are they actively allowing the other groups to lead?

Does this organization have a reputation for supporting the best practices of local organizers in a hands-off manner, instead of silencing local activists to fit the greater national message?

Does this organization have a reputation for supporting women of color rather than co-opting their work?

If you can't answer yes to each of these questions, simply don't donate or volunteer, and make it clear to them exactly why you won't. Make a pledge to refuse to work with any organization that doesn't prioritize marginalized leadership or voices or directly address racism and its effects on economic and social power structures. If every person vows to only support nonprofits and political groups that prioritize and elevate women and queer people of color, especially in their own communities and regions, reproductive health and rights groups will be forced to look at their own teams and campaigns and acknowledge the white privilege that has kept them in power even as the rights they claim to be dedicated to protecting eroded under their leadership.

Roe was a national decision that was immediately attacked on a state front by legislative restrictions, an attack that successfully stole abortion access from poor women and women of color years before the threat of *Roe* being overturned became a reality. We can no longer afford to keep taking a national approach to reproductive health and rights that continues to segregate political action and power from the communities that are the most impacted.

"National reproductive health and rights groups have created a culture of movement building placing us all on the defense, not the offense. Our work can no longer be reactive but must be strategic. Otherwise we will remain vulnerable as a conglomerate of movements and our various bases even more vulnerable, " said Cherisse Scott, CEO and founder of SisterReach in Tennessee. "The real threat of losing *Roe* offers an opportunity for us to start again, and this time with women and queer people of color in every aspect of leadership, including in philanthropy, research, strategy, and movement building. "

A list of reproductive justice groups follows, broken down by region. New groups are also being created every day, and SisterSong, SisterReach, New Voices for Reproductive Justice, and National Asian Pacific American Women's Forum (NAPAWF) are doing regionally based organizing and mobilization, which need sustained financial support to continue their important work.

Donating, volunteering, and otherwise supporting reproductive justice groups are the most impactful actions a person can take in a post-*Roe* America. These groups have been and continue to be the force doing much of the grassroots work in their communities, which have always been the hardest hit by restrictions.

Western/Mountain

Colorado Doula Project

https://www.coloradodoulaproject.com/

Colorado Organization for Latina Opportunity and Reproductive Rights (COLOR)

PO Box 40991, Denver, CO 80204
303-393-0382
https://www.colorlatina.org/
info@colorlatina.org

Indigenous Women Rising

505-398-1990
https://www.iwrising.org/
indigenouswomenrising@gmail.com

Young Women United

309 Gold St. SW, Albuquerque, NM 87102
505-831-8930

201 N. Church, Suite 320, Las Cruces, NM 88001
575-526-7964

https://youngwomenunited.org

Strong Families New Mexico/Forward Together

400 Gold Ave. SW, Suite 900, Albuquerque, NM 87102
505-842-8070
https://forwardtogether.org/
info@forwardtogether.org

Forward Together

300 Frank H. Ogawa Plaza, Suite 700, Oakland, CA 94612
510-663-8300

5020 NE Martin Luther King Jr. Blvd., Portland, OR 97214
510-663-8300, ext. 348

https://forwardtogether.org/
info@forwardtogether.org

Black Women for Wellness

PO Box 292516, Los Angeles, CA 90029
323-290-5955
http://www.bwwla.org
info@bwwla.com

California Latinas for Reproductive Justice

PO Box 861766, Los Angeles, CA 90086
213-270-5258
https://californialatinas.org/
info@clrj.org

Southern

SPARK Reproductive Justice Now

PO Box 89210, Atlanta, GA 30312
404-331-3250
http://www.sparkrj.org/
info@sparkrj.org

SisterLove

PO Box 10558, Atlanta, GA 30310-1731
404-505-7777
https://www.sisterlove.org/
info@sisterlove.org

Lift Louisiana

PO Box 792063, New Orleans, LA 70179
504-484-9636
http://liftlouisiana.org/

Women with a Vision

1226 N. Broad St., New Orleans, LA 70119
504-301-0428
http://wwav-no.org/

SisterReach

2725 Kirby Rd., Suite 15, Memphis, TN 38119
901-614-9906
http://sisterreach.org

BirthStrides

Memphis, TN
https://www.birthstrides.org/
https://www.birthstrides.org/contact.html

Afiya Center

Dallas, TX
972-629-9266
https://theafiyacenter.org/
info@theafiyacenter.org

South Texans for Reproductive Justice

https://www.facebook.com/SoTX4ReproJustice/
sotx4rj@gmail.com

Eastern/Midwest

Illinois Caucus for Adolescent Health

719 S. State St., Floor 4, Chicago, IL 60605
312-427-4460
https://www.icah.org
info@icah.org

New Voices for Reproductive Justice

New Voices Pittsburgh, 5987 Broad St., Pittsburgh, PA 15206
412-363-4500
http://www.newvoicespittsburgh.org/
info@newvoicespittsburgh.org

New Voices Cleveland

2200 Fairhill Rd., Cleveland, OH 44120
412-363-4500
info@newvoicespittsburgh.org

New Voices Philadelphia

3853 Lancaster Ave., Philadelphia, PA 19104
412-363-4500
info@newvoicespittsburgh.org

Restoring Our Own Through Transformation (ROOTT)

Columbus, OH
614-398-1766
https://www.roott.org/

IndyFeminists

https://www.facebook.com/IndyFems

National

Advocates for Youth

1325 G St. NW, Suite 980, Washington, DC 20005
202-419-3420
http://www.advocatesforyouth.org/
http://www.advocatesforyouth.org/about-us/contact

Black Mamas Matter Alliance

1237 Ralph David Abernathy Blvd., Atlanta, GA 30310
https://blackmamasmatter.org/
info@blackmamasmatter.org

Black Women's Health Imperative

55 M St. SE, Suite 940, Washington, DC 20003
202-787-5931
https://www.bwhi.org/
info@bwhi.org

In Our Own Voice/National Black Women's Reproductive Justice Agenda

1012 14th St. NW, Suite 450, Washington, DC 20005
202-545-7660
http://blackrj.org/

Interfaith Voices for Reproductive Justice

http://iv4rj.org/
https://www.facebook.com/IV4RJ/
interfaith4rj@gmail.com

National Asian Pacific American Women's Forum (NAPAWF)

773-251-8440
https://www.napawf.org/
info@napawf.org

National Latina Institute for Reproductive Health

212-422-2553
http://latinainstitute.org/en
http://latinainstitute.org/es
HumanResources@latinainstitute.org

Native American Women's Health Education Resource Center

PO Box 572, Lake Andes, SD 57356-0572
605-487-7072
http://www.nativeshop.org/

SisterSong

1237 Ralph David Abernathy Blvd., Atlanta, GA 30310
404-756-2680
https://www.sistersong.net/
info@sistersong.net

Women Engaged

https://www.womenengaged.org/
info@womenengaged.org

7

Knowing Your Comfort Zone

Why Civil Disobedience?

Access to abortion and birth control isn't just a health care issue or an economic issue, it's also a civil rights issue, and like every civil rights battle, gains are often made through acts of civil disobedience, or working outside the legal framework. Married people officially gained the right to access birth control only after Estelle Griswold, the executive director of the Planned Parenthood League of Connecticut, opened a clinic and began offering contraception in direct opposition to the 1960s state law forbidding it. That right was extended to single people in 1972 after Bill Baird was arrested in 1967 for purposely flaunting the Massachusetts law and publicly providing contraceptives to an unmarried woman during a college lecture. The Clergy Consultation Service on Abortion spent much of the 1960s and early '70s prior to the *Roe* decision assisting pregnant people in finding safe abortions either from legal or illegal providers throughout the country and across the borders, and there were groups like Jane's Collective that provided the service themselves even at the risk of their own arrest.

Today people are highlighting a number of issues through acts of civil disobedience. North Carolina had weekly mass arrests at their state capitol during Moral Mondays protests, while the Black Lives Matter movement physically closed highways with their bodies. And of course when Brett Kavanaugh was appointed to the Supreme Court hundreds of activists were arrested—some multiple times—for interrupting his hearing, protesting in the Hart Building when it became clear the Senate Judiciary was not going to investigate charges of past sexual assault—some protestors even blocked the stairs prior to Kavanaugh's swearing-in ceremony.[28] As our society recedes further into racism, sexism, xenophobia, and classism, opposing the power structure through nonviolent means grows more imperative.

"If *Roe* is overturned or gutted, it is certain that some states will propose and enact new abortion bans. Again, nonviolent civil disobedience should remain on the table, this time targeting state and municipal-level lawmakers," writes Erin Matson, the cofounder of the reproductive rights group ReproAction, in *Teen Vogue.*[29] "We must remember that while in several contexts abortion rights supporters lack immediate political power—in spite of the fact that nearly seven in ten Americans do not want to see *Roe* overturned—we always retain the power of using our bodies to slow or stop the machinery of state repression."

Matson adds, "Ultimately, it is up to activists to decide—are we willing to break convention if lobbying fails? Are we willing to strategically expose ourselves to the risk of arrest? And if we are not, are we willing to look into the eyes of the future generations who will be incarcerated for abortions, miscarriages, and pregnancy complications?"

ReproAction is a growing network of state-based activists that conducts political events, teach-ins, and other direct actions to increase access to abortion and birth control services. They currently have national campaigns as well as individual campaigns in DC, Virginia, Missouri, Arkansas, and Wisconsin. You can join up with or financially support ReproAction to increase their national and local reach.

ReproAction

https://reproaction.org/
https://reproaction.org/contact-us/
https://donatenow.networkforgood.org/reproaction

Is Civil Disobedience Right for Me?

What are you willing to do to make sure you, the people you know, or even total strangers have access to contraception and abortion care—especially once more abortion options become illegal? Are you willing to be arrested if you participate in direct action or nonviolent protest? Is helping someone obtain abortion pills worth a potential prison sentence? Would you drive a teen to another state to get an abortion if that drive makes you an abortion "facilitator" and a federal criminal?

You may believe you are willing to risk everything to help someone get an abortion—and that may very well be what is needed in some cases in a post-*Roe* America. But make sure that you've really thought out all of the consequences of such a radical approach.

These are the questions you should be asking yourself now, before the laws are put in place.

Am I the Only One Who Can Help?

One small silver lining of the Trump era is the way it has energized so many people to actively resist the political agenda. There are more activists, donors, candidates and protesters than there have been in decades, and that means lots of people who can work together and step in when and where people are needed.

But in certain geographic areas it is and will continue to be harder to find those with the ability and privilege to do resistance work. For example, with the Trump administration's increasing militarization of ICE and border security, checkpoints into and out of America will be more scrutinized than ever before. With a population that in many cases is literally trapped in places like the Rio Grande Valley or Las Cruces, where undocumented people can neither leave the country for services nor go further into the US for care, the need for additional action (and people who have the willingness and ability to act) may be much greater than in New York City or the Bay Area.

Maybe you have a very specific skill set. You might be medically trained, have a legal background, or maybe you've done counseling or social work or you are a member of the clergy. These are people who will add a lot of value to the movement, especially if it turns out civil disobedience is the way to proceed.

Ask yourself if you are the only person who can do the thing you are considering doing, or if there are a number of people like you who are planning to step up. Then ask yourself what sort of risk you may be running and see how those factors balance out.

Do I Like to Work Alone or with Groups?

It's almost impossible to be a solitary activist these days, but there are spaces where you can manage. Letter-writing campaigns, social media campaigns, information distribution, and fund-raising can all be accomplished in a fairly solitary environment. But realize you will still need to work with other people in some form—they are unavoidable. If you are comfortable with one-on-one interaction and just don't enjoy group settings, a practical support action (driving patients, lending out a space for them to stay, etc.) or Plan B distribution might be a good way to balance the two.

If you are a person who thrives in a group setting, consider activities like clinic escorting, protesting (in appropriate venues), lobbying at the capital, or other forms of abortion action trainings.

Is My Privacy Important?

If we get to a point where abortion is mostly or completely illegal, that means we are also at a point where if you do offer any sort of assistance, you can expect to be targeted by those who oppose abortion. This will happen regardless of whether your activism is legal or not, and it is already happening to those who support abortion patients and clinics.

Are you ready to have abortion opponents looking for your name or your address? Would you be okay with photos or videos of you being shared on social media, either with or without your name attached? Are you worried about losing your job if your employer gets ID'ed and harassed? Will you be uncomfortable if people mention the names of your children or in some other way show that they know about your personal life as a means of trying to intimidate you?

These are not hypotheticals. Each and every one of these examples are commonplace for abortion providers, clinic owners, clinic escorts, even some well-known abortion rights activists. And if *Roe* is overturned, the attacks will only intensify.

Am I Worried About My Family?

Do you need to be concerned about your family's physical safety if you become completely invested in abortion access when *Roe* is overturned? Hopefully not. However, there is a lot more to protecting your family than just ensuring their physical safety. In the '80s–'90s Rescue Movement days, providers and others associated with clinics reported their own children being verbally harassed by strangers and in some cases even followed by anti-abortion activists when they were in public, such as at their schools. More recently, abortion opponents picketed a clinic landlord's children's elementary school to try to get him to stop renting to one provider (that landlord eventually sold the building after years of constant harassment).

Privacy can never be completely guaranteed, and you simply have to prepare yourself for the absolute worst-case scenario. If you are worried about how your children or other family members might be targeted because of your actions, the best decision is to find a different way to be involved.

What Would Happen if I Were in Jail?

Is your family dependent upon you financially? Are you the care-taker either for children or for other relatives? Would you lose a job or relationship if you were imprisoned for any length of time? Would it be impossible for you to find a new job, or rent or buy a home with a possible criminal charge on your record? Are you willing to lose your ability to vote if that charge ends up being a felony? Could it be used against you in a custody situation? Is there someone else who can pay your bills or feed your pets?

Some of these questions may seem serious, others far-fetched. But they all need to be considered before you decide how much you are willing to give up when it comes to civil disobedience. An arrest for a peaceful demonstration would still impact your life in ways you may not have considered. An arrest for something far more serious, like being an accessory to an illegal abortion, is some-thing else. For communities of color, the likelihood and severity of punishment is increased regardless of the peacefulness of the action due to the internal racial bias of our police and judicial system. It may be even more dangerous for those who are accused of helping someone procure an illegal abortion, since the groundwork for jailing "accomplices" is already in place.

In Pennsylvania, one mother was given a sentence of up to eighteen months in prison for giving her daughter misoprostol to end her pregnancy when the two were unable to find an affordable nearby clinic to use. This happened while abortion was still legal in that state. Imagine what the consequences may be once abortion is made illegal—and consider them all carefully before you act.[30]

Would My Partner and Family Support Me?

Once you have finished asking yourself all of these questions, go back and ask them of the people you live with. If your partner/parent/roommate/etc. is unable to support you in your actions, definitely rethink your plans. Getting more aggressively involved in abortion access while laws are being overturned has the potential to be emotionally and financially exhausting, and if you do not have a support network (either because they don't support your activism on an emotional level or because they believe they are unable to take up your responsibilities if necessary), you need to know that and come up with alternative ways to take action.

Above all else, if you do not feel comfortable enough with your partner or family to even ask these questions, that means you should consider a different way to support patients seeking abortion care.

Do I Fit the "Profile"?

Unsurprisingly, the best people to commit acts of civil disobedience or conscientious lawbreaking are often white. Because communities of color are already in many cases living under a police state and are bearing the greatest burden of the racist enforcement of current laws, civil disobedience is one of the biggest places where white allies can step in and have the most impact politically.

When it comes to potentially illegal activities such as bringing abortion-inducing medicines through a border checkpoint or helping a teen cross state lines if CIANNA is ever passed into law, the best candidate to take these risks will likely be white, more specifically white clergy, middle-aged or retired white women, or, in small communities, active churchgoers. It should be the people most likely to inspire trust in and tamp down the suspicion of those who might later investigate them. And it should also be the people the police are most likely to overlook, and the ones who would make the most sympathetic public cases in the media if they were discovered and arrested.

It should also be someone familiar with and prepared to adhere to all other laws when taking on a potentially illegal action. For example, if a person were to travel with non-prescribed pharmaceuticals in their possession, they would be advised to be abundantly careful about any other laws they could be breaking that could cause the car or the person to be searched. That means knowing the state laws, such as whether marijuana possession is a crime, if it is illegal to talk on a cell phone when driving, even seatbelt laws. It would also be important to ensure that they don't speed, that there is no vehicular defect (like a broken tail light) that could cause a cop to pull them over, and that they obey all traffic lights and signs.

Be sure to take all of those things into account and think very long and hard before making any decisions.

What Can I Specifically Do to Protest Abortion Restrictions in a Meaningful Way?

Sit-ins, or the refusal to leave the state capitol or another legislative area in protest, are one of the most frequently used tactics for civil disobedience against abortion restrictions. In 2013 over sixty activists were arrested in the state house in North Carolina after Republican legislators tried to sneak abortion restrictions in as a last-minute amendment on a bill that was drafted to protect the state from "sharia law."[31] The protest worked and the bill failed, but unfortunately the same restrictions were then added into a new bill—this time about motorcycle safety. That one passed.

More recently activists flooded the capitol to try to stop the confirmation of Supreme Court justice Brett Kavanaugh, President Donald Trump's replacement for Justice Anthony Kennedy. More than two hundred people were arrested on just the first day of Kavanaugh's confirmation hearing.

"This country has a long history of men co-opting the bodies of those without power—women, people of color, immigrants, refugees, LGBTQ people, people with low incomes, and intersections of all these identities—to make white men with wealth even more powerful," said Jennifer Epps-Addison, the president of the Center for Popular Democracy Action Network, in a press statement following her arrest, after she was removed from the hearing room for disrupting the judiciary proceedings. "We can't let this trend continue with the nomination of Brett Kavanaugh. He would erode access to health care, good jobs, and safe housing. I put my body on the line so that Kavanaugh doesn't do it for me."

As Kavanaugh's confirmation became less of a sure thing—especially as news of potential sexual assault was revealed—civil disobedience became even more important. Activists cornered senators, demanding to be heard and to tell their own stories of assault. Over three hundred protesters were arrested at a "Cancel Kavanaugh" event the day the Judiciary Committee agreed to put his nomination forward. Another hundred were arrested the next day, when the Senate voted to end the debating period, and on the day of the Senate vote a massive sit-in was held outside, while other protesters repeatedly interrupted the vote until they were removed from the room.[32]

These types of sit-ins don't need to be relegated to capitol buildings, either. Blocking or disrupting traffic or marching or demonstrating in front of businesses owned by anti-abortion lawmakers can be effective, too.

South Korean women took a novel approach to protesting abortion bans and helping increase abortion access—a pill protest. In order to convince the government to allow legal abortion, 125 women publicly took an abortion-inducing medication in defiance of current law, with thirty other women in attendance taking a vitamin in solidarity. Because abortion-inducing medication cannot be detected by any medical test, the police couldn't determine who actually took illegal medication and who did not, and the women were able to avoid arrest.[33]

Of course, civil disobedience is just one potential illegal act that someone might feel pushed to commit in a post-*Roe* America. There is also inducing and self-managing your own abortion. The next chapter will provide details on how to do that.

8

What to Know About Self-Managed Abortion Care with Abortion Pills and/or Herbs

Two days after President Donald Trump's inauguration, an editor from the United Kingdom approached me with an assignment—reporting on the likelihood of DIY (self-induced, "do-it-yourself") abortion taking over the country now that the federal government was under Republican control. It didn't take me long to learn that it was a topic at the front of everyone's mind. In April 2017 Women Help Women announced the launch of an online support service called Self-Managed Abortion: Safe and Supported (SASS) to offer information and counseling to those trying to end their pregnancies through abortion-inducing medications outside a clinical setting. As SASS's US spokesperson Susan Yanow told the *Guardian*, "People are not being advised to use the pills. They're being advised if they've already decided to use the pills. What drives this project is the knowledge that women have been managing this on their own."[34]

Those who want to end a pregnancy but either can't access a clinic or prefer to manage their own abortions have been using herbs and abortion pills since long before Trump's surprise electoral win. Herbal abortions have existed for as long as there have been midwives, medicine women, and pregnancy. Today's herbal abortion attempts are often far less effective due to misleading or incorrect information on the Internet and no medically vetted, detailed directions on how to use herbs correctly that the general public can easily access. Herbs also tend to require action as early as possible in the pregnancy and are a long-term commitment since they take time to work.

Using medication (mifepristone plus misoprostol or misoprostol alone) to effectively induce a miscarriage, however, is a much more recent (and effective) option. Mifepristone (RU-486) was approved by the FDA for use in the US in 2000 and offered as a medication-only option for terminating a pregnancy outside an abortion clinic. As part of a protocol developed first by the FDA and later streamlined by medical professionals through their own clinical use and more than a decade of research, patients were now able to obtain medicine in the clinic and take the dose of mifepristone there, then take misoprostol home to finish the termination in private. Current research shows that medication abortion can and is being used to easily and safely end pregnancies independent of a clinic and with minimal risk to a patient—at least, minimal medical risk. The biggest health risk for self-managed abortion care using abortion pills is that those who attempt to induce their own abortions may not seek out medical assistance in the rare case that there is a complication, fearing a doctor or hospital may then report them to law enforcement.

Again, to be clear, multiple studies from mainstream medical journals state that medication abortion conducted independent of a provider is a safe and effective means of ending a pregnancy—as long as the person terminating is not forced to hide their actions out of fear of legal punishment. It is the criminal code—not the medications themselves—that makes self-managed abortion care risky.

The following sections are reprints of information found on the Internet or taken from medical sources, and are simply a compilation of what information has been published regarding herbal and medication abortions in a nonclinical setting. This is not meant to encourage any decisions regarding abortion care. In many states in the US it is illegal to purchase medications online from outside the country, and in some states it is illegal to purposely terminate a pregnancy if you are not a medical provider or if you are doing it outside a hospital or clinic. However, it is not illegal to research or to share scientific and medical information, especially when that information is about health care that may affect more than half of the population.

This is only information, and not legal or medical advice. If a person were seeking information about self-managing an abortion using medications and herbs, this is the type of information that they would find by searching the Internet.

Herbal Abortion

It isn't easy to find information online about inducing miscarriage with herbs, and googling brings up a lot of nonspecific information ("ingest a lot of Vitamin C" or "insert parsley into your vagina"). Sometimes that information conflicts with other sources and some instructions can be potentially dangerous. According to those with experience in herbal abortions, there are a lot of misconceptions on the Internet, especially when it comes to how and when herbs should be used.

In general best practices, using herbs to try to induce a miscarriage must be done as soon as a person believes they may be pregnant in order to have any potential success, and even then there is no guarantee that it will work. According to Sister Zeus, the reference point for most of the at-home herbal abortion information on the Internet (but again, not a medically vetted or endorsed site), if an abortion hasn't been successful by about six weeks (two weeks after the period should have arrived), it's unlikely it will work at all.[35]

By sorting through multiple websites one does find a few commonalities, usually involving the use of parsley. One site suggests that as soon as a person realizes their period is late, that person should insert fresh parsley into the vagina, removing and replacing it with new sprigs every twelve hours, while also taking a tincture of between two and six tablespoons of a parsley infusion every four hours (a tincture should be made by adding one ounce parsley stems to two and a half cups of boiling water, removing the water from the heat, and then allowing the mixture to steep for one to two hours). In addition, a person should also ingest five hundred milligrams of vitamin C every hour, maxing out at six thousand milligrams a day.

As you can see, even these instructions are still frustratingly imprecise, and the results are only partially guaranteed, which is why so few people manage to successfully induce miscarriages using herbs. Even more alarming is the assumption that just because something is "herbal" rather than medication based, it can't harm you.

In Argentina, where an August 2018 attempt to legalize abortion in the first trimester failed to pass the senate, a woman died just days after attempting to induce her own miscarriage using herbs. According to reports, the thirty-four-year-old woman named Elizabeth already had a two-year-old and, unable to obtain an abortion in Argentina, attempted to induce labor by inserting parsley into her vagina. When an infection developed, she was afraid to go to a hospital out of fear of jail for attempting her own abortion, waiting until she developed sepsis before seeking care. Her uterus was removed, but she died anyway, another victim of the country's abortion ban.[36]

Remember—herbal doesn't automatically mean safe, either in miscarriage induction or in any other setting.

Medication Abortion

Unlike herbal abortion methods, which can be unreliable, long, labor intensive, and potentially ineffective or dangerous, medication abortion has been extensively studied. Misoprostol alone is effective in ending a pregnancy before twelve weeks 80 to 85 percent of the time. Mifepristone plus misoprostol is effective in ending a pregnancy before ten weeks 95 to 98 percent of the time.

Medication abortion as it is conducted in a clinic is actually a combination of the two medications—two hundred milligrams of mifepristone and eight hundred micrograms of misoprostol. Mifepristone will reduce the progesterone in a person's body by blocking progesterone receptors, ending the pregnancy. Misoprostol causes contractions, expelling from the womb the products of conception. Misoprostol is taken after the mifepristone, with the time interval depending on whether people place the tablets vaginally or buccally (between the cheek and gums).

People have also learned that miscarriage can be induced by using Misoprostol alone, although that is a bit less effective than the combination of the two medications. Those who research abortion-inducing medications often find that accessing misoprostol is easier than locating mifepristone and using the two medications together.

Where People Find Medications

Many people are likely to look online in order to find websites where they can either purchase misoprostol or mifepristone plus misoprostol in a "combipack," or find information on where to purchase those medicines. The website www.abortionpillinfo.org is one place where information can be found. If a person were to click on "Information about abortion pills" and then the question "How can I find abortion pills?" they would learn the following:

- That abortion in the first twelve weeks of pregnancy can be done safely using misoprostol alone (80 to 85 percent effective) or mifepristone plus misoprostol (95 to 98 percent effective). Abortion pills cause a miscarriage if used correctly.

- Misoprostol is available in pharmacies, with a prescription. Misoprostol is used to prevent ulcers in people with conditions like arthritis that require them to take nonsteroidal anti-inflammatory (NSAID) medication long-term.
- Misoprostol is available from some Internet veterinary supply stores and veterinarians, as it is used to treat ulcers and arthritis in dogs.
- Misoprostol is available over the counter in many Latin American countries.
- Online pharmacies in Canada sell misoprostol inexpensively, and it has been reported that some may not require a prescription.
- Combination packs of mifepristone and misoprostol together are also available on the Internet.

In October 2017 a study was conducted to determine how reliable it was to get abortion pills from online pharmacies outside the US. A report on which websites were found to sell authentic medicines can be found on the Plan C website at https://plancpills.org/need-pills#options at the link "Report Card" and is also printed later in this chapter. The average cost of mifepristone plus misoprostol from these sites was reported to be $85–$200.

According to the Plan C site:

> Online pharmacies—A Google search for "buy abortion pills online" will give many options for purchasing products. In early 2017, we ordered from sixteen different sites and received pills from fourteen of them . . .
>
> . . . All of the pills we received contained the labeled

active ingredients. Some of these sites accept credit cards, others require wiring money from a bank account or Western Union. The cost of the pills, including shipping, averages about $200 for an abortion "kit" containing both mifepristone and misoprostol. Buying misoprostol (Cytotec) alone may be less expensive (but is less effective than using both mifepristone and misoprostol). None of the websites we ordered from asked for a prescription.

ORDERING ABORTION PILLS ONLINE:
Results of a September 2017 "Mystery Shopper Study"
by Plan C and Gynuity Health Projects

The information below summarizes results of a mystery shopper study done by Plan C and Gynuity Health Projects in early 2017. At that time, all of the websites listed shipped real pills. Because these online pharmacy services are unregulated, there is no way to assess the authenticity or quality of the products they provide now. But, but we have no reason to suspect that the quality of pills they ship now would be different. Please visit planpills.org/faq for more information about the legality of self-use of abortion pills.

Website URL	Overall Score	Price, including shipping	Price	Ship Time	Product Quality
http://macrobioticstoner.com/my-secret-bodega/	*CURRENTLY INACTIVE*				
http://daynighthealthcare.com	A-	$235.00	●	●	●
http://abortionpillrx.co	B+	$230.00	●	●	●
http://abortionpillsrx.com	B+	$360.00	●	●	●
http://abortionrx.com	B	$239.00	●	●	●
http://drugspillsmart.com	B	$206.00	●	●	●
http://nopregnancy.net	B	$239.00	●	●	●
http://uspharmacy24.com	B-	$239.00	●	●	●
http://zeepharmacy.biz	C	$289.00	●	●	●
http://mtpkit24.com	D	$175.00	●	●	●
http://onlineabortionpillrx.com	D	$147.00	●	●	●

Source: Murtagh C, Wells E, Raymond EG, Coeytaux F, Winikoff B. Exploring the Feasibility of Obtaining Mifepristone and Misoprostol from the Internet. Contraception. Published online October 11, 2017. http://www.sciencedirect.com/science/article/pii/S0010782417304754

Please note that our findings reflect purchases made in early 2017. Because these online pharmacy services are unregulated, there is no way to assess the authenticity or quality of the products they are providing currently, but we have no reason to suspect that the quality of pills they ship now would be different.

Also, be aware that certain states—Hawaii, Maine, New York, Oregon, and Washington State—are currently allowing abortion pills by mail through the TelAbortion Study. Please visit www.telabortion.org for further information if you live in one of those states.

How Are Mifepristone and Misoprostol Used to End a Pregnancy?

These instructions are replicated from the Women Help Women website, an open-sourced information-sharing site about World Health Organization protocols (https://consult.womenhelp.org/en/page/401/how-should-i-take-the-pills):

> These instructions are for a pregnancy that is up to ten weeks (seventy days). The evidence suggests that mifepristone plus misoprostol is very safe and effective to ten weeks. After twelve weeks, there is a higher chance of a complication and the medicines are used differently.
>
> 1. Mifepristone should be swallowed with a glass of water.
>
> 2. Twenty-four hours later the woman should put four pills of misoprostol buccally (between the gum and the cheek).
>
> She should put two tablets into her mouth, between her gum and cheek, on the left side and two more tablets between the gum and cheek, on the right side.
>
> All four pills should be left in the mouth for approximately thirty minutes to dissolve. Women shouldn't eat

or drink anything while the pills are dissolving. Anything left in the mouth after thirty minutes should be swallowed. Before and after using the misoprostol she can eat and drink normally, but should not use drugs or alcohol; she needs to pay attention to her body.

How Is Misoprostol Alone Used to End a Pregnancy?

Again, according to Women Help Women (https://consult.women-help.org/en/page/434/how-should-i-take-the-misoprostol-pills):

These instructions are for a pregnancy that is up to twelve weeks (eighty-four days). These instructions are based on the recommendations of the World Health Organization. After twelve weeks, there is a higher chance of a complication and the medicines are used differently.

A woman will need a total of twelve pills of two hundred micrograms each.

1. A woman should put four pills of two hundred micrograms (in total eight hundred micrograms) misoprostol under the tongue. Do not swallow the pills for at least thirty minutes until the tablets are dissolved! (She can swallow her saliva, but NOT the pills. After thirty minutes it is okay to swallow what remains of the pills.)

2. After three hours she should put another four pills of misoprostol under the tongue. Do not swallow the pills for at least thirty minutes, until the tablets are dissolved.

3. After three hours she should put another four pills of misoprostol under the tongue again for a third time. Do not swallow the pills for at least thirty minutes, until the tablets are dissolved.

In between the doses of misoprostol, a woman can eat and drink normally.

The success rate is approximately 84 percent.

This means that eight to nine women of every ten women who use misoprostol correctly will have a safe abortion after this procedure.

Can People Share Information About Using Abortion Pills?

While conducting an abortion outside a clinic setting may not be legal in all circumstances, sharing open-sourced information is always legal. Please be aware that this is publicly available information based on the World Health Organization (WHO) protocol, and is not meant to encourage a person to induce a termination of pregnancy.

These graphics are available for reprint and can be shared online, as printouts or handouts, posters, pamphlets, or in any other form. Feel free to copy and distribute them on campuses, on bulletin boards, at political marches or demonstrations, or any place you think it would be good to get the information out to the general public.

The originals can be found at the Women Help Women website: https://consult.womenhelp.org/en/page/434/how-should-i-take-the-misoprostol-pills

https://consult.womenhelp.org/en/page/117640/whw-safe-abortion-with-misoprostol-english2-pdf

Stickers encouraging people to learn more about safe use of abortion pills can be found at https://abortionpillinfo.org/en/page/352/want-to-help. These can also be reprinted and circulated.

(https://womenhelp.org/en/page/646/how-to-use-abortion-pills-misoprostol-and-mifepristone-at-home)

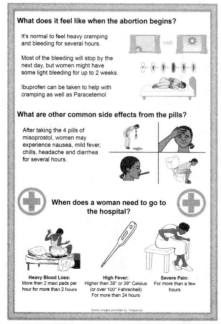

(https://womenhelp.org/en/page/646/how-to-use-abortion-pills-misoprostol-and-mifepristone-at-home)

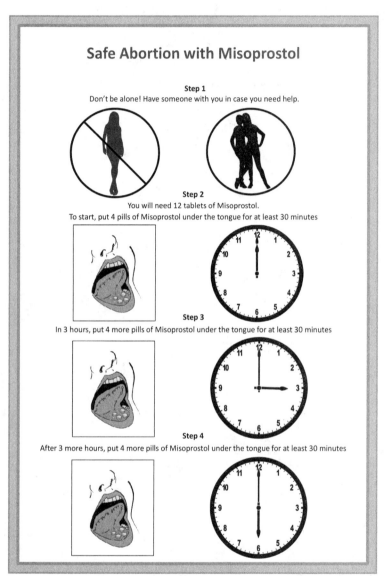

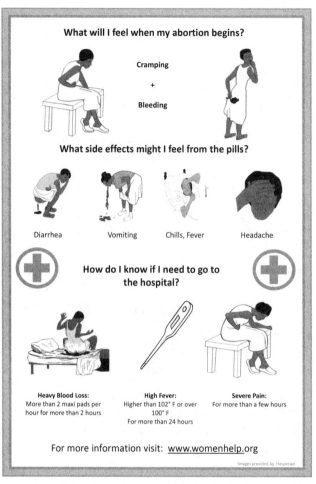

(https://womenhelp.org/it/media/inline/2015/12/22/whw_after_abortion_english.pdf)

Aftercare

Information on post-abortion care is also available online. A very simple protocol can be found at Women Help Women (womenhelp.org):

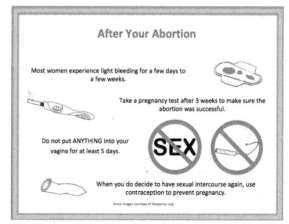

(https://womenhelp.org/it/media/inline/2015/12/22/whw_after_abortion_english.pdf)

Medical Risks

According to an article published in the *BMJ* in a study of one thousand women in Ireland who accessed medication abortion via Women on Web (www.womenonweb.org/en/i-need-an-abortion) because abortion was illegal in their country, nearly 95 percent of them were successful in ending their pregnancies without surgical intervention. Less than 10 percent of the patients reported symptoms that were alarming enough to suggest they should seek out medical advice, and there were no deaths.[37]

Public information about potential medical risks and symptoms of a possible complication can be found at the Women Help Women site at https://consult.womenhelp.org/en/page/417/what-to-do-in-case-of-emergency.

The information on the page reads as follows:

> Complications after medical abortion are rare, and include severe bleeding and infection. You should go to the doctor

or hospital if you have any of the signs of complication below:

- Severe bleeding (more than two or three pads used every hour for more than two or three hours)
- Severe abdominal pain that isn't relieved with painkillers or continues for two to three days after taking the pills
- Fever over 39° or 38° for more than twenty-four hours (over 101° F)
- Abnormal vaginal discharge

The risk of a complication is low (two to five women in every one hundred), and the need for emergency care (that might be needed in case the woman suffers from heavy bleeding) is extremely low (one in every two thousand women). However, to make the process as safe as possible, it is important to be near medical care in case of an emergency or a complication throughout the process of abortion. If a woman lives far from medical care, she should use the medicines where she can access medical care, preferably within one or two hours. She should also plan how she would get to medical care (by car, taxi, or in case of emergency by ambulance).

If possible, the woman should choose a hospital or doctor where she knows that women having miscarriages are treated respectfully.

If a woman seeks medical attention, she does not have to say she used medicines. She can say she is having a miscarriage. The symptoms and treatment of a complication of miscarriage are exactly the same as those of abortion.

Misoprostol cannot be detected in the blood or any bodily fluids within a few hours after use. Even if a hospital claims that they can check to see if a woman took medicines to cause the miscarriage, it is not true.

How Can Medical Risks Be Minimized?

If a person has begun a self-managed abortion outside a clinical setting and has questions but doesn't want to seek out medical help at this point, there are other options available to them. If they are in the US and need assistance, they should go to SASS and fill out the contact form at https://consult.womenhelp.org/en/contact-sass. This is a secure portal and there will be no electronic trail after the Q and A session. All questions are answered by skilled counselors from Women Help Women (womenhelp.org) who speak English and Spanish and are located outside the US.

Legal Risks

There are multiple legal risks that can come with self-inducing an abortion, and not just for the person who is terminating the pregnancy. Even with *Roe* in place, nearly two dozen people have been jailed for various crimes associated with allegedly inducing abortions, ranging from murder, homicide, and feticide to failure to report a death or properly dispose of remains, child endangerment or negligence, and being in possession of a drug without a prescription.

Unsurprisingly, it is people of color who tend to get the most severe punishments. Because prosecutors and other law enforcement officials typically pursue the "crime" of self-induced abortion at their discretion, racial bias becomes a large factor in deciding who should be investigated and to what extent they should be charged.

"Whether they are choosing to end a pregnancy or continue one, low-income women and women of color are more likely to be the target of investigations and prosecutions, as they are less likely to be able to access private medical care and more likely to regularly encounter police and other government officials in their day-to-day lives. In the post-*Roe* world, women themselves, and low-income women and women of color in particular, are at more risk of criminal prosecution for abortion and other pregnancy outcomes than at any other point in history," explains the National Institute for Reproductive Health in their report, *When Self-Abortion is a Crime: Laws That Put Women at Risk.*[38]

Those who may be seen as "assisting" in a self-induced abortion could face charges as well. One Pennsylvania mother was jailed for providing abortion-inducing medications to her daughter because there was no nearby clinic.[39] Other potential charges could include "unlawful termination of pregnancy" for someone who may live at the same address or whose computer or phone was used to purchase medicines, or "accessory" charges if they are found to have helped cover up an illegal abortion during an investigation.

According to the Self-Induced Abortion (SIA) Legal Team report *Roe's Unfinished Promise*, "There are seven states with laws directly criminalizing self-induced abortions, ten states with laws criminalizing harm to fetuses that lack adequate exemptions for the pregnant person, and fifteen states with criminal abortion laws that have been and could be misapplied to people who self-induce. There are also a number of laws deployed when no other legal authorization to punish can be found (obscure laws like disposal of human remains or concealing a birth), which have led to at least twenty arrests for [self-induced abortion] and criminal investigations in twenty states for alleged self-induced abortions since 1973."[40]

There is little doubt that as abortion becomes more illegal and inaccessible, more people will go to jail if they are discovered conducting or assisting in a self-managed abortion. If you need legal help or wish to support those who will assist in legal defense for these cases, consider reaching out to the Self-Induced Abortion (SIA) Legal Team:

SIA LEGAL TEAM
844-868-2812 (legal help line)
https://www.sialegalteam.org
info@SIALegalTeam.org

What People Self-Managing Their Abortion Care Need to Know

While the laws differ from state to state and will get even more extreme as *Roe* is dismantled and potentially overturned, none of this will change the fact that being able to determine your own medical care—including if and when you want to carry a pregnancy to term—is a human right. That also includes a person's right to health care for whatever that person's circumstances warrant. No person should ever feel the need to avoid follow-up care because of fear of an arrest. According to a video on the SIA website:

- A person has the right to talk to a health care provider before, during, and after a self-managed abortion—but they also have the right to provide as much or as little detail as they choose.
- That includes hospital staff, emergency room doctors, and anyone else who may ask questions about recent medical actions.
- Doctors state that there is no difference between how they treat complications from a miscarriage and how they treat complications from an abortion, meaning there is no need for a person to clarify which may be occurring.

- Doctors admit there is no actual test that can show if a person has ingested medications meant to induce a miscarriage.
- There are no laws that require hospitals to report suspected abortions to law enforcement.
- Some states even impose penalties on health care providers who violate a person's privacy by releasing personal health information without patient consent.
- However, because not all medical professionals are clear on the laws, or on the importance of maintaining doctor/patient confidentiality, a patient should always only provide the information they feel comfortable with sharing.

We will discuss how to minimize other potential legal risks in greater detail in chapter 10.

Why Can't We Just Have Abortion Pills Online in the US?

With the current laws and political climate, at this point it is almost impossible to successfully create a central, telemedicine-style self-managed abortion care network in the US for a number of reasons. While it isn't illegal to share information about abortion protocols, and in many cases it isn't illegal to self-induce an abortion, the two being offered together without legal backing offers much greater risk. The multi-state TelAbortion Study mentioned earlier in this chapter is an example of how medication abortion could easily be done remotely, but because of state restrictions it has been impossible so far to extend nationally. But that doesn't mean people aren't trying to see if such a network can be created, and how long it can stay active.

In 2018, a new website went live called Aid Access, which claims to offer consultation for pregnant people who either cannot or choose not to go to an abortion clinic to end a pregnancy. After the consultation, according to the site, "A licensed doctor will use the information provided by you and his/her best clinical judgment to determine whether you can use abortion pills without risk." If the provider approves the request, a package containing mifepristone and misoprostol will be mailed to the address you provide within ten days.

Aid Access is run by Rebecca Gomperts of Women on Waves/Women on Web. Gomperts is a reproductive rights activist who is already supplying medications in countries where abortion is completely illegal. She believes her actions remain legal because the FDA allows medication to be imported for personal use. Still there are some concerns beyond just the legality, such as the possibility that the medication will not get to a user in a timely manner and before the person is too far along gestationally to use it properly, or that the private information being gathered will somehow be leaked, hacked, or otherwise confiscated and turned over to law enforcement, published online, or in any other way used nefariously. It also must be stressed that in some states, using these medications outside a clinic setting continues to be against the law, even if the importing of the drugs is not.

Gomperts claims more than six hundred people have been assisted by the site as of October 2018, but it is unclear if—now that it is more publicly known—it will even still exist by the time you read this book. If not, you can be certain another one will pop up to replace it.

AidAccess as of August 2018 can be reached at www.aidaccess.org.

9

So You Want to Be the Next "Jane"

"Bring back Jane!"

That has been the call of many abortion supporters since hearing Trump would get to add another justice bent on ending legal abortion to the Supreme Court. Luckily, abortion techniques have vastly progressed since the Janes were providing illegal abortions in the late 1960s and early '70s. That means people seeking to end their pregnancies outside a clinic setting are far more likely to turn to medications than medical devices.

Yet there will probably always be some people looking for ways to terminate a pregnancy without the use of medications. This chapter provides information on menstrual extractions and early vacuum aspirations for those who are truly insistent on "bringing back Jane" and offering non-medication abortion outside a legal clinical setting.

Who Was "Jane"?

The Jane Collective was a group of mostly white women from the Chicago area who first offered counseling and referrals and later trained to provide first- and second-trimester abortions prior to legalization in 1973. The Janes—all in their late teens and twenties—started out by using doctors or other medical professionals and simply acting as the go-between for pregnant people and the providers, but they eventually realized that they could easily do D&Cs (dilation and curettage, where the cervix is opened with dilators then the uterus is gently scraped with an instrument to remove the embryo or fetus as well as additional products of conception like placenta and uterine lining) themselves. This offered them not just a chance to eliminate how many people were involved that could be susceptible to a police investigation, but also to do lower-cost and even free abortions since there was no doctor to pay.

The Janes were forced to work under multiple layers of secrecy to protect themselves and their patients from the law. They shared a phone number through posters, fliers, and word of mouth, telling people who were pregnant and didn't want to be to call and leave a callback number, as well as the date of their last period. The Janes would return calls afterward with instructions on where to meet. The meeting area was just the first step—the patient would then wait for transportation to another secret location, and it was there that the abortion would be performed.

Most of the Janes had no professional medical background. Instead, they learned first from their original doctors and then later from each other. According to NPR, which profiled the Jane Collective in an article in early 2018, the group believes they performed about eleven thousand first- and second-trimester abortions in the four years they operated before the *Roe* decision came down and abortion was legalized in the country.[41]

For more information about the Janes, read Laura Kaplan's book *The Story of Jane: The Legendary Underground Feminist Abortion Service*. Kaplan, a former Jane, provides a fascinating look into the history and legacy of the radical group—one that is even more compelling as the country returns to a pre-*Roe* era.

How Were Abortions Done Pre-Roe?

The coat hanger became and for some reason remains the ubiquitous symbol of the illegal abortion, and it's true that some women may have used that, but it was just one of many ways that pregnant people attempted to end their pregnancies pre-*Roe*.

Kate Manning, author of *My Notorious Life*, highlighted many of the most popular pre-*Roe* home abortion remedies in a *New York Times* column in 2013. "WHY would a woman put a leech inside her body, in the most private of female places? Why would she put cayenne pepper there? Why might a woman swallow lye? Gunpowder? Why would a woman hit herself about the abdomen with a meat pulverizer? A brickbat? Throw herself down the stairs? Why would she syringe herself, internally, with turpentine? Gin? Drink laundry bluing? Why might she probe herself with a piece of whalebone? A turkey feather? A knitting needle? Why would she consume medicine made of pulverized Spanish fly? How about powdered ergot, a poisonous fungus? Or strychnine, a poison? Why would she take a bath in scalding water? Or spend the night in the snow?" Manning asked. "Because she wanted to end a pregnancy. Historically, women have chosen all those methods to induce abortion."[42]

While dangerous DIY home abortion approaches using tools, corrosives, and toxins were commonplace before *Roe* (and unfortunately are still attempted in times of complete desperation today, as we learned from the 2015 arrest of a woman who tried to do her own abortion at home using a coat hanger[43]) so were actual medical procedures done by trained professionals and even enthusiastic activists.

D&C abortion was how the women of Jane performed their abortions, but other activists also worked outside the medical profession complex and offered abortions via menstrual extractions—a type of early manual vacuum aspiration.

Unlike a D&C, menstrual extractions didn't require that the cervix be dilated, making it far simpler for someone without extensive medical training to perform them. Because there is no curettage, there is less likelihood of a hemorrhage or puncture, too.

In California, a group of women began meeting to conduct "self-help clinics" to do menstrual extractions, teaching each other to insert speculums and look at their own cervixes. Soon after, they adapted a manual aspirator that would allow them to essentially suction out menstrual lining and blood all at once at the beginning of a period, or, if a period was delayed because of possible early pregnancy, simply remove the lining and fertilized egg all at once.

The tool and technique was developed by Carol Downer and Lorraine Rothman, who took a standard plastic cannula and syringe, then modified it in order to ensure there would be enough container for a full menses to fit in and that there would be no issue with air accidentally being pumped back into the uterus, where it could cause a potential embolism. With their new kits they believed they could do extraction and very early abortion in a safer, less uncomfortable manner, eliminating the sharp tools and the lack of anesthetic that came from traditional illegal D&Cs, where abortion providers refused to give patients medications so they could leave more quickly if there were police or other problems.

What to Know About Menstrual Extractions

The process is done with a device called a Del Em, which nonmedical professionals have been able to build at home. According to Carol Downer, one of the originators of the American practice, menstrual extraction should always be done with others, and never on yourself. "The tabloids and the electronic media have labeled menstrual extraction 'self-abortion' or 'do-it-yourself abortion' but these terms are misleading," Downer explains in her 1992 book *A Woman's Book of Choices: Abortion, Menstrual Extraction, RU-486*, coauthored with Rebecca Chalker. "First of all, due to the location of the uterus, it is virtually impossible for a woman to do ME on herself. To do the procedure safely and correctly, a woman needs the help of one or more women who are trained and experienced in ME."

The most significant physical risk of menstrual extraction is the possibility of infection from unsterile equipment or otherwise introducing bacteria into the uterus. Downer suggests in her book that a person doing menstrual extractions do them multiple times on non-pregnant people in order to gain experience before ever attempting it on a person who may be pregnant.

How Can a Person Build a Del Em?

Below is an image of items needed for crafting the Del Em, provided by Carol Downer via her website Women's Health Specialists (https://www.womenshealthspecialists.org/self-help/menstrual-extraction/).

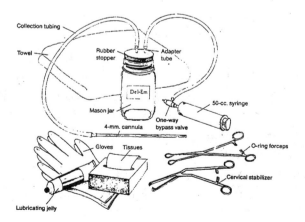

What Are the Instructions for Doing a Menstrual Extraction?

A person can easily find instructions for doing a menstrual extraction online. Full information, including illustrations, is available at http://womenshealthinwomenshands.com/PDFs/MenstrualExtraction.pdf, which is a reprint of the detailed guide published in *A New View of Women's Bodies*, a now out-of-print book published by the Federation of Women's Health Centers in 1981.

The following information was found at http://www.skepticfiles.org/atheist2/selfabor.htm and was allegedly first published in a pamphlet called *Womenpower—Do It Yourself Abortion—Time's Up!*

How to Perform a Menstrual Extraction (ME)

1) Supplies first: Betadine, speculum, "Del Em" ME equipment, latex gloves, alcohol, Valerian or Motrin, copy of *When Birth Control Fails*, small four millimeter and five millimeter cannulas, flashlight, mirror, pillows.

2) Before proceeding, with the help of your group, check to see if you're pregnant or not. ME can be done on nonpregnant women. Look at your cervix and see if it has changed in color or texture. Have a member of your self-help group perform a pelvic exam as well. Make sure it is someone who has felt your cervix before. See if your cervix feels enlarged or softer to her. Have you had any morning sickness? For how long? Study your most recent menstrual cycle. You do this by counting the number of weeks that have passed since your last normal period. If you are late, this might be a sign

that you are pregnant. If you think you might be more than eight weeks pregnant, *do not* proceed with this method.

3) Lie back on a low bed or futon and, with your legs spread, get comfortable. You may want someone to hold your legs for you. Definitely have someone by your side to assist you with whatever you might want (water, abdominal massage, Motrin, an extra pillow) during the extraction.

4) Although the vagina is not a sterile area, bacteria should never enter the os, cervix, or uterus or else you run the risk of infection. With the speculum in place, so that your cervix can be easily seen by the person who will be holding the cannula, and using tongs that have been boiled until sterile to hold a Betadine soaked cotton swab, cleanse the cervix and the vaginal canal.

5) Touching only the two or so inches furthest from the end of the cannula that will enter the cervix, carefully put the cannula inside the vagina (do not let it touch the vaginal walls either; remember the vagina is not a sterile field) and slowly insert it into the exterior os. After you have put the cannula into the os about three-quarters of an inch, you will begin to feel resistance, as if the cannula will not go any further. You have reached the inner os or the entrance to the uterus. You may feel cramping at this point because both the os and the uterus are muscles. The uterus may also recede into the body making it hard to continue. This is normal as well. Continue to push, with a gentle insistence, until you feel something give and the level of resistance reduce; the cannula has entered the uterus.

6) It is time to attach the rest of the Del Em apparatus to the cannula. Before doing so, remove all the air from a Del Em jar using your one-way valve syringe. This will provide the right amount of suction needed to detach early-first-trimester menses and fetal tissue from the uterine wall. Attach the tubing to the cannula and begin to move it in a semi-slow, back-and-forth rotating fashion in the uterus. Remain in one area until you feel the texture of the uterus go from soft and mushy to hard and ribbed or ridge-like. Then repeat the same motions in another part of the uterus. You will see blood and, if you are pregnant, a white, pudding-like substance (fetal tissue) in the tubing. Continue to do this until you no longer feel (through your "eleventh finger," the cannula) any softness in the uterus nor see any blood or fetal tissue in the tubing. Remove the cannula. Mission accomplished.

Where Can I Find the Tools for Making a Del Em?

Many of the tools can be found through medical supply stores. One woman, meanwhile, provides her own experience online on her blog of building one at home and for minimal cost primarily by obtaining items from local stores and a pet supply company. Writing at the *Reproductive Right Blog* (the-reproductive-right.blogspot.com) the woman explains that after purchasing a speculum off eBay, she then found the rest of the supplies much closer to home, including a mason jar, a rubber sink stopper, tubing, and a one-way value in a pet store's fish department, and a spray bottle tube for a cannula. She then bought a meat injector and removed the needle to serve as her syringe. Cut down the stopper if it is too large for the jar, she writes, then create two small holes for the tubing. After inserting the tubing and creating an airtight seal around the holes, add the valve to one end and then the syringe. Add the cannula to the other and test your device on a glass of water to be certain it works, she advises.[44]

What's a Manual Vacuum Aspiration?

A manual vacuum aspiration (MVA) is similar to a menstrual extraction but can be done until later gestation (usually up to fourteen weeks). Unlike a menstrual extraction, a series of dilators is used to slowly and incrementally open the cervix, allowing a larger cannula to be inserted, which by extension means a more developed pregnancy can be terminated in this manner.

The following instructions are meant only for trained medical professionals and were found in Médecins Sans Frontières (MSF), which "has been producing medical guides for over twenty-five years to help practitioners in the field. The contents of these guides are based on scientific data collected from MSF's experience, the World Health Organization (WHO), other renowned international medical institutions and medical and scientific journals." The instructions can be found at https://medicalguidelines.msf.org/viewport/EONC/english/9-5-manual-vacuum-aspiration-mva-20316948.html, under the section "9.5 Manual Vacuum Aspiration." Instructions pick up after placing the speculum in the patient.

Dilation

Dilate the cervix if the cervical canal cannot accommodate the cannula appropriate for gestational age (or the size of the uterus). Dilation should be smooth and gradual:

—With one hand, pull the forceps attached to the cervix and keep traction in order to bring the cervix and the uterine body into the best possible alignment.

—With the other hand, insert the smallest diameter dilator; then switch to the next larger dilator. Continue in this way, using the next size dilator each time, until obtaining dilation appropriate to the cannula to be inserted, without ever relaxing the traction on the cervix.

—Insert the dilator through the internal os. A resistance may be felt: this indicates that there is no need to advance the dilator any further. This resistance is not necessarily felt. In such case, it can be assumed that the internal os has been penetrated when the dilator has been inserted five centimeters beyond the external os.

—Do not force the cervix with the dilators (risk of rupture or perforation, especially when the uterus is very retro- or anteverted).

Aspiration

—Attach the prepared (i.e., under vacuum) sterile syringe to the chosen cannula.

—Maintain traction on the cervix with one hand.

—With the other hand, gently insert the cannula into the uterine cavity. Rotating the cannula while applying gentle pressure facilitates insertion. Slowly and cautiously push the cannula into the uterine cavity until it touches the fundus.

—Release the valves on the syringe to perform the aspiration. The contents of the uterus should be visible through the syringe (blood and the whitish products of conception).

—Hold the syringe by the tube (not the plunger) once a vacuum has been established in the syringe and the cannula has been inserted into the uterus; otherwise, the plunger can go back in, pushing the aspirated tissue or air back into the uterus.

—Carefully (risk of perforation) suction all areas of the uterus, gently rotating the cannula back and forth 180°. Take care not to break the vacuum by pulling the cannula out of the uterine cavity.

—If the syringe is full, close the valves, disconnect the syringe from the cannula, empty the contents, re-establish the vacuum, and reconnect the syringe to the cannula and continue the procedure.

—Stop when the uterus is empty, as indicated by a foamy, reddish-pink aspirate, with no tissue in the syringe. It is also possible to assess the emptiness of the uterus by passing the cannula over the surface of the uterus: if the surface feels rough, or it feels as if the uterus is contracting around the cannula, assume that the evacuation is complete.

—Close the valve, detach the syringe and then remove the cannula and the forceps. Check for bleeding before removing the speculum.

In a surgical setting, aspiration can be done using a cannula connected to the electric suction machine, with a maximum pressure of eight hundred millibars.

Examining the aspirated contents

To confirm that the uterus has been emptied, check the presence and quantity of debris, estimating whether it corresponds to the gestational age.

The debris consists of villi, fetal membranes, and, beyond nine weeks, fetal fragments. To inspect the tissues visually, place them in a compress or strainer, and rinse them with water.

Where Would I Find Equipment if I Wanted to Perform MVA?

Because MVA should only be conducted by trained professionals, most equipment can only be found through medical retailers. There are rare occasions that abortion tools can be discovered in places like rummage shops or other unique stores (for example, I found dilators and a speculum at an art fair in a "Strange Items" boutique display).

MVA kits can also be purchased through some websites, which can be found by googling keywords like "Menstrual extraction kits" or "MVA kits" or "MVA tools." One such complete kit was found on the online retail site https://www.alibaba.com, which offers disposable MVA kits for anywhere between ten and fifty dollars apiece, depending on the number purchased. Note: this retailer has not been verified; this is only an explanation of how a person would find kits online.

What Are the Risks of Doing Non-Medication Abortion Outside Clinics?

According to the Janes, they never had a patient die, but they did have to occasionally send them to the emergency room for follow-up care—dealing with complications that included excessive bleeding or incomplete abortion. Of course that was fifty years ago, and using a curettage, which is not in any of the practices above.

Still, unlike medication-induced abortion, these other procedures introduce obvious medical risks. Not having properly and completely sterilized equipment means a possibility of bacterial infection even if the abortion itself is a complete success, and few people have antibiotics just lying around for treatment. While a medication abortion can be done solely by the pregnant person if they choose, these non-medication techniques require at least one other person to be involved in the procedure, opening up more legal risks, too. And while medication abortion doesn't require any experience, MVA and even menstrual extraction requires extensive practice to complete safely, something that would be difficult to obtain outside a medical setting.

Are MVA and ME safer than introducing a long, sharp object into the womb through the cervix in order to start a miscarriage? Or ingesting toxic poisons or inserting them into the uterus? No doubt. But with medications in existence that can safely be used to end a pregnancy, "safer than douching with lye" really shouldn't be our standard anymore.

If a person were to decide to try to undertake abortion outside a legal clinic setting after the first trimester, the simplest and least dangerous way to undertake that process would simply be to attempt a miscarriage with the same medications used for medication abortion. The major difference between the protocol earlier in the pregnancy and later in the pregnancy would be the amount of time and medication necessary, and the amount of support a person would require to go through the abortion.

One abortion provider with over twenty years of experience suggested that in their opinion mifepristone and misoprostol alone in multiple doses would work. In such a situation, a person would want to take one dose of mifepristone, then wait thirty-six hours, then take four hundred micrograms of misoprostol every three hours until completion. This method would likely be able to end a pregnancy at any gestation. Also, according to them, this would be the "the safest route to go" if the options are using medication or attempting an invasive procedure outside a clinic setting. They suggested having an experienced doula involved as a support person in this case to assist with the process.

Can I Get Arrested for Providing an Abortion if I'm Not a Doctor?

Yes. Absolutely. Even with abortion legal, abortion opponents are fiercely charging those who help a person end a pregnancy outside an approved clinical setting. Jennifer Whalen's 2014 arrest for helping her daughter obtain medicine to end her pregnancy put her in jail with a felony for "offering medical consultation about abortion without a medical license" as well as misdemeanors for endangering the welfare of a child, dispensing drugs without being a pharmacist, and assault.

According to the *New York Times* in 2014, "In thirty-nine states, it's against the law to perform an abortion if you're not a doctor. In some of the remaining states, you are still required to be a medical professional (a midwife, nurse, or physician assistant). In New York, you can do your own abortion in the first two trimesters, but only if you're following a doctor's advice. About a quarter of states also still have old laws that make it a crime to help someone else with a self-induction. In a law passed in 1845, for example, Massachusetts calls for a sentence of up to seven years for assisting."[45]

Massachusetts revoked their law in the summer of 2018 and New York is currently looking to remove theirs as well. But be certain that when *Roe* falls, wherever abortion is made illegal, the biggest focus will be on arresting those who provide clandestine abortions. That means increased legal danger for anyone helping a person obtain medicines, assisting in non-medication procedures, or helping minors bypass laws around parental consent.

With this risk in mind, the next chapter will discuss tactics for keeping your actions secure and private.

10

Avoiding Surveillance in a Post-Roe America

Even with abortion technically legal in the United States, those who terminate their pregnancies outside the inconsistent and often medically unnecessary governmental parameters can find themselves facing time in jail. As more states add more barriers—or end legal abortion altogether—that rate of prosecution will only increase.

In an age of endless information on the Internet and social media channels that can reach across state lines and around the globe, it is easier than ever to find information, medication, and other forms of medical assistance if you want to end a pregnancy or help someone who needs an abortion. But that's a double-edged sword, too, since it's also much easier to find evidence to prosecute someone who is working outside the officially sanctioned rules for termination.

This chapter is all about how to stay secure when it comes to finding abortion information, self-managing abortion care, or assisting someone else in terminating a pregnancy. It also includes safety tips for those who may be setting up new activist organizations in underserved areas of the US, or for those who may want to donate or be involved with organizations but don't want to be identified as supporters.

How to Have an Abortion without Leaving an Electronic Trail

Not leaving an electronic trail when researching or obtaining an abortion isn't just something for a person to consider once abortion is illegal. For a significant number of pregnant people, even obtaining a legal abortion is something they would like to keep as private as possible, and they may prefer not to have a partner, friends, or family members know about the pregnancy or procedure.

In January 2017, the *Cut*'s Lisa Ryan wrote a very detailed article called "How to Plan an Abortion in the Surveillance State," that offers a number of best practices that could be used regardless of a person's reason for wanting to keep their abortion a secret.

Ryan suggests simple steps like "Don't send private messages on your work computer" or "Get a disposable phone" and recommends using encrypted texting apps like Signal—which you can set to wipe your text messages after a certain period of time so they cannot be used as evidence later on. You can also create a separate, secret e-mail that will only be used for arranging the abortion, or even better, do everything offline to be sure that there is no electronic trail at all. She also advises using a completely private browser like Tor, which passes your search through multiple servers, making it far more difficult for someone to track your search engine history or browsing activity.[46]

Using Your Phone as Your Go-To Tool

Of course, if it comes to seeking an abortion or organizing to help others do so, it would be almost impossible to do absolutely everything offline. In that case, it may work best to use your phone as your sole tool—from secure texting and phone calls via Signal to web browsing only on your smartphone (and on public Wi-Fi) and creating separate e-mail addresses that all can be accessed via mobile. There is some benefit to keeping everything all in one place—especially if you keep your phone secure and clear your cache frequently in case of anyone searching your phone or, even worse, police seizing it.

Here are some tips on good phone security practices taken from both the ACLU's "Freedom of the Press Foundation"[47] and a cyber-security specialist who works in abortion access spaces. These tips offer good advice for anyone who needs extra security from potential government surveillance.

> *Encrypt your phone.* Having an encrypted phone means that your data will not be readable to anyone when your phone is powered down, and even if a copy is made of your phone data, it won't be readable without your code. This requires using a pin or pass phrase to unlock your device, which might seem like a lot of work at first, but it's worth it, and you will get used to it. iPhones and other Apple mobile devices are encrypted by default. For Androids and other devices, go to the "privacy and security" sections of their settings. Note that encrypting your phone may put it out of commission for ten to thirty minutes during setup.
>
> *Lock your phone with a complex pass code.* Change your settings so your phone locks immediately after sleep, and immediately after you press the power button. While this doesn't encrypt your phone (it's always unencrypted while it's on, especially on Android), it will prevent anyone from accessing and using your apps. It's not recommended that you use fingerprint, face ID, or anything biometric to lock

your phone—facial recognition can be tricked with some photos, fingerprints hacked remotely, and police don't need permission to unlock a phone using biometrics.[48]

Prevent your SMS apps from showing the full text of a message while the phone is locked. No one should be able to read your communications with friends, or two-factor authentication codes, without opening the app first. These can be found in the "notifications" section of most phones' settings.

Lock your SIM card. Set a PIN to control access to your SIM data and cellular network use. A SIM card may still be unlocked by your carrier, but locking it locally protects against people who grab your card from you.

Practice good login hygiene. Use strong pass phrases, two-factor authentication, and different passwords for different accounts with the help of a password manager.

Protect your mobile service account. Take the time to properly lock down the account you have with your mobile carrier. Some people think of it as an afterthought, but it's alarmingly easy for anyone to take over your phone number, SIM card, and eventually, all mobile communications if such accounts aren't secured. Visit your provider's website to create a strong pass phrase and/or backup PIN for your account. Then call your provider and have a representative put a "security notice" on your account, saying something to the effect of "No one can make any changes to my account unless they give you the pass phrase/PIN first."

Limit porting requests on your phone number. Call your phone carrier and ask them to limit or lock out porting requests on your number, preventing someone else from putting in a request that would forward your messages to their phone.

Keep a list of all the accounts that are important to you. Having a list of accounts that need to be addressed in the event of compromise will save you time and worry.

Burst the cloud! Frequently delete your browsing history from your web browsing apps via their settings. If you're a Google services user, prune (or better yet, disable) your "web and web activity." iPhone users must prevent messaging apps from syncing data to iCloud. We know it might seem scary, but unlinking your phone and mac computers from iCloud is the best way to protect your data from prying eyes. Journalists, activists, and concerned citizens usually want to sync photos and videos to the cloud as soon as they take them, and that's okay! However, consider using another cloud-based service that gives you more control over how, when, and where you sync your data—something better than iCloud.

Use good device hygiene. Be careful using accounts that are logged in on multiple devices, like the unlocked family iPad on the coffee table that has your iMessage logged in. Are your iMessage or WhatsApp accounts logged in on a computer that someone else has access to? Ensuring you log out of shared devices can help prevent any issues.

Use "two-factor" on your accounts, especially critical accounts like e-mail that hold the keys to most other services you use. This means that after you log in to a service, it will request either via a text message, app message, or physical token a second form of confirmation that this is indeed you. This can be turned on in your privacy settings and is one of the most important things you can do to thwart entry to your accounts if someone gets ahold of your password.

Avoiding Open Phone Lines

Not everyone is going to go out and buy burner phones so they can organize or find an abortion in a post-*Roe* America, and sometimes you just have to work with the phone options you have. That's fine, as long as you are working with end-to-end encrypted calls.

This matters because of something called "third-party doctrine," which is the basis of legal authority for institutions to request information from your phone company or any other third party to whom you have given your data. Phone companies typically respond to subpoena requests and give a variety of rich and unfortunately detailed information about the calls, texts, and location information given to their service. This is why, when possible, we opt for communication methods and technologies that do not keep this kind of enriched information.

The Electronic Frontier Foundation offers many tips regarding making secure encrypted voice calls in their Surveillance Self-Defense tool kit, which can be accessed at https://ssd.eff.org. The most important advice they offer is a reminder that most of our most common calls aren't nearly as private as we think they are. After all, these companies will be obligated to respond to government requests like wiretaps or subpoena.

> Beware! Most popular VoIP [voice over Internet protocol] providers, such as Skype and Google Hangouts, offer transport encryption so that eavesdroppers cannot listen in, but *the providers themselves are still potentially able to listen in.* Depending on your threat model, this may or may not be a problem.
>
> Some services that offer end-to-end encrypted VoIP calls include:

- WhatsApp
- Signal
- Jitsi
- Silent Phone
- Zphone

In order to have end-to-end encrypted VoIP conversations, both parties must be using the same (or compatible) software.[49]

According to one abortion cybersecurity specialist, services like Signal keep vastly less information than your phone company that could potentially be requested by law enforcement or other parties. For example, Signal only keeps the time two numbers first made contact (not the cadence, content, or time of any messages) and the last time the user logged in. WhatsApp uses Signal protocol, and both apps can be set up to have messages evaporate after a set amount of time, and can be used for voice calls.

Why Is This Necessary?

Abortion is still legal in this country in every state, yet we still have multiple examples of people being investigated for potential illegal abortion whenever a pregnant person shows up in an emergency room with excessive bleeding, or a discarded fetus is found. Because of the current anti–abortion rights climate, district attorneys and prosecutors have excessive discretion to decide whether or not to pursue an investigation over a poor birth outcome, and local police are going to greater extents to find the person who gave birth when-ever a miscarried fetus is discovered.

Already just in 2018 we have seen two extremely disturbing examples of law enforcement going to new lengths when it comes to investigating miscarriage. In Augusta, Georgia, a city coroner claimed he would be using a DNA database in an attempt to locate the parent of an approximately twenty-week-gestation fetus found in the city's sewer system—allegedly just to "unite" the deceased fetus with its family, but critics suspected his motives were to search out a possible crime.[50] And just months later medical examiners combed the flight records of a plane that landed in New York to determine who miscarried in the airplane bathroom, leaving behind an approximately five-month-gestation fetus in the toilet—an incident first investigated as a "potential botched abortion."[51]

When miscarriages are investigated, the first thing that police do is check the text messages, e-mails, web browser history, search engine caches, and any other electronic communication they believe may hold a hint as to whether it was indeed a medical accident, or if the pregnant person may have sought a way to end the pregnancy—or was even just unhappy about being pregnant. This is especially dangerous for those who may lack prenatal care, the poor, those who are younger, and those who may have substance abuse or mental health issues or physical health issues, since they are at higher risk for poor pregnancy outcomes. Even if the miscarriage is completely natural, investigators could consider a visit to an abortion clinic website, a text from weeks prior showing ambivalence to the pregnancy, or an e-mail to an online drug site suspicious enough to press charges.

Whether online, over the phone, or in person, when it comes to protecting yourself, limit all of your discussions about your medical decisions and your pregnancy status in general only to those you are completely sure are trustworthy and supportive. Of those who have been arrested for allegedly inducing their own miscarriages, it is often someone they know—a family member, a neighbor, or someone related to those people—who initiates an investigation by informing law enforcement about a suspicious birth outcome.

How to Work with Others in a Secure Environment

Securing your own electronic footprint and communications is one thing. But what if you want to work with others, either across state lines or international lines? That means making sure everyone follows the same security protocols, and only working with people you are certain are doing it, and who have similar goals as you do.

At *A Womb of One's Own*, the writer refers to this secure and vetted group as a "network of trust." She says:

> What is a "network of trust"? Put simply, this is a group of women who want to help each other to ensure that people in their group of friends will be able to make reproductive decisions regardless of legal restrictions.
>
> If you already know your friends to be pro-choice, you may believe it would be easy to build these networks. However, even pro-choice people can sometimes be hesitant to break the law in order to support the cause … It is important to only allow people into your networks of trust that you believe will keep your secrets safe. While the vast majority of what you will be doing is legal, allowing people into your networks of trust who are not, themselves, trustworthy can create a host of problems.[52]

A "network of trust" isn't just for activities around self-managed abortion care or the medical side of abortion, but it is also imperative if you plan to do any sort of organizing around abortion access post-*Roe*. Being positive that you can trust everyone in your network is just as important when it comes to actions that are completely legal, since allowing someone into your network who isn't trustworthy doesn't just add to the potential legal consequences but can create a dangerous and volatile activist environment too.

Protection from Anti-Abortion Infiltration

Perhaps the most well-known recent incident of letting someone into a network of trust, only to have it abused, is the multiyear infiltration of David Daleiden, the anti-abortion activist who pretended to be a "tissue procurement" professional in order to get access to meetings and events with abortion providers across the country. His edited videos obtained while secretly recording conversations with medical providers—conversations in which Daleiden himself often asked leading questions in an effort to try to egg providers into potentially breaking laws—are a more egregious example of how abortion opponents can infiltrate even the most secure environments.

But for every Daleiden there are many other activists trying to make other inroads into your network of trust—from sending e-mails asking questions in the hopes you might offer advice that is illegal to interacting with you on social media in order to move further into your group of activists. As abortion becomes more restricted, vetting the people you let into your network will become even more vital.

Stay Secure Online

This should be a given, but always be extremely careful of anything you say in e-mail, even if the person sending the e-mail is someone you know. E-mail accounts can be hacked, or someone could even create an e-mail almost identical to—but not quite—the address of the friend in question. We often see what we expect to see, so always play it safe. This is especially important if you or others in your network have public e-mail addresses associated with your work as activists. You can absolutely never be too cautious online.

It is just as important to be vigilant on social media sites. If you plan on posting any information about your activities on Facebook, be absolutely certain that you know every person you allow to be your friend. It is not uncommon for people to set up fake accounts in order to infiltrate a friend circle of people they may see as political enemies, and far too often people will accept friend requests of strangers simply because they have a number of friends in common already. If you have not physically met the person, consider checking in with one of your common friends to ensure they know the person in real life. If it turns out none of your mutual friends know where the person came from, either, there is a pretty good chance you are dealing with a fake account trying to get access to your network.

Vetting Your Contacts

If you have decided to start a new organization—a practical support group for those seeking terminations, a new political action group, or an escorting team at a new clinic or an EC delivery service—you are going to need other volunteers to help you. Here are a few tips for making sure the people you bring on aren't actually trying to sabotage your efforts.

First, the easiest way to make sure your network is safe is to use people you already know and trust. Next, get word-of-mouth recommendations. Expand your current network to a friends-of-friends basis. Again, these should be people that your first volunteers already trust and are prepared to vouch for. Finally, if you do end up expanding to new volunteers who aren't firsthand acquaintances, be sure to vet their Internet presence. A person willing to work in reproductive rights or justice is highly unlikely to have no history whatsoever. Do a Google search, ask if they have social media accounts you can examine. And yes, if necessary, say no to them. It is always better to have too few volunteers doing the work than to have someone in your organization who may be trying to bring it down from the inside.

Protecting Yourself When the Worst Happens

Let's be honest—try as hard as you might, bad stuff still happens. Maybe despite all of your security and all of your vetting, you did end up with an abortion opponent in your personal network. It could have been that coworker from your last job that you stayed in touch with but never talked politics with, or maybe that one cousin who always sends you chain e-mails about angel prayers. Whatever happened, now you've realized that the protesters outside the clinic you are defending are now calling you by your first and last name, or maybe your new boss is getting harassing phone calls demanding you be fired. How do you cope?

Hopefully, before it gets to this point, you have already put some precautions in place to protect your personal information. If you have registered websites, consider paying additional fees to block your name and contact information from being published. If you do register without privacy, considering using a PO Box and setting up a Google voice number for registration in order to avoid giving away your home address.

Your home address and phone number are often stored online and can come up in search engines, too. To remove them, you can go to websites like Spokeo (http://www.spokeo.com/opt_out/new) or Whitepages (https://support.whitepages.com/hc/en-us/articles/115010106908-How-do-I-edit-or-remove-a-personal-listing-) and follow their instructions for opting out. There are also services that can do this for a fee, like DeleteMe or PrivacyDuck.

When it comes to keeping your address private, the most important thing to do is pay attention to your social media. Don't take photos of your home, especially if it shows an address, and be careful about how much identifying information is out there on Facebook, Instagram, or Twitter that could give away your neighborhood simply based on local restaurants or businesses you frequent. Always turn off geotagging to eliminate extra metadata on your photos or check-ins, and be cognizant about putting up things like routes from runs on Runkeeper or other fitness apps that could easily give away your home address.

Also make sure that your employer information is hidden. As more people are networking professionally using LinkedIn, that can be an easy way for someone to find out your current employer, so consider that when thinking about what information you want online. Consider removing your employer information from your Facebook profile, too.

Of course none of this matters if your employer info can be easily accessed though a news search. If there are professional press releases in trade publications or elsewhere, removing your Internet footprint may be far more work than you can accomplish on your own. Take the precautions you can, but don't beat yourself up if you can't do it all.

Dealing with a Cyberattack

Finally, sometimes it isn't just you getting attacked, it's your entire organization. Abortion opponents have allegedly already executed cyberattacks on large reproductive rights organizations. In 2015 an anti-abortion hacker claimed responsibility for a security breech on the Planned Parenthood website, obtaining e-mail addresses and other

Planned Parenthood databases.[53] The National Network of Abortion Funds was attacked a year later, with a distributed denial of service attack (DDOS) that shut down its abortion Bowl-a-Thon fund-raiser after attempting to create billions of dollars in fake donations. The hackers also accessed donor e-mails, sending spoofed anti-abortion e-mails with racist language to the real abortion fund donors.[54]

So what should you do to prepare for a potential cyberattack? Most "attacks" result from credentials, or log-in information to the services you use, being disclosed in public breaches of other services. This is why it's important to use long passwords, passwords that differ from each other in case one service you use is compromised, and a two-factor method to ensure that even your password is not enough to access your information.

The first thing to do for any web presence is have an emergency plan that includes a backup of your website, in case you need to revert because hackers put up their own site or inserted inappropriate images into yours. Make sure to back up any information in your databases frequently as well, so a potential wipe won't be as devastating.

Be sure to have all of the information you need to contact your web host immediately in order to get the site fixed—whether it requires taking it offline until it can be restored or even longer to see how intense any breach might be. It's also highly recommended to use an online protection service that can help filter the fake traffic meant to crash your site by overwhelming it with "users" (i.e., a distributed denial of service attack). Many of these services are available for cheap or free for nonprofits or individual users. Some of the ones available for nonprofits include Cloudflare and Google Shield.

If everyone in your organization uses e-mail addresses hosted on the domain, be sure that they have alternate addresses they can use until it can be determined that the original addresses weren't compromised. Also, have a game plan for how to connect with each other to alert all of the volunteers about the hack, especially if you are worried that your electronic communication may no longer be safe.

Why Hard Copies Matter

Finally, remember to keep physical copies of information that you will use on a regular basis, rather than relying solely on the Internet, your computer, or your phone. Viruses can wipe out hard drives. Your phone could get confiscated. Websites can get hacked. If you have procedures, resource lists, maps and addresses, or other info you use regularly, consider making hard copies and keeping them somewhere safe. Or even take notes here, in this book.

Less than a hundred years ago, it was a crime in the United States to publicize information about abortion or birth control. In Ireland, it was illegal until 2018 to offer public information about abortion services outside the country—only doctors could do so, and only to their patients.

Will the US make publishing and accessing abortion information a crime if abortion itself becomes illegal? The idea seems very unlikely. But that doesn't mean that an anti-abortion administration couldn't find ways to make that information less available through financial coercion of Internet providers or restrictions on content allowed in publicly funded institutions like libraries, public university computer labs, or wireless networks in nonprofit agencies. And even if the government does keep its hands off abortion information access, we can't be certain that anti-abortion tech activists won't continue their cyberattacks on websites with abortion content.

So, just to be safe, when in doubt, print it out.

Resource Guide

Clinics, political action groups, abortion funds, and practical support networks are listed below and grouped by state. First listed are all the clinics in the state, alphabetized by city. After that is a listing of any abortion direct support (abortion funds or practical support groups), followed by any reproductive justice, reproductive rights, or other activist or political groups directly working on abortion rights and access. Following the state guide is a list of national organizations.

This information is also available and updated in an interactive map at www.postroehandbook.com.

Notes

- This guide includes the latest date a person can get a clinic abortion in each state, but not every clinic will offer services that late. Contact the clinic directly for their info.
- If a clinic is designated "medication only," there is no non-medication option, and it only provides services for the first nine weeks of a pregnancy.
- Members of the Abortion Care Network—a network of high-quality independent abortion care providers—are signified with a *.
- American Medical Services has clinics in several states, but has been flagged as potentially unsafe. Because of that, they are not included on this list.

State Resources

Alabama (abortion available in the state until twenty-one weeks six days' gestation)

CLINICS

Planned Parenthood—Birmingham Health Center
1211 27th Pl. S., Birmingham, AL
205-322-2121
https://www.plannedparenthood.org/health-center/alabama/birmingham/35205/
birmingham-center-3253-90330

✱Alabama Women's Center
4831 Sparkman Dr. NW, Huntsville, AL
866-536-2231
http://www.alabamawomenscenter.com/

Planned Parenthood—Mobile Health Center (medication only)
717 Downtowner Loop W., Mobile, AL
251-342-6695
https://www.plannedparenthood.org/health-center/alabama/mobile/36609/mobile-
center-2911-90330

Reproductive Health Services of Montgomery
811 S. Perry St., Montgomery, AL
800-277-0156
https://www.rhs4choice.com/

✱West Alabama Women's Center Inc.
535 Jack Warner Pkwy., Tuscaloosa, AL
800-616-2383
http://www.wa-wc.com/

POLITICAL, FUNDING, AND PRACTICAL SUPPORT GROUPS

Access Reproductive Care Southeast (ARC Southeast)
855-227-2475
https://www.arc-southeast.org/

Yellowhammer Fund
https://yellowhammerfund.org/
https://www.paypal.com/us/fundraiser/charity/2728256

Alabama Reproductive Rights Advocates (ARRA)
2824 Hunterwood Dr. SE, Decatur, AL
865-465-9793
http://alabamareproductiverightsadvocates.com
http://alabamareproductiverightsadvocates.com/thelindadfoundation/
lindadfoundation@gmail.com

Greater Birmingham NOW
https://taihicks.wixsite.com/gbnow
now.birmingham@gmail.com

P.O.W.E.R. House (Montgomery, Alabama)
https://montgomeryareareproductivejusticecoalition.wordpress.com/
montgomeryareaprojustice@gmail.com

Planned Parenthood Southeast Advocates
https://www.plannedparenthoodaction.org/planned-parenthood-southeast-advocates

Alaska (abortion available in the state until thirteen weeks six days' gestation)

CLINICS

Planned Parenthood—Anchorage Health Center
4001 Lake Otis Pkwy. #101, Anchorage, AK
800-769-0045
https://www.plannedparenthood.org/health-center/alaska/anchorage/99508/
    anchorage-health-center-3254-91810

Planned Parenthood—Fairbanks Health Center
1867 Airport Way #160b, Fairbanks, AK
800-769-0045
https://www.plannedparenthood.org/health-center/alaska/fairbanks/99701/fairbanks-
    health-center-2603-91810

Planned Parenthood—Juneau Health Center
3231 Glacier Hwy., Juneau, AK
800-769-0045
https://www.plannedparenthood.org/health-center/alaska/juneau/99801/juneau-
    health-center-3865-91810

Planned Parenthood—Soldotna Health Center (medication only)
130 E. Redoubt Ave., Soldotna, AK
800-769-0045
https://www.plannedparenthood.org/health-center/alaska/soldotna/99669/
 soldotna-health-center-2604-91810

POLITICAL, FUNDING, AND PRACTICAL SUPPORT GROUPS

Planned Parenthood Votes Northwest and Hawaii
https://www.plannedparenthoodaction.org/planned-parenthood-votes-northwest-and-hawaii

Alaska National Organization for Women
https://www.facebook.com/pg/NOWAlaska/about/
alaskanow@gmail.com

Northwest Abortion Access Fund (NWAAF) (Northwest and Hawaii)
https://nwaafund.org/travelhelp/

Arizona *(abortion available in the state until twenty-three weeks six days' gestation)*

CLINICS

Planned Parenthood—Flagstaff Health Center (medication only)
2500 S. Woodlands Village Blvd. #12, Flagstaff, AZ
855-207-7526
https://www.plannedparenthood.org/health-center/arizona/flagstaff/86001/flagstaff-
 health-center-2566-90030

Acacia Women's Center
1615 E. Osborn Rd., Phoenix, AZ
602-462-5559
http://www.acaciawomenscenter.com/

✱Camelback Family Planning
4141 N. 32nd St. #105, Phoenix, AZ
877-966-2337
https://www.camelbackfamilyplanning.com/

✱Desert Star Family Planning
1526 W. Glendale Ave. #109, Phoenix, AZ
480-447-8857
http://www.desertstarfp.com/

✱Family Planning Associates Medical Group
1331 North 7th St. #225, Phoenix, AZ
602-553-0440
https://fpamg.com/

Planned Parenthood—Glendale Health Center
5771 W. Eugie Ave., Glendale, AZ
602-277-7526
https://www.plannedparenthood.org/health-center/arizona/glendale/85304/glendale-
health-center-3963-90030

Planned Parenthood—New Tempe Health Center
1837 E. Baseline Rd., Tempe, AZ
602-277-7526
https://www.plannedparenthood.org/health-center/arizona/tempe/85283/
new-tempe-regional-health-center-4256-90030

Planned Parenthood—Tucson Women's Center
5240 E. Knight Dr., Suite 112, Tucson, AZ
520-408-7526

POLITICAL, FUNDING, AND PRACTICAL SUPPORT GROUPS

NARAL Pro-Choice Arizona
http://www.prochoicearizona.org/

Pro-Choice Arizona
4141 N. 32nd St., Suite 105, Phoenix, AZ
602-258-4091
info@prochoicearizona.org

Planned Parenthood Advocates of Arizona
http://advocatesaz.org/

Arizona NOW
https://www.facebook.com/AZNOW/

AZ Clinic Defense Force
https://www.facebook.com/azclinicdefenseforce/
azclinicdefenceforce@gmail.com

National Asian Pacific American Women's Forum—Arizona Chapter
https://www.napawf.org/arizonachapter.html
arizonaleaders@napawf.org

Abortion Fund of Arizona
Phoenix, Arizona
602-327-5166
http://www.abortionfundofaz.org/

Arkansas *(abortion is available in the state until twenty-one weeks' gestation)*

CLINICS

Planned Parenthood—Fayetteville Health Center (medication only)
3729 N. Crossover Rd., Suite 107, Fayetteville, AR
855-841-7526
https://www.plannedparenthood.org/health-center/arkansas/fayetteville/72703/
    fayetteville-health-center-2972-90740

✱Little Rock Family Planning
4 Office Park Dr., Little Rock, AR
800-272-2183
https://lrfps.com/

Planned Parenthood—Little Rock Health Center (medication only)
5921 W. 12th St., Little Rock, AR
855-841-7526
https://www.plannedparenthood.org/health-center/arkansas/
    fayetteville/72703/fayetteville-health-center-2972-90740

POLITICAL, FUNDING, AND PRACTICAL SUPPORT GROUPS

ReproAction—Arkansas state affiliate
https://reproaction.org/take-action/?ss=963#listing

Arkansas Abortion Support Network (AASN) (Little Rock)
501-712-0671
https://www.arabortionsupport.org

Planned Parenthood Great Plains Votes
http://www.ppgpvotes.org/

California (abortion is available in the state until the point of viability, or between twenty-four and twenty-six weeks' gestation)

CLINICS

Planned Parenthood—Alhambra Health Center
330 S. Garfield Ave. #300, Alhambra, CA
626-798-0706
https://www.plannedparenthood.org/health-center/california/alhambra/91801/
alhambra-health-center-3561-90090

Planned Parenthood—Anaheim Health Center
303 W. Lincoln Ave. #105, Anaheim, CA
714-922-4100
https://www.plannedparenthood.org/health-center/california/anaheim/92805/
anaheim-health-center-2284-90160

Planned Parenthood—Antioch Health Center
1104 Buchanan Rd., Antioch, CA
925-754-4550
https://www.plannedparenthood.org/health-center/california/antioch/94509/antioch-
health-center-2573-90200

Women's First Choice
51 N. 5th Ave., Arcadia, CA
626-616-3768
http://www.womansfirstchoice.com/

FPA Women's Health—Bakersfield
2500 H St., Bakersfield, CA
661-633-5266
http://www.fpawomenshealth.com/locations/bakersfield-ca-2/

＊Pro-Choice Medical Center: Dr. Josepha Seletz
99 N. La Cienega Blvd., Beverly Hills, CA
310-247-8745
http://www.prochoicemedical.com/

Planned Parenthood—Burbank Health Center
916 W. Burbank Blvd., Burbank, CA
800-576-5544
https://www.plannedparenthood.org/health-center/california/burbank/91506/
burbank-health-center-2236-90070

FPA Women's Health—Canoga Park
7023 Owensmouth Ave., Canoga Park, CA
877-883-7264
http://www.fpawomenshealth.com/locations/5447/

Planned Parenthood—Canoga Park Health Center
21001 Sherman Way #9, Canoga Park, CA
800-576-5544
https://www.plannedparenthood.org/health-center/california/canoga-park/91303/
canoga-park-health-center-2235-90070

❋Women's Health Specialists—Chico
1469 Humboldt Rd. #200, Chico, CA
530-891-1911
https://www.womenshealthspecialists.org/

Planned Parenthood—Chico Health Center
3100 Cohasset Rd., Chico, CA
530-342-8367
https://www.plannedparenthood.org/health-center/california/chico/95973/chico-
health-center-2770-90200

Planned Parenthood—Chula Vista Health Center
1295 Broadway #201, Chula Vista, CA
888-743-7526
https://www.plannedparenthood.org/health-center/california/chula-vista/91911/
chula-vista-center-2328-90110

Planned Parenthood—Clearlake Health Center
14671 Olympic Dr., Clearlake, CA
707-995-2261
https://www.plannedparenthood.org/health-center/california/clearlake/95422/
clearlake-health-center-4068-90200

Planned Parenthood—Coachella Health Center
49-111 California 111 #6A, Coachella, CA
888-743-7526
https://www.plannedparenthood.org/health-center/california/coachella/92236/
coachella-center-2186-90110

Planned Parenthood—Concord Health Center
2185 Pacheco St., Concord, CA
925-676-0300
https://www.plannedparenthood.org/health-center/california/concord/94520/
concord-health-center-3269-90200

Planned Parenthood—Costa Mesa Health Center
601 W. 19th St., Costa Mesa, CA
714-922-4100
https://www.plannedparenthood.org/health-center/california/costa-mesa/92627/
    costa-mesa-health-center-2286-90160

FPA Women's Health—Downey
8635 Firestone Blvd. #100, Downey, CA
562-862-5121
http://www.fpawomenshealth.com/locations/downey-ca/

Planned Parenthood—El Cajon Health Center
1685 E. Main St. #301, El Cajon, CA
888-743-7526
https://www.plannedparenthood.org/health-center/california/el-cajon/92021/
    el-cajon-center-2329-90110

Planned Parenthood—Imperial Valley Health Center
1463 S. 4th St., El Centro, CA
760-594-9100
https://www.plannedparenthood.org/health-center/california/el-centro/92243/
    imperial-valley-health-center-4182-90110

Planned Parenthood—El Cerrito Health Center
320 El Cerrito Plaza, El Cerrito, CA
510-527-5806
https://www.plannedparenthood.org/health-center/california/el-cerrito/94530/
    el-cerrito-health-center-3940-90200

Planned Parenthood—El Monte Health Center
4786 Peck Rd., El Monte, CA
800-576-5544
https://www.plannedparenthood.org/health-center/california/el-monte/91732/
    el-monte-health-center-2322-90070

Planned Parenthood—Escondido Center
347 W. Mission Ave., Escondido, CA
888-743-7526
https://www.plannedparenthood.org/health-center/california/escondido/92025/
    escondido-center-2331-90110

Planned Parenthood—Eureka Health Center
3225 Timber Fall Ct., Eureka, CA
707-442-5700
https://www.plannedparenthood.org/health-center/california/eureka/95503/eureka-
    health-center-2301-90200

Planned Parenthood—Fairfield Health Center
1325 Travis Blvd., Fairfield, CA
707-429-8855
https://www.plannedparenthood.org/health-center/california/fairfield/94533/
 fairfield-health-center-2700-90200

FPA Women's Health—Fresno
165 N. Clark St., Fresno, CA
559-233-8657
http://www.fpawomenshealth.com/locations/fresno-ca/

Planned Parenthood—Family First Health Center
6095 N. First St., Fresno, CA
559-446-1515
https://www.plannedparenthood.org/health-center/california/fresno/93710/family-
 first-health-center-2365-90130

Planned Parenthood—Fulton Street Health Center
650 N. Fulton St., Fresno, CA
559-488-4900
https://www.plannedparenthood.org/health-center/california/fresno/93728/fulton-
 street-health-center-2364-90130

Planned Parenthood—Gilroy Health Center
760 Renz Ln., Gilroy, CA
408-847-1739
https://www.plannedparenthood.org/health-center/california/gilroy/95020/gilroy-
 health-center-2433-90130

FPA Women's Health—Glendale
372 Arden Ave. #200, Glendale, CA
818-502-1341
http://www.fpawomenshealth.com/locations/glendale-ca/

Planned Parenthood—Glendora Health Center
130 W. Route 66 #100, Glendora, CA
626-798-0706
https://www.plannedparenthood.org/health-center/california/glendora/91740/
 glendora-health-center-4070-90090

Women's Health Specialists—Grass Valley
120 Richardson St., Grass Valley, CA
800-714-8151
https://www.womenshealthspecialists.org/

Planned Parenthood—Hayward Health Center
1032 A St., Hayward, CA
510-300-3800
https://www.plannedparenthood.org/health-center/california/hayward/94541/
    hayward-health-center-4150-90130

Planned Parenthood—Lakewood Health Center
5525 Del Amo Blvd., Lakewood, CA
800-576-5544
https://www.plannedparenthood.org/health-center/california/lakewood/90713/
    lakewood-health-center-2359-90070

FPA Women's Health—Long Beach
2777 Long Beach Blvd. #200, Long Beach, CA
562-595-5653
http://www.fpawomenshealth.com/locations/long-beach-ca/

Planned Parenthood—Long Beach Health Center
2690 Pacific Ave. #370, Long Beach, CA
800-576-5544
https://www.plannedparenthood.org/health-center/california/long-beach/90806/
    long-beach-health-center-3945-90070

Alliance Women's Medical Group
1930 Wilshire Blvd. #500, Los Angeles, CA
213-353-4971
http://alliancewomensmedicalgroup.biz/

FPA Women's Health—Los Angeles (Downtown)
601 S. Westmoreland Ave., Los Angeles, CA
213-738-7283
http://www.fpawomenshealth.com/locations/los-angeles-downtown-ca/

Her Smart Choice
2226 E. Cesar E. Chavez Ave., Los Angeles, CA
323-685-4747
http://www.hersmartchoice.com/

My Choice Medical Center—Los Angeles
4903 W. Pico Blvd. #202, Los Angeles, CA
866-397-3070
http://www.mychoicemedicalcenter.com/

Planned Parenthood—Dorothy Hecht Health Center
8520 S. Broadway, Los Angeles, CA
800-576-5544
https://www.plannedparenthood.org/health-center/california/los-angeles/90003/
dorothy-hecht-health-center-2465-90070

Planned Parenthood—East Los Angeles Health Center
5068 Whittier Blvd., East Los Angeles, CA
800-576-5544
https://www.plannedparenthood.org/health-center/california/los-angeles/90022/
east-los-angeles-health-center-3375-90070

Planned Parenthood—Hollywood Health Center
1014 N. Vermont Ave., Los Angeles, CA
800-576-5544
https://www.plannedparenthood.org/health-center/california/
los-angeles/90029/hollywood-health-center-2466-90070

Planned Parenthood—S. Mark Taper Foundation Center for Medical Training
400 W. 30th St., Los Angeles, CA
800-576-5544
https://www.plannedparenthood.org/health-center/california/los-angeles/90007/
s.-mark-taper-foundation-center-for-medical-training-3862-90070

Planned Parenthood—Madera Health Center
500 E. Almond Ave., Madera, CA
559-675-1133
https://www.plannedparenthood.org/health-center/california/madera/93637/madera-
health-center-2363-90130

FPA Women's Health—Mission Hills
10200 Sepulveda Blvd., Suite 200, Mission Hills, CA
818-893-6949
http://www.fpawomenshealth.com/locations/mission-hills-ca/

Planned Parenthood—Mission Viejo
26137 La Paz Rd. #200, Mission Viejo, CA
714-922-4100
https://www.plannedparenthood.org/health-center/california/mission-viejo/92691/
mission-viejo-health-center-2288-90160

FPA Women's Heath—Modesto
2030 Coffee Rd. #1, Modesto, CA
800-338-1361
http://www.fpawomenshealth.com/locations/modesto-ca/

Planned Parenthood—Modesto Health Center
1431 McHenry Ave. #100, Modesto, CA
209-578-0443
https://www.plannedparenthood.org/health-center/california/modesto/95350/
modesto-health-center-2527-90130

Planned Parenthood—Moreno Valley Health Center
12900 Frederick St., Suite C, Moreno Valley, CA
888-743-7526
https://www.plannedparenthood.org/health-center/california/moreno-valley/92553/
moreno-valley-center-2188-90110

Planned Parenthood—Mountain View Health Center
225 San Antonio Rd., Mountain View, CA
650-948-0807
https://www.plannedparenthood.org/health-center/california/mountain-view/94040/
mountain-view-health-center-2310-90130

Planned Parenthood—Napa Health Center
1735 Jefferson St., Napa, CA
707-252-8050
https://www.plannedparenthood.org/health-center/california/napa/94559/napa-
health-center-2702-90200

Planned Parenthood—North Highlands Health Center
5700 Watt Ave., North Highlands, CA
916-332-5715
https://www.plannedparenthood.org/health-center/california/north-high-
lands/95660/north-highlands-health-center-2201-90130

FPA Women's Health—Oakland
400 29th St. #301, Oakland, CA
510-899-7099
http://www.fpawomenshealth.com/locations/oakland-ca/

Family Planning Specialist Medical Group
200 Webster St. #100, Oakland, CA
510-268-3720
https://familyplanningspecialists.com/

Planned Parenthood—East Oakland/Coliseum Health Center
8480 Enterprise Way, Oakland, CA
510-746-4700
https://www.plannedparenthood.org/health-center/california/oakland/94621/east-
oakland---coliseum-health-center-4188-90130

Planned Parenthood—West Oakland Health Center
1682 7th St., Oakland, CA
510-300-3800
https://www.plannedparenthood.org/health-center/california/oakland/94607/
west-oakland-4090-90130

Planned Parenthood—Orange Health Center
700 S. Tustin St., Orange, CA
714-922-4100
https://www.plannedparenthood.org/health-center/california/orange/92866/orange-
health-center-3264-90160

FPA Women's Health—Oxnard
1700 Lombard St. #110, Oxnard, CA
805-822-5879
http://www.fpawomenshealth.com/locations/oxnard-ca/

Stanford Family Planning
Garden Level, Suite W0050, 900 Blake Wilbur Dr., Palo Alto, CA
650-725-6079
https://obgyn.stanford.edu/divisions/family_planning.html

Planned Parenthood—Pasadena Health Center
1045 N. Lake Ave., Pasadena, CA
626-798-0706
https://www.plannedparenthood.org/health-center/california/pasadena/91104/
pasadena-health-center-3265-90090

Planned Parenthood—Pittsburg Health Center
3715 Railroad Ave., Suite B, Pittsburg, CA
925-439-1237

FPA Women's Health—Pomona
1996 Indian Hill Blvd., Pomona, CA
909-626-2463
http://www.fpawomenshealth.com/locations/pomona/

Planned Parenthood—Pomona Health Center
1550 N. Garey Ave., Pomona, CA
800-576-5544
https://www.plannedparenthood.org/health-center/california/pomona/91767/
pomona-health-center-2208-90070

Planned Parenthood—Rancho Mirago Family Planning Center
71777 San Jacinto Dr. #202, Rancho Mirago, CA
888-743-7526
https://www.plannedparenthood.org/health-center/california/rancho-mirage/92270/
rancho-mirage-family-planning-center-2325-90110

*Women's Health Specialists—Redding
1901 Victor Ave., Redding, CA
530-221-0193
https://www.womenshealthspecialists.org/

Planned Parenthood—Redding Health Center
2935 Bechelli Ln., Suite A, Redding, CA
530-351-7100
https://www.plannedparenthood.org/health-center/california/redding/96002/
redding-health-center-2376-90200

Planned Parenthood—Redwood City Health Center
2907 El Camino Real, Redwood City, CA
650-503-7810
https://www.plannedparenthood.org/health-center/california/redwood-city/94061/
redwood-city-health-center-4129-90130

Planned Parenthood—Central Richmond Health Center
340 Marina Way, Richmond, CA
510-232-1250

Planned Parenthood—Hilltop-Richmond Health Center
2970 Hilltop Mall Rd. #307, Richmond, CA
510-222-5290
https://www.plannedparenthood.org/health-center/california/richmond/94806/
hilltop-richmond-health-center-2791-90200

FPA Women's Health—Riverside
3660 Park Sierra Dr., Suite 202, Riverside, CA
951-637-2100
http://www.fpawomenshealth.com/locations/riverside-ca/

Planned Parenthood—Riverside Health Center
3772 Tibbetts St., Riverside, CA
888-743-7526
https://www.plannedparenthood.org/health-center/california/riverside/92506/
riverside-health-center-2187-90110

Planned Parenthood—Roseville Health Center
729 Sunrise Ave. #900, Roseville, CA
916-781-3310
https://www.plannedparenthood.org/health-center/california/roseville/95661/
roseville-health-center-2197-90130

FPA Women's Health—Sacramento
2322 Butano Dr. #205, Sacramento, CA
916-483-2885
http://www.fpawomenshealth.com/locations/sacramento-ca/

Planned Parenthood—B Street Health Center
201 29th St., Sacramento, CA
916-446-6921
https://www.plannedparenthood.org/health-center/california/sacramento/95816/b-
street-health-center-2200-90130

Planned Parenthood—Fruitridge Health Center
5385 Franklin Blvd., Suites A–D, Sacramento, CA
916-452-7305
https://www.plannedparenthood.org/health-center/california/sacramento/95820/
fruitridge-health-center-2198-90130

Planned Parenthood—Salinas Health Center
316 N. Main St., Salinas, CA
831-758-8261
https://www.plannedparenthood.org/health-center/california/salinas/93901/salinas-
health-center-2228-90130

FPA Women's Health—San Bernardino
855 E. Hospitality Ln., San Bernardino, CA
909-885-0282
http://www.fpawomenshealth.com/locations/san-bernardino-ca/

Planned Parenthood—San Bernardino Health Center
1873 Commercenter W., San Bernardino, CA
909-890-5511
https://www.plannedparenthood.org/health-center/california/san-bernardino/92408/
san-bernardino-health-center-2282-90160

FPA Women's Health—San Diego (Downtown)
1625 E. Main St., Suite 202, El Cajon, CA
858-547-7100
http://www.fpawomenshealth.com/locations/san-diego-downtown-ca/

FPA Women's Health—San Diego (North)
1625 E. Main St., Suite 202, El Cajon, CA
858-547-7100
http://www.fpawomenshealth.com/locations/san-diego-north-ca/

Planned Parenthood—College Avenue Sarah Weddington Center
4575 College Ave., San Diego, CA
888-743-7526
https://www.plannedparenthood.org/health-center/california/san-diego/92115/
college-avenue-sarah-weddington-center-2324-90110

Planned Parenthood—Euclid Avenue Parker Health Center
220 Euclid Ave. #30, San Diego, CA
888-743-7526
https://www.plannedparenthood.org/health-center/california/san-diego/92114/
euclid-avenue-parker-center-2334-90110

Planned Parenthood—First Avenue Family Planning Michelle Wagner Center
2017 1st Ave., Suites #100 and #301, San Diego, CA
888-743-7526
https://www.plannedparenthood.org/health-center/california/san-diego/92101/
first-avenue-specialty-services-michelle-wagner-center-4036-90110

Planned Parenthood—Kearny Mesa Health Center
7526 Clairemont Mesa Blvd., San Diego, CA
888-743-7526
https://www.plannedparenthood.org/health-center/california/san-diego/92111/
kearny-mesa-center-2332-90110

Planned Parenthood—Mira Mesa Health Center
10737 Camino Ruiz Medical Mall #220, San Diego, CA
888-743-7526
https://www.plannedparenthood.org/health-center/california/san-diego/92126/
mira-mesa-center-2333-90110

Planned Parenthood—Mission Bay Mimi Brien Health Center
Columbia Mission Bay Hospital
4501 Mission Bay Dr. #1c and 1d, San Diego, CA
888-743-7526
https://www.plannedparenthood.org/health-center/california/san-diego/92109/
mission-bay-mimi-brien-health-center-2330-90110

Women's Community Clinic
1735 Mission St., San Francisco, CA
415-379-7800
http://womenscommunityclinic.org/

Planned Parenthood—San Francisco Health Center
1650 Valencia St., San Francisco, CA
415-821-1282
https://www.plannedparenthood.org/health-center/california/san-francisco/94110/
san-francisco-health-center-3997-90200

✱Women's Options Center
2356 Sutter St., San Francisco, CA
415-353-7003
https://www.ucsfhealth.org/programs/womens_options_center/

Planned Parenthood—Eastside Health Center
3131 Alum Rock Ave., San Jose, CA
408-729-7600
https://www.plannedparenthood.org/health-center/california/san-jose/95127/east-
side-health-center-2435-90130

Planned Parenthood—San Jose Health Center
1691 The Alameda, San Jose, CA
408-287-7526
https://www.plannedparenthood.org/health-center/california/san-jose/95126/san-
jose-health-center-3263-90130

Planned Parenthood—San Luis Obispo
743 Pismo St., San Luis Obispo, CA
888-898-3806
https://www.plannedparenthood.org/health-center/california/san-luis-obispo/93401/
san-luis-obispo-center-2252-90170

Planned Parenthood—San Mateo Health Center
29 Baywood Ave., San Mateo, CA
650-235-7940
https://www.plannedparenthood.org/health-center/california/san-mateo/94402/san-
mateo-health-center-4104-90130

Planned Parenthood—San Rafael Center
2 H St., San Rafael, CA
415-459-4907
https://www.plannedparenthood.org/health-center/california/san-rafael/94901/san-
rafael-health-center-4114-90200

Planned Parenthood—San Ramon Health Center
200 Porter Dr. #200, San Ramon, CA
925-838-2108
https://www.plannedparenthood.org/health-center/california/san-ramon/94583/san-
ramon-health-center-2572-90200

✳Her Choice Women's Clinic
1155 West Central Ave., Suite 214, Santa Ana, CA
714-966-9094
http://www.herchoiceclinic.com/

FPA Women's Health—Santa Ana
1901 N. Tustin Ave., Santa Ana, CA
657-859-5463
http://www.fpawomenshealth.com/locations/santa-ana-ca/

Planned Parenthood—Santa Ana Health Center
1421 17th St., Santa Ana, CA
714-922-4100
https://www.plannedparenthood.org/health-center/california/santa-ana/92705/santa-
ana-health-center-2287-90160

Planned Parenthood—Santa Barbara Health Center
518 Garden St., Santa Barbara, CA
888-898-3806
https://www.plannedparenthood.org/health-center/california/santa-barbara/93101/
santa-barbara-center-3268-90170

Planned Parenthood—Westside Health Center
1119 Pacific Ave. #200, Santa Cruz, CA
831-426-5550
https://www.plannedparenthood.org/health-center/california/santa-cruz/95060/west-
side-health-center-2232-90130

Planned Parenthood—Santa Maria Health Center
415 E. Chapel St., Santa Maria, CA
888-898-3806
https://www.plannedparenthood.org/health-center/california/santa-maria/93454/
santa-maria-center-2250-90170

FPA Women's Health—Santa Monica
12304 Santa Monica Blvd. #116, Santa Monica, CA
310-820-8084
http://www.fpawomenshealth.com/locations/santa-monica/

Planned Parenthood—Santa Monica Health Center
1316 3rd Street Promenade #201, Santa Monica, CA
800-576-5544
https://www.plannedparenthood.org/health-center/california/santa-monica/90401/
santa-monica-health-center-2476-90070

Planned Parenthood—Santa Rosa Health Center
1140 Sonoma Ave., Bldg. 3, Santa Rosa, CA
707-527-7656
https://www.plannedparenthood.org/health-center/california/santa-rosa/95405/san-
ta-rosa-health-center-3990-90200

Planned Parenthood—Seaside Health Center
625 Hilby Ave., Seaside, CA
831-394-1691
https://www.plannedparenthood.org/health-center/california/seaside/93955/seaside-
health-center-2233-90130

Planned Parenthood—South Bay Health Center
14623 Hawthorne Blvd. #300, South Bay, CA
800-576-5544
https://www.plannedparenthood.org/health-center/california/lawndale/90260/south-
bay-health-center-2477-90070

Planned Parenthood—Eastland Plaza Health Center
678 N Wilson Way, Suite G, Stockton, CA
209-466-2081
https://www.plannedparenthood.org/health-center/california/stockton/95205/east-
land-plaza-health-center-2529-90130

Planned Parenthood—North Stockton Health Center
4555 Precissi Ln., Stockton, CA
209-477-4103
https://www.plannedparenthood.org/health-center/california/stockton/95207/north-
stockton-health-center-2528-90130

FPA Women's Health—Temecula
41715 Winchester Rd. #204, Temecula, CA
951-296-0454
http://www.fpawomenshealth.com/locations/temecula-ca/

Planned Parenthood—Thousand Oaks Center
1200 W. Hillcrest Dr., Thousand Oaks, CA
888-898-3806
https://www.plannedparenthood.org/health-center/california/thousand-oaks/91320/
thousand-oaks-center-3851-90170

FPA Women's Health—Torrance
3655 Lomita Blvd. #400, Torrance, CA
310-373-1042
http://www.fpawomenshealth.com/locations/torrance-ca/

Planned Parenthood—Ukiah Health Center
1165 S. Dora St., Suite A, Ukiah, CA
707-462-4303
https://www.plannedparenthood.org/health-center/california/ukiah/95482/ukiah-
health-center-4034-90200

Planned Parenthood—Vacaville Health Center
600 Nut Tree Rd. #210, Vacaville, CA
707-317-2111

Planned Parenthood—Vallejo Health Center
990 Broadway St., Vallejo, CA
707-643-4545
https://www.plannedparenthood.org/health-center/california/vallejo/94590/vallejo-
health-center-2699-90200

My Choice Medical—Van Nuys
7232 Van Nuys Blvd. #202, Van Nuys, CA
866-397-3070
http://www.mychoicemedicalcenter.com/

Planned Parenthood—Van Nuys Health Center
7100 Van Nuys Blvd. #108, Van Nuys, CA
800-576-5544
https://www.plannedparenthood.org/health-center/california/van-nuys/91405/
van-nuys-health-center-2234-90070

Planned Parenthood—Ventura Health Center
5400 Ralston St., Ventura, CA
888-898-3806
https://www.plannedparenthood.org/health-center/california/ventura/93003/
ventura-center-2251-90170

Planned Parenthood—Victorville Health Center
15403 Park Ave. E, Victorville, CA
760-245-9500
https://www.plannedparenthood.org/health-center/california/victorville/92391/
victorville-health-center-4082-90160

Planned Parenthood—Vista Isabella Health Center
1964 Via Centre, Vista, CA
888-743-7526
https://www.plannedparenthood.org/health-center/california/vista/92081/
vista-isabella-health-center-4186-90110

Planned Parenthood—Walnut Creek Health Center
1357 Oakland Blvd., Walnut Creek, CA
925-935-3010
https://www.plannedparenthood.org/health-center/california/walnut-creek/94596/
walnut-creek-health-center-2571-90200

Planned Parenthood—Watsonville Health Center
398 S Green Valley Rd., Watsonville, CA
831-724-7525
https://www.plannedparenthood.org/health-center/california/watsonville/95076/
watsonville-health-center-2229-90130

Planned Parenthood—Westminster Health Center
14372 Beach Blvd., Westminster, CA
714-922-4100
https://www.plannedparenthood.org/health-center/california/westminster/92683/
westminster-health-center-2285-90160

Planned Parenthood—Whittier Health Center
7655 Greenleaf Ave., Whittier, CA
800-576-5544
https://www.plannedparenthood.org/health-center/california/whittier/90602/
whittier-health-center-2358-90070

Planned Parenthood—Woodland Health Center
520 Cottonwood St. #10, Woodland, CA
530-662-4646
https://www.plannedparenthood.org/health-center/california/woodland/95695/
woodland-health-center-2375-90130

Planned Parenthood—Yuba City Health Center
430 Palora Ave., Suite G, Yuba City, CA
530-674-2603
https://www.plannedparenthood.org/health-center/california/yuba-city/95991/yuba-
city-health-center-2374-90130

POLITICAL, FUNDING, AND PRACTICAL SUPPORT GROUPS

Forward Together
300 Frank H. Ogawa Plaza, Suite 700, Oakland, CA
510-663-8300
https://forwardtogether.org/

California Latinas for Reproductive Justice
PO Box 861766, Los Angeles, CA
213-270-5258
info@clrj.org

Black Women for Wellness
PO Box 292516, Los Angeles, CA
323-290-5955
http://www.bwwla.org
info@bwwla.com

National Asian Pacific American Women's Forum—Bay Area Chapter
https://www.napawf.org/bayareachapter.html
bayareachapter@napawf.org

National Asian Pacific American Women's Forum—Los Angeles Chapter
https://www.napawf.org/lachapter.html
LAchapter@napawf.org

National Asian Pacific American Women's Forum—San Diego Chapter
https://www.napawf.org/sandiegochapter.html
sandiegochapter@napawf.org

NARAL Pro-Choice California
335 South Van Ness Ave., San Francisco, CA
415-890-1020
https://prochoicecalifornia.org/
info@prochoicecalifornia.org

California RCRC (Religious Coalition for Reproductive Choice)
1460 Pelham Rd., 106-G, Seal Beach, CA
http://rcrc.org/affiliates/
mlarson.telfords@gmail.com

California NOW
916-442-3414
http://www.canow.org/
info@canow.org

Access Women's Health Justice (Oakland)—Funding and practical support
Oakland, CA
800-376-4636 (English); 888-442-2237 (Spanish)
http://accesswhj.org/

LA For Choice (clinic escorting)
https://la4choice.org/
LA4Choice@gmail.com

Justice Fund (San Jose)
1605 The Alameda, San Jose, CA
775-688-5560, ext. 244
http://www.plannedparenthood.org/mar-monte/

Women's Health Specialists—Women in Need Fund (Sacramento)
1442 Ethan Way, Suite 100, Sacramento, CA
530-891-1911
https://www.womenshealthspecialists.org/

Planned Parenthood Affiliates of California
http://www.ppactionca.org/

Planned Parenthood Advocacy Project of Los Angeles County
http://www.ppactionca.org/local-info/los-angeles/

Planned Parenthood Advocates Mar Monte
http://www.ppactionca.org/local-info/mar-monte/

Community Action Fund of Planned Parenthood Orange and San Bernardino Counties
http://www.ppactionca.org/local-info/orange-san-bernardino/

Planned Parenthood Acton Fund of the Pacific Southwest
http://www.ppactionca.org/local-info/san-diego-riverside-imperial/

Planned Parenthood Central Coast Action Fund
http://www.ppactionca.org/local-info/central-coast/

Planned Parenthood Advocates of Pasadena and San Gabriel Valley
http://www.ppactionca.org/local-info/pasadena-and-san-gabriel-valley/

Planned Parenthood Northern California Action Fund
http://www.ppactionca.org/local-info/northern-california/

Colorado (abortion is available in this state until viability, about twenty-four to twenty-six weeks' gestation, or later based on individual cases)

CLINICS

Planned Parenthood—Alamosa Health Center
1560 12th St. #7, Alamosa, CO
719-589-4906
https://www.plannedparenthood.org/health-center/colorado/alamosa/81101/
  alamosa-2153-90210

Planned Parenthood—Aurora Center
1284 S. Abilene St., Aurora, CO
303-671-7526
https://www.plannedparenthood.org/health-center/colorado/aurora/80012/aurora-
  2489-90210

✽Boulder Abortion Clinic (note: this clinic will provide third-trimester abortions on an individual basis)
1130 Alpine Ave., Boulder, CO
800-535-1287
http://www.drhern.com/

✽Boulder Valley Women's Health Center—Boulder
2855 Valmont Rd., Boulder, CO
303-442-5160
http://www.boulderwomenshealth.org/services/abortion-care

Planned Parenthood—Boulder Health Clinic
2525 Arapahoe Ave., Suite C-200, Boulder, CO
303-447-1040
https://www.plannedparenthood.org/health-center/colorado/boulder/80302/
  boulder-2488-90210

Planned Parenthood—Colorado Springs Westside
3480 Centennial Blvd., Colorado Springs, CO
719-475-7162
https://www.plannedparenthood.org/health-center/colorado/colorado-springs/
  80907/colorado-springs-westside-3967-90210

Comprehensive Women's Health
Address available after booking an appointment
Denver, CO
720-810-5442
https://cwhccolorado.com/

*Partners in Women's Health
4500 E. 9th Ave., Suite 700, Denver, CO
303-399-3315
http://www.piwhdenver.com/

Planned Parenthood—Denver Stapleton Health Center
7155 E. 38th Ave., Denver, CO
303-321-2458
https://www.plannedparenthood.org/health-center/colorado/denver/80207/
    denver-stapleton-3543-90210

Planned Parenthood—Durango Health Center
46 Suttle St., Durango, CO
970-247-3002
https://www.plannedparenthood.org/health-center/colorado/durango/81303/
    durango-2174-90210

Healthy Futures for Women
300 E. Hampden Ave., Suite 201, Englewood, CO
303-647-3517
http://www.healthyfuturesforwomen.com/

Planned Parenthood—Fort Collins Health Center
825 S. Shields St., Suites 4–7, Fort Collins, CO
970-493-0281
https://www.plannedparenthood.org/health-center/colorado/fort-collins/80521/
    fort-collins-4087-90210

Planned Parenthood—Glenwood Springs Health Center
50923 Hwy. 6, Glenwood Springs, CO
970-945-8631
https://www.plannedparenthood.org/health-center/colorado/glenwood-springs/
    81601/glenwood-springs-2172-90210

Planned Parenthood—Greeley Health Center
3487B W. 10th St., Greeley, CO
970-352-4762
https://www.plannedparenthood.org/health-center/colorado/greeley/80634/
    greeley-2173-90210

Planned Parenthood—Littleton Health Center
131 W. County Line Rd., Littleton, CO
303-798-0963
https://www.plannedparenthood.org/health-center/colorado/littleton/80129/
    littleton-2485-90210

*Boulder Valley Women's Health Center—Longmont
82 21st Ave., Suite C, Longmont, CO
303-416-5914
https://www.boulderwomenshealth.org/

Planned Parenthood—Steamboat Springs Health Center
111 11th St. #102, Steamboat Springs, CO
970-879-2212
https://www.plannedparenthood.org/health-center/colorado/steamboat-springs/
    80487/steamboat-springs-2168-90210

POLITICAL, FUNDING, AND PRACTICAL SUPPORT GROUPS

Colorado Doula Project
https://www.coloradodoulaproject.org/

Colorado Organization for Latina Opportunity and Reproductive Rights [COLOR]
PO Box 40991, Denver, CO
303-393-0382
https://www.colorlatina.org/
info@colorlatina.org

NARAL Pro-Choice Colorado
PO Box 22485, Denver, CO
303-394-1973
https://prochoicecolorado.org/about/contact/

Colorado RCRC (Religious Coalition for Reproductive Choice)
PO Box 102464, Denver, CO
720-744-2672
www.corcrc.org
corcrc1@gmail.com

Planned Parenthood Votes Colorado
https://www.plannedparenthoodaction.org/planned-parenthood-votes-colorado

Northern Colorado NOW (Fort Collins)
http://www.noconow.org
info@noconow.org

Reproductive Equality Fund of the Boulder Valley Women's Health Center (Boulder)
2855 Valmont Rd., Boulder, CO
303-440-9320, ext. 26
https://abortionfunds.org/fund/reproductive-equality-fund-of-the-boulder-valley-
women%C2%90s-health-center/

Women's Freedom Fund
https://www.womensfreedomfund.org/for-patients/
support@womensfreedomfund.org

Connecticut (abortion is available in clinics in this state until viability, about twenty-four to twenty-six weeks' gestation)

CLINICS

Planned Parenthood—Bridgeport Health Center
4697 Main St., Bridgeport, CT
203-366-0664
https://www.plannedparenthood.org/health-center/connecticut/bridgeport/06606/
bridgeport-center-4275-90220

Planned Parenthood—Danbury Health Center
44 Main St., Danbury, CT
203-743-2446
https://www.plannedparenthood.org/health-center/connecticut/danbury/06810/
danbury-center-2539-90220

Planned Parenthood—Danielson Health Center
87 Westcott Rd., Danielson, CT
860-774-0533
https://www.plannedparenthood.org/health-center/connecticut/danielson/06239/
danielson-center-2218-90220

Planned Parenthood—Enfield Health Center
111 Hazard Ave., Enfield, CT
860-741-2197
https://www.plannedparenthood.org/health-center/connecticut/enfield/06082/
enfield-center-2219-90220

✽Hartford GYN Center
1 Main St., Suite N1, Hartford, CT
800-877-6335
http://thewomenscenters.com/hartfordgyncenter/

Planned Parenthood—Hartford North Center
1229 Albany Ave., Hartford, CT
860-728-0203
https://www.plannedparenthood.org/health-center/connecticut/hartford/06112/
    hartford-north-center-2220-90220

Planned Parenthood—West Hartford Health Center
1030 New Britain Ave., West Hartford, CT
860-953-6201
https://www.plannedparenthood.org/health-center/connecticut/west-hartford/06110/
    west-hartford-center-2216-90220

Planned Parenthood—Manchester Center
319B Main St., Manchester, CT
860-643-1607
https://www.plannedparenthood.org/health-center/connecticut/manchester/06040/
    manchester-center-2221-90220

Planned Parenthood—Meriden Center
26 Women's Way, Meriden, CT
203-238-0542
https://www.plannedparenthood.org/health-center/connecticut/meriden/06451/
    meriden-center-2543-90220

Planned Parenthood—New Haven Center
345 Whitney Ave., New Haven, CT
203-503-0450
https://www.plannedparenthood.org/health-center/connecticut/new-haven/06511/
    new-haven-center-3271-90220

Planned Parenthood—New London Center
45 Franklin St., New London, CT
860-443-5820
https://www.plannedparenthood.org/health-center/connecticut/new-london/06320/
    new-london-center-2223-90220

Planned Parenthood—Norwich Center
12 Case St., Norwich, CT
860-889-5211
https://www.plannedparenthood.org/health-center/connecticut/norwich/06360/
    norwich-center-2217-90220

Planned Parenthood—Old Saybrook Center
263 Main St., Old Saybrook, CT
860-388-4459
https://www.plannedparenthood.org/health-center/connecticut/old-saybrook/06475/
    old-saybrook-center-2225-90220

Planned Parenthood—Stamford Center
35 Sixth St., Stamford, CT
203-327-2722
https://www.plannedparenthood.org/health-center/connecticut/stamford/06902/
stamford-center-2536-90220

Planned Parenthood—Torrington Center
249 Winsted Rd., Torrington, CT
860-489-5500
https://www.plannedparenthood.org/health-center/connecticut/torrington/06790/
torrington-center-2222-90220

Planned Parenthood—Waterbury Center
969 W. Main St., Waterbury, CT
203-753-2119
https://www.plannedparenthood.org/health-center/connecticut/waterbury/06708/
waterbury-center-2540-90220

Planned Parenthood—Willimantic Health Center
1548 W. Main St., Willimantic, CT
860-423-8426
https://www.plannedparenthood.org/health-center/connecticut/willimantic/06226/
willimantic-center-2224-90220

POLITICAL, FUNDING, AND PRACTICAL SUPPORT GROUPS

NARAL Pro-Choice Connecticut
1 Main St., Suite T4, Hartford, CT
203-787-8763
info@prochoicect.org

RCRC of Connecticut (Religious Coalition of Reproductive Choice)
c/o Temple Emanuel of Greater New Haven
150 Derby Ave., Orange, CT
646-533-2192
Rcrcofct@aol.com

Planned Parenthood Votes! Connecticut
https://www.plannedparenthoodaction.org/planned-parenthood-votes-connecticut

Connecticut NOW
https://www.facebook.com/CTNOWChapter/

Delaware (abortion can be obtained in clinics in this state until fifteen weeks six days' gestation)

CLINICS

Planned Parenthood—Dover Center
805 S. Governors Ave., Dover, DE
302-678-5200
https://www.plannedparenthood.org/health-center/delaware/dover/19901/dover-center-2896-90240

Planned Parenthood—Wilmington Center
625 N. Shipley St., Wilmington, DE
302-655-7293
https://www.plannedparenthood.org/health-center/delaware/wilmington/19801/wilmington-center-de-3272-90240

POLITICAL, FUNDING, AND PRACTICAL SUPPORT GROUPS
Planned Parenthood Advocacy Fund of Delaware
https://ppadvocacydelaware.org/
https://www.facebook.com/pg/plannedparenthooddelaware/
https://www.facebook.com/PPAdvocacyDE

Florida (abortion is available in clinics until around twenty-four to twenty-six weeks' gestation)

CLINICS

✳All Women's Health Center of Orlando Inc.
431 Maitland Ave., Altamonte Springs, FL
888-257-2262
http://www.floridaabortion.com/profile/all-womens-health-center-of-orlando-altamonte-springs

Planned Parenthood—Boca Raton Health Center
8177 Glades Rd., Bay 25, Boca Raton, FL
561-226-4116
https://www.plannedparenthood.org/health-center/florida/boca-raton/33434/boca-raton-health-center-3863-90320

Office of Dr. Philip F. Waterman II MD FACOG
650 Del Prado Blvd. #100, Cape Coral, FL
239-574-8200
http://www.philipwatermanmd.com/

✱All Women's Health Center of Clearwater
28960 US Hwy. 19 N. #110, Clearwater, FL
800-827-0082
http://www.floridaabortion.com/locations/clearwater.shtml

Woman's Health Centers—Bread and Roses Health Center
1560 S. Highland Ave., Clearwater, FL
727-446-2690
http://www.tampabayabortionclinics.com/

Fort Lauderdale Abortion Clinic
2001 W. Oakland Park Blvd., Fort Lauderdale, FL
877-966-3673
http://www.womenscenter.com/fort_lauderdale_womens_center.html

✱Fort Meyers Women's Health Center
3900 Broadway Blvd., Bldg. C, Fort Meyers, FL
239-936-4494
800-733-4494
https://www.floridaabortion.com/profile/ft-myers-womens-health-center/

A Woman's World Medical Center
503 S. 12th St., Fort Pierce, FL
800-226-1506
http://www.awwmc.com/

✱All Women's Health Center of Gainesville
1135 NW 23rd Ave., Suite N, Gainesville, FL
800-869-0440
http://www.floridaabortion.com/profile/all-womens-health-center-of-gainesville

✱Bread and Roses Women's Health Center
1233 NW 10th Ave., Gainesville, FL
844-490-2660
http://www.breadroses.com/

A Woman's Choice of Jacksonville
4131 University Blvd. S., Bldg. 2, Jacksonville, FL
800-298-8874
https://www.awomanschoiceinc.com/awc-jacksonville/

✳All Women's Health Center of Jacksonville
1545 Huffingham Rd., Jacksonville, FL
800-733-2755
http://www.floridaabortion.com/profile/all-womens-health-center-of-jacksonville

Planned Parenthood—Jacksonville Health Center
5978 Powers Ave., Jacksonville, FL
904-399-2800
https://www.plannedparenthood.org/health-center/florida/jacksonville/32217/
    jacksonville-health-center-3278-90320

Planned Parenthood—Kissimmee Health Center
610 Oak Commons Blvd., Kissimmee, FL
407-246-1788
https://www.plannedparenthood.org/health-center/florida/kissimmee/34741/
    kissimmee-health-center-4144-90300

✳Lakeland Women's Health Center
4444 S. Florida Ave., Lakeland, FL
800-733-7541
http://www.floridaabortion.com/profile/lakeland-womens-health-center

A Woman's Care
68 NE 167th St., Miami, FL
305-947-0885
http://www.awomanscare.com/

Eve Women's Medical Center—Kendall Plaza
8603 S. Dixie Hwy., Suite 102, Miami, FL
305-670-9797
http://www.eveabortioncarespecialists.com/

Eve Women's Medical Center—79th Ave.
3900 NW 79th Ave. #575, Miami, FL
305-591-2288
http://www.eveabortioncarespecialists.com/

Planned Parenthood—Golden Glades-Miami Health Center
585 NW 161 St. Suites 200–300, Miami, FL
305-830-4111
https://www.plannedparenthood.org/health-center/florida/miami/33169/golden-
    glades-miami-health-center-4183-90320

Planned Parenthood—Jean Shehan Health Center
1378 Coral Way, 4th Floor, Miami, FL
305-285-5535
https://www.plannedparenthood.org/health-center/florida/miami/33145/jean-shehan-
    health-center-3369-90320

University of Miami—Department of Obstetrics & Gynecology—Reproductive
Health Services Clinic
1400 NW 12th Ave., Miami, FL
305-243-2984
http://obgyn.med.miami.edu/reproductive-health

Planned Parenthood—Naples Center
1425 Creech Rd., Naples, FL
239-262-0301
https://www.plannedparenthood.org/health-center/florida/naples/34103/naples-
center-3294-90300

Women and Teens Healthcare
16876 NE 19th Ave., North Miami Beach, FL
305-895-5555
https://womenandteens.com/

Ocala Women's Center
108 NW Pine Ave., Ocala, FL
877-622-5234
http://www.womenscenter.com/ocala_womens_center.html

✱All Women's Health Center of Orlando
1800 Pembrook Dr. #300, Orlando, FL
800-203-2135
http://www.floridaabortion.com/profile/all-womens-health-center

EPOC Abortion Clinic
609 Virginia Dr., Orlando, FL
877-376-2227
http://www.womenscenter.com/epoc_clinic.html

Orlando Women's Center/Abortion Clinic
1103 Lucerne Ter., Orlando, FL
877-692-2273
http://www.womenscenter.com/orlando_womens_center.html

Planned Parenthood—Downtown Orlando Health Center
726 S. Tampa Ave., Orlando, FL
407-246-1788
https://www.plannedparenthood.org/health-center/florida/orlando/32805/
downtown-orlando-health-center-3275-90300

Planned Parenthood—Pembroke Pines Health Center
263 N. University Dr., Pembroke Pines, FL
954-989-5747
https://www.plannedparenthood.org/health-center/florida/pembroke-pines/33024/
pembroke-pines-health-center-3917-90320

Aastra Women's Center
10 SW 44th Ave., Plantation, FL
954-792-9198
http://www.aastrawomenscenter.com/

✳Michael Benjamin, MD BSSI
7777 N. University Dr. #102, Fort Lauderdale, FL
954-720-7777
http://drbenjamin.com/

Venice Woman's Health Center: Azima Ali MD
21178 Olean Blvd., Suite C, Port Charlotte, FL
941-629-3646
http://www.swflwomensclinic.com/home

✳All Women's Health Center of Sarasota
2700 S. Tamiami Trl. #5, Sarasota, FL
800-347-7066
http://www.floridaabortion.com/profile/all-womens-health-center-of-sarasota/

Planned Parenthood—Sarasota Health Center
736 Central Ave., Sarasota, FL
941-953-4060
https://www.plannedparenthood.org/health-center/florida/sarasota/34236/saraso-
ta-health-center-2189-90300

✳All Women's Health Center—St. Petersburg
4131 Central Ave., St. Petersburg, FL
800-736-6656
http://www.floridaabortion.com/profile/all-womens-health-center-st-petersburg/

Woman's Health Centers—St. Petersburg Health Center
3401 66th St. N., St. Petersburg, FL
727-381-6620
http://www.tampabayabortionclinics.com/

Planned Parenthood—Martin County Health Center
1322 NW Federal Hwy., Emerald Plaza, Stuart, FL
772-692-2023
https://www.plannedparenthood.org/health-center/florida/stuart/34994/martin-
county-health-center-2269-90320

North Florida Women's Health
1345 Cross Creek Cir., Tallahassee, FL
850-877-3183
http://aboutabortion.org/

✱All Women's Health Center of North Tampa
14498 University Cove Pl., Tampa, FL
800-733-7907
http://www.floridaabortion.com/profile/all-womens-health-center-of-north-tampa/

✱All Women's Health Center of Tampa
3330 W. Kennedy Blvd., Tampa, FL
800-736-0505
http://www.floridaabortion.com/profile/all-womens-health-center-of-tampa

Planned Parenthood—Tampa Health Center
8068 N. 56th St., Tampa, FL
813-980-3555
https://www.plannedparenthood.org/health-center/florida/tampa/33617/tampa-
     health-center-2247-90300

Woman's Health Centers—Tampa Health Center
2010 E. Fletcher Ave., Tampa, FL
813-977-6176
http://www.tampabayabortionclinics.com/

Women's Center of Hyde Park/Tampa Abortion Clinic
502 S. Magnolia Ave., Tampa, FL
855-214-9964
http://www.womenscenter.com/womens_center_hyde_park.html

Planned Parenthood—Wellington Health Center
10111 Forest Hill Blvd., Suite 340, Wellington, FL
561-296-4919
https://www.plannedparenthood.org/health-center/florida/wellington/33414/
     wellington-health-center-4066-90320

Presidential Women's Center
100 Northpoint Pkwy., West Palm Beach, FL
800-273-3047
https://presidentialcenter.com/

POLITICAL, FUNDING, AND PRACTICAL SUPPORT GROUPS

The Florida Latina Advocacy Network (FL LAN)
http://latinainstitute.org/en/florida

Planned Parenthood Alliance of Florida Affiliates
https://www.plannedparenthoodaction.org/florida-alliance-planned-parenthood-affiliates

Florida NOW
https://flnow.org/

Broward Women's Emergency Fund
1965 S. Ocean Dr. #17, Hallandale Beach, FL
http://bwefund.org/

Central Florida Women's Emergency Fund
PO Box 536522, Orlando, FL
http://cflwef.org/
http://cflwef.org/donate.html

Emergency Medical Assistance Inc.
PO Box 33552, Palm Beach Gardens, FL
561-271-5164
http://www.emawpb.org/

North Florida Justice Fund
Jacksonville, FL
904-399-2800, ext. 133
https://abortionfunds.org/fund/north-florida-justice-fund/

Roe Fund
736 Central Ave., Sarasota, FL
941-567-3800
https://abortionfunds.org/fund/roe-fund/

W.O.M.E.N.
PO Box 82184, Tampa, FL
813-973-8524
https://abortionfunds.org/fund/w-o-m-e-n/

Women's Emergency Network
PO Box 566392, Miami, FL
305-670-2266
http://www.wen-online.org/

Georgia *(abortion can be obtained at clinics in this state until twenty-two weeks' gestation)*

CLINICS

A Preferred Women's Health—Atlanta
519 Forest Pkwy., Suite 100, Atlanta, GA
404-758-9900
http://www.apwhc.com/

✱Atlanta Women's Center
235 W. Wieuca Rd., NE, Atlanta, GA
800-877-6332
http://thewomenscenters/atlantawomenscenter/

✱carafem
1800 Peachtree St. NW, Suite 800, Atlanta, GA
877-828-8915
https://carafem.org/

Dunwoody Women's Medical Group
3114 Mercer University Dr., Suite 100, Atlanta, GA
800-586-9790
http://www.dunwoodywomensmedicalgroup.com/

✱Feminist Women's Health Center
1924 Cliff Valley Way NE, Atlanta, GA
800-877-6013
http://www.feministcenter.org/en/

✱Summit Medical Associates—Atlanta
1874 Piedmont Ave. NE 500-E, Atlanta, GA
800-537-2985
https://www.summitcenters.com/atlanta-abortion-clinic/

A Preferred Women's Health—Augusta
2903 Professional Pkwy., Augusta, GA
706-228-4545
http://www.apwhc.com/

Columbus Women's Health Organization
3850 Rosemont Dr., Columbus, GA
706-323-8363
http://columbuswomenshealth.com/

Planned Parenthood—Gwinnett Health Center (medication only)
798 Lawrenceville Suwanee Rd., Suite 300, Lawrenceville, GA
404-688-9300
https://www.plannedparenthood.org/health-center/georgia/lawrenceville/30043/
gwinnett-center-2271-90330

Planned Parenthood—Cobb Health Center (medication only)
220 Cobb Pkwy. N., Suite 500, Marietta, GA
404-688-9300
https://www.plannedparenthood.org/health-center/georgia/marietta/30062/
cobb-center-2270-90330

Savannah Medical Clinic
120 E. 34th St., Savannah, GA
800-247-4424
http://savannahmedicalclinic.com/

POLITICAL, FUNDING, AND PRACTICAL SUPPORT GROUPS

SisterSong
1237 Ralph David Abernathy Blvd., Atlanta, GA
404-756-2680; 866-750-7733
https://www.sistersong.net/
info@sistersong.net

SPARK Reproductive Justice Now
PO Box 89210, Atlanta, GA
404-331-3250
http://www.sparkrj.org/
info@sparkrj.org

SisterLove
PO Box 10558, Atlanta, GA
404-505-7777
https://www.sisterlove.org/
info@sisterlove.org

National Asian Pacific American Women's Forum—Atlanta Chapter
https://www.napawf.org/atlantachapter.html
atlantaleaders@napawf.org

NARAL Pro-Choice Georgia
202-973-3000
http://prochoicegeorgia.org
georgia@prochoiceamerica.org

Access Reproductive Care—Southeast (ARC Southeast)
PO Box 7354, Atlanta, GA
855-227-2475
http://www.arc-southeast.org/

Planned Parenthood Southeast Advocates
https://www.plannedparenthoodaction.org/planned-parenthood-southeast-advocates

Georgia NOW
https://www.georgia-now.org/

Women in Need Fund
75 Piedmont Ave. NE, Suite 800, Atlanta, GA

Hawaii (abortion is available in clinics until thirteen weeks six days' gestation)

CLINICS

Planned Parenthood—Honolulu Health Center
1350 S. King St., Suite 310, Honolulu, HI
808-589-1149
https://www.plannedparenthood.org/health-center/hawaii/honolulu/96814/
honolulu-health-center-2951-91810

Planned Parenthood—Kahului Health Center
140 Hoohana St., Suite 303, Maui, HI
808-871-1176
https://www.plannedparenthood.org/health-center/hawaii/kahului/96732/maui-
health-center-2950-91810

POLITICAL, FUNDING, AND PRACTICAL SUPPORT GROUPS

Northwest Abortion Access Fund (NWAAF) (Northwest and Hawaii)
https://nwaafund.org/travelhelp/
866-692-2310, ext. 3

Planned Parenthood Votes Northwest and Hawaii
2001 E. Madison St., Seattle, WA
https://www.plannedparenthoodaction.org/planned-parenthood-votes-northwest-
and-hawaii
ppaction@ppvnh.org

Idaho (abortion is available at clinics in this state until fifteen weeks six days' gestation)

CLINICS

Planned Parenthood—Boise Health Center (medication only)
3668 North Harbor Ln., Boise, ID
800-769-0045
https://www.plannedparenthood.org/health-center/idaho/boise/83703/boise-health-center-2939-91810

Planned Parenthood—Meridian Health Center
2112 E. Franklin Rd., Meridian, ID
800-769-0045
https://www.plannedparenthood.org/health-center/idaho/meridian/83642/meridian-health-center-4105-91810

Planned Parenthood—Twin Falls Health Center (medication only)
200 Second Ave. N., Twin Falls, ID
800-769-0045
https://www.plannedparenthood.org/health-center/idaho/twin-falls/83301/twin-falls-health-center-2938-91810

POLITICAL, FUNDING, AND PRACTICAL SUPPORT GROUPS

Northwest Abortion Access Fund (NWAAF) (Northwest and Hawaii)
https://nwaafund.org/travelhelp/
866-692-2310, ext. 3

Planned Parenthood Votes Northwest and Hawaii
2001 E. Madison St., Seattle, WA
https://www.plannedparenthoodaction.org/planned-parenthood-votes-northwest-and-hawaii
ppaction@ppvnh.org

Planned Parenthood Advocates of Greater Washington and North Idaho
https://www.plannedparenthoodaction.org/planned-parenthood-advocates-greater-washington-and-north-idaho

Idaho NOW
https://www.facebook.com/SWIdahoNOW/

Illinois (abortion is available in this state until viability, about twenty-four to twenty-six weeks' gestation)

CLINICS

Planned Parenthood—Aurora Health Center
3051 E. New York St., Aurora, IL
630-585-0500
https://www.plannedparenthood.org/health-center/illinois/aurora/60504/aurora-health-center-3483-90430

Planned Parenthood—Fairview Heights Health Center (medication only)
Lakeland Square
4529 N. Illinois St., Belleville, IL
618-277-6668
https://www.plannedparenthood.org/health-center/illinois/belleville/62226/fairview-heights-health-center-2712-90770

Planned Parenthood—Champaign Health Center (medication only)
302 E. Stoughton St., Suite 2, Champaign, IL
217-359-8022
https://www.plannedparenthood.org/health-center/illinois/champaign/61820/champaign-health-center-3283-90430

Women's Health Practice
2125 S. Neil St., Champaign, IL
217-356-3736
http://www.womenshealthpractice.com/

American Women's Medical Center
2744 N. Western Ave., Chicago, IL
773-772-7726
http://www.americanwomensmedicalcenter.com/

✳Chicago Women's Health Center
1025 W. Sunnyside, Suite 201, Chicago, IL
773-935-6126
http://www.chicagowomenshealthcenter.org/

Family Planning Associates—Downtown Chicago
659 W. Washington Blvd., Chicago, IL
312-462-1846
http://fpachicago.com/about-us/downtown-chicago-abortion-clinic/

Family Planning Associates—Northwest Chicago
4341 N. Milwaukee Ave., Chicago, IL
773-362-5465
http://fpachicago.com/northwest-chicago-womens-health-clinic/

Michigan Avenue Center for Health
2415 S. Michigan Ave., Chicago, IL
877-674-0100
http://www.michiganavenuecenterforhealth.com/

Planned Parenthood—Austin Health Center (medication only)
5937 W. Chicago Ave., Chicago, IL
773-287-2020
https://www.plannedparenthood.org/health-center/illinois/chicago/60651/
austin-health-center-2265-90430

Planned Parenthood—Loop Health Center (medication only)
18 S. Michigan Ave., 6th Floor, Chicago, IL
877-200-7745
https://www.plannedparenthood.org/health-center/illinois/chicago/60603/loop-
health-center-3286-90430

Planned Parenthood—Near North Health Center
1200 N. LaSalle St., Chicago, IL
312-266-1033
https://www.plannedparenthood.org/health-center/illinois/chicago/60610/near-
north-health-center-2474-90430

Planned Parenthood—Roseland Health Center
11250 S. Halsted St., Chicago, IL
877-200-7745
https://www.plannedparenthood.org/health-center/illinois/chicago/60628/roseland-
health-center-2263-90430

Ryan Center Clinic
5758 S. Maryland Ave., Chicago, IL
773-834-9995
http://familyplanning.uchicago.edu/page/ryan-center

✱Women's Aid Center
4801 Peterson Ave. #609, Chicago, IL
800-998-4751
http://www.womensaidcenter.com/

Planned Parenthood—Decatur Health Center (medication only)
3021 N. Oakland Ave., Decatur, IL
217-877-6474
https://www.plannedparenthood.org/health-center/illinois/decatur/62526/decatur-
health-center-3282-90430

American Women's Medical Center—Des Plaines
110 S. River Rd. #7, Des Plaines, IL
847-294-9614
http://www.americanwomensmedicalcenter.com/

Access Health Clinic
1700 75th St., Downers Grove, IL
800-403-3033
http://www.accesshealthcenter.net/

Planned Parenthood—Englewood Health Center (medication only)
6059 S. Ashland Ave., Chicago, IL
773-434-3700
https://www.plannedparenthood.org/health-center/illinois/chicago/60636/
englewood-health-center-2264-90430

Aanchor Health Center
1186 Roosevelt Rd., Glen Ellyn, IL
888-910-4400
http://www.aanchorhealthcenter.com/

✱Hope Clinic for Women
1602 21st St., Granite City, IL
618-451-5722
http://www.hopeclinic.com/

Planned Parenthood—Ottawa Health Center (medication only)
612 Court St., Ottawa, IL
815-433-4111
https://www.plannedparenthood.org/health-center/illinois/ottawa/61350/ottawa-
health-center-2631-90430

✱Whole Women's Health of Peoria
7405 N. University St., Peoria, IL
309-691-9073

✱carafem Chicago Health Center
4711 Golf Rd., Suite 920, Skokie, IL
855-SAY-CARA
carafem.org/location/carafem-health-center-chicago

Planned Parenthood—Springfield Health Center
601 N. Bruns, Springfield, IL
217-544-2744
https://www.plannedparenthood.org/health-center/illinois/springfield/62702/
springfield-health-center-3284-90430

✱Advantage Health Care Ltd.
203 W. Irving Park Rd., Wood Dale, IL
888-795-1515
http://advantagehealthcareltd.com/

POLITICAL, FUNDING, AND PRACTICAL SUPPORT GROUPS

Illinois Choice Action Team
1333 W. Devon Ave. #253, Chicago IL
312-458-9169
info@ilchoiceactionteam.org

ICAT Clinic Escorts
1333 W. Devon Ave. #253, Chicago, IL
312-458-9169
escorts@ilchoiceactionteam.org

Illinois Caucus for Adolescent Health
719 S. State St., Floor 4, Chicago, IL
312-427-4460, ext. 234
https://www.icah.org
info@icah.org

Illinois RCRC (Religious Coalition for Reproductive Choice)
c/o UTUUC (or Unity Temple)
875 Lake St., Oak Park, IL
www.rcrcil.blogspot.com
rcrc_il@hotmail.com

Planned Parenthood Illinois Action
https://www.plannedparenthoodaction.org/planned-parenthood-illinois-action

National Asian Pacific American Women's Forum—Chicago Chapter
https://www.napawf.org/chicagochapter.html
chicagochapter@napawf.org

Illinois NOW
http://ilnow.org/

Chicago Abortion Fund
333 W. North Ave. Ste. 267, Chicago, IL
312-663-0338
http://www.chicagoabortionfund.com/

Planned Parenthood of Illinois Reproductive Justice Fund
18 S. Michigan Ave., 6th Floor, Chicago, IL
800-230-7526
https://www.plannedparenthood.org/planned-parenthood-illinois

Midwest Access Fund (MAC) (Chicago)—Practical Support
847-750-6224
https://midwestaccesscoalition.org/
info@midwestaccesscoalition.org

Indiana (abortion is available in clinics in this state until thirteen weeks six days' gestation)

CLINICS

Planned Parenthood—Bloomington Health Center
421 S. College Ave., Bloomington, IN
812-336-0219
https://www.plannedparenthood.org/health-center/indiana/bloomington/47403/
    bloomington-health-center-2639-90500

✱ Clinic for Women
3607 W. 16th St., Suite B-2, Indianapolis, IN
800-545-2400
http://clinic4women.net/

Planned Parenthood—Georgetown Health Center
8590 Georgetown Rd., Indianapolis, IN
317-872-3115; 800-230-7526
https://www.plannedparenthood.org/health-center/indiana/indianapolis/46268/
    georgetown-health-center-2870-90500

Women's Med Indianapolis
1201 N. Arlington Ave., Indianapolis, IN
800-382-9029
http://www.womensmed.com/

Planned Parenthood—Lafayette Health Center (medication only)
964 Mezzanine Dr., Lafayette, IN
765-446-8078
https://www.plannedparenthood.org/health-center/indiana/lafayette/47905/lafayette-health-center-2669-90500

Planned Parenthood—Merrillville Health Center
8645 Connecticut St., Merrillville, IN
219-769-3500
https://www.plannedparenthood.org/health-center/indiana/merrillville/46410/merrillville-health-center-2923-90500

POLITICAL, FUNDING, AND PRACTICAL SUPPORT GROUPS

IndyFeminists
https://www.facebook.com/IndyFems

All Options Pregnancy Resource Center
1014 Walnut St., Bloomington, IN
812-558-0089
https://alloptionsprc.org/

Indiana RCRC (Religious Coalition for Reproductive Choice)
PO Box 723, Lafayette, IN
317-721-5386
https://www.facebook.com/ircrc/
info@ircrc.org

Planned Parenthood Advocates of Indiana and Kentucky
https://www.plannedparenthoodaction.org/planned-parenthood-advocates-indiana-and-kentucky-inc

Indiana NOW
https://www.facebook.com/IndianaNOW/

Hoosier Abortion Fund (via All Options Pregnancy Center)
1014 S. Walnut, Bloomington, IN
812-558-0089
http://alloptionsprc.org

Iowa (abortion is available in clinics up to twenty-one weeks six days' gestation)

CLINICS

Planned Parenthood—Ames Health Center (medication only)
2530 Chamberlain St., Ames, IA
877-811-7526
https://www.plannedparenthood.org/health-center/iowa/ames/50014/ames-center-2385-90380

Planned Parenthood—Cedar Falls Health Center (medication only)
2520 Melrose Dr., Suite L, Cedar Falls, IA
877-811-7526
https://www.plannedparenthood.org/health-center/iowa/cedar-falls/50613/cedar-falls-center-2866-90380

Planned Parenthood—Council Bluffs Health Center (medication only)
1604 2nd Ave., Council Bluffs, IA
877-811-7526
https://www.plannedparenthood.org/health-center/iowa/council-bluffs/51501/council-bluffs-health-center-3683-90380

Planned Parenthood—Rosenfield Center
1000 E. Army Post Rd., Des Moines, IA
877-811-7526
https://www.plannedparenthood.org/health-center/iowa/des-moines/50315/rosenfield-center-2386-90380

✱The Emma Goldman Clinic
227 N. Dubuque St., Iowa City, IA
800-848-7684
http://www.emmagoldman.com/information/abortion.html

Planned Parenthood—Iowa City Health Center
850 Orchard St., Iowa City, IA
877-811-7526
https://www.plannedparenthood.org/health-center/iowa/iowa-city/52246/iowa-city-health-center-2470-90380

POLITICAL, FUNDING, AND PRACTICAL SUPPORT GROUPS

NARAL Pro-Choice Iowa
202-973-3000
iowa@prochoiceamerica.org

Planned Parenthood Voters of Iowa
https://www.plannedparenthoodaction.org/planned-parenthood-voters-iowa

Iowa NOW
http://www.iowanow.org/

deProsse Access Fund of the Emma Goldman Clinic
227 N. Dubuque St., Iowa City, IA
319-337-2111
http://emmagoldman.com/

Iowa Abortion Access Fund
PO Box 721, Cedar Rapids, IA
http://www.iaafund.org/

Kansas (Abortion is available in clinics until twenty-one weeks six days' gestation)

CLINICS

Center for Women's Health
4840 College Blvd., Overland Park, KS
800-733-2404
http://www.hodesnauser.com/

Planned Parenthood—Comprehensive Health Services
4401 W. 109th St. #100, Overland Park, KS
913-345-1400
https://www.plannedparenthood.org/health-center/kansas/overland-park/66211/
comprehensive-health-center-2594-90740

Planned Parenthood—Wichita Health Center (medication only)
2226 E. Central, Wichita, KS
316-263-7575
https://www.plannedparenthood.org/health-center/kansas/wichita/67214/
wichita-health-center-2876-90741

✱South Wind Women's Health Center Wichita (Trust Women)
5107 E. Kellogg Dr., Wichita, KS
316-260-6934
http://www.southwindwomenscenter.org/

POLITICAL, FUNDING, AND PRACTICAL SUPPORT GROUPS

Trust Women PAC
PO Box 3222, Wichita, KS
316-425-3215
http://www.trustwomenpac.org/

Planned Parenthood Great Plains Votes
http://www.ppgpvotes.org/

Peggy Bowman Second Chance Fund
PO Box 1093, Lawrence, KS
785-760-3959
http://www.secondchancefund.net/

Kentucky (abortion is available in clinic until twenty-one weeks six days' gestation)

CLINICS

✱EMW Women's Surgical Center
136 W. Market St., Louisville, KY
502-589-2124; 800-626-3512
http://www.emwwomens.com/

POLITICAL, FUNDING, AND PRACTICAL SUPPORT GROUPS

A Fund, Inc.
PO Box 221286, Louisville, KY
http://kyafund.org/

Kentucky Health Justice Network
PO Box 4761, Louisville, KY
855-576-4576
http://www.kentuckyhealthjusticenetwork.org/

Kentucky RCRC (Religious Council for Reproductive Choice)
PO Box 4065, Louisville, KY
866-606-0988
www.krcrc.org
info@krcrc.org

Planned Parenthood Advocates of Indiana and Kentucky
https://www.plannedparenthoodaction.org/planned-parenthood-advocates-
indiana-and-kentucky-inc

Kentucky NOW
https://www.facebook.com/KentuckyNOW

Every Saturday Morning (clinic escorting)
https://everysaturdaymorning.net/
everysaturdaymorning@gmail.com

Louisiana (abortion is available in clinics until twenty weeks' gestation)

CLINICS

Delta Clinic of Baton Rouge
756 Colonial Dr., Baton Rouge, LA
225-923-3242
http://iguana-workspace.com/dcbr/

✱Hope Medical Group for Women
210 Kings Hwy., Shreveport, LA
800-448-5004
http://www.hopemedical.com/

Women's Health Care Center
2701 General Pershing St., New Orleans, LA
504-899-6010
http://www.womenshealthcarecenter.com/

POLITICAL, FUNDING, AND PRACTICAL SUPPORT GROUPS

Lift Louisiana
PO Box 792063, New Orleans, LA
504-484-9636
http://liftlouisiana.org/

Women with a Vision
1226 N. Broad St., New Orleans, LA
504-301-0428
http://wwav-no.org/

Louisiana NOW
https://www.facebook.com/groups/LouisianaNOW/

Plan B NOLA (New Orleans Area)
504-264-3656
https://www.planbnola.com/

New Orleans Abortion Fund
PO Box 770141, New Orleans, LA
504-363-1112
http://neworleansabortionfund.org/

Maine (abortion is available in clinic up to eighteen weeks six days' gestation)

CLINICS

✱Maine Family Planning—Abortion Care: Center for Reproductive Health
43 Gabriel Dr., Augusta, ME
207-922-3222

✱Mabel Wadsworth Health Center
700 Mt. Hope Ave. #420, Bangor, ME
800-948-5337
https://www.mabelwadsworth.org/

Maine Family Planning (medication only)
68 Mt. Hope Ave., Bangor, ME
207-922-3440

Maine Family Planning—Calais Center (medication only)
43 Union St., Calais, ME
207-853-8930

Maine Family Planning—Damariscotta Center (medication only)
767 Main St., Damariscotta, ME
207-563-1224

Maine Family Planning—Dexter Center (medication only)
311 Corinna Rd., Dexter, ME
207-924-7383

Maine Family Planning—Ellsworth Center and Primary Care (medication only)
248 State St. #3a, Ellsworth, ME
207-812-7030

Maine Family Planning—Farmington Center (medication only)
193 Front St., Farmington, ME
207-778-4553

Maine Family Planning—Fort Kent Center (medication only)
139 Market St., Fort Kent, ME
207-402-3220

Maine Family Planning—Houlton Center (medication only)
91 Military St., Suite B, Houlton, ME
207-254-4050

Maine Family Planning—Lewiston Center (medication only)
179 Lisbon St., Lewiston, ME
207-795-4007

Maine Family Planning—Machias Center (medication only)
247 Main St. #2, Machias, ME
207-402-3230

Maine Family Planning—Norway Center (medication only)
9 Marston St., Norway, ME
207-743-2066

Maine Family Planning—Presque Isle Center (medication only)
5 Martin St., Presque Isle, ME
207-768-3062

Planned Parenthood—Portland Health Center
443 Congress St., 2nd Floor, Portland, ME
207-797-8881
https://www.plannedparenthood.org/health-center/maine/portland/04101/portland-
health-center-2940-91770

Maine Family Planning—Rockland Center (medication only)
22 White St. #101, Rockland, ME
207-594-3114

Maine Family Planning—Rumford Center (medication only)
218 Penobscot St., Rumford, ME
207-364-3960

Maine Family Planning—Skowhegan Center (medication only)
188 Madison Ave., Skowhegan, ME
207-612-5000

Maine Family Planning—Waterville Center (medication only)
18 Silver St., Waterville, ME
207-509-3267

POLITICAL, FUNDING, AND PRACTICAL SUPPORT GROUPS

Mable Wadsworth Center
700 Mount Hope Ave., Suite 420, Bangor, ME
207-947-5337
https://www.mabelwadsworth.org/get-involved/

Planned Parenthood Maine Action Fund
https://www.plannedparenthoodaction.org/planned-parenthood-maine-action-fund

Maryland (abortions are available in clinic until twenty-two weeks' gestation, and a later abortion can be obtained at ACO in Bethesda)

CLINICS

Planned Parenthood—Annapolis Health Center
929 West St. #305, Annapolis, MD
410-576-1414
https://www.plannedparenthood.org/health-center/maryland/annapolis/21401/
   annapolis-health-center-2834-90620

✱Whole Women's Health of Baltimore
7648 Belair Rd., Nottingham, MD
410-661-2900

Planned Parenthood—Baltimore City Health Center
330 N. Howard St., Baltimore, MD
410-576-1414
https://www.plannedparenthood.org/health-center/maryland/baltimore/21201/
   baltimore-city-health-center-3292-90620

Potomac Family Planning—Hillcrest Clinic
5602 Baltimore National Pike #600, Baltimore, MD
800-427-2813
http://potomacfamilyplanning.com/

✻ACO Bethesda (late-second- and third-trimester abortions available on an
    individual basis)
10401 Old Georgetown Rd., Suite 104, Bethesda, MD
888-684-3599
http://abortionclinics.org/clinics/bethesda-maryland.html

✻carafem
5530 Wisconsin Ave., Chevy Chase, MD
855-211-1030; 877-708-2423
https://carafem.org/

Planned Parenthood—Easton Health Center (medication only)
8579 Commerce Dr. #102, Easton, MD
410-576-1414
https://www.plannedparenthood.org/health-center/maryland/easton/21601/easton-
    health-center,-md-2830-90620

Planned Parenthood—Gaithersburg Health Center (medication only)
19650 Clubhouse Rd. #104, Gaithersburg, MD
301-208-1300
https://www.plannedparenthood.org/health-center/maryland/gaithersburg/20879/
    gaithersburg-center-2493-90230

Potomac Family Planning—Hagerstown Clinic
160 W. Washington St. #100, Hagerstown, MD
800-773-9140
http://potomacfamilyplanning.com/

Femi-Care Surgery Center
66 Painters Mill Rd. #106, Owings Mill, MD
443-394-0523
https://femicaresurgery.com/

Potomac Family Planning—Rockville Clinic
966 Hungerford Dr. #24, Rockville, MD
800-260-CHOICE (2464)
http://potomacfamilyplanning.com/

Gynemed Surgery Center
17 Fontana Ln. #201, Rosedale, MD
877-686-8220
https://www.gynemed.org/

Silver Spring Family Planning
1111 Spring St., Silver Spring, MD
240-691-4390
http://www.silverspringwomenscare.com/

Planned Parenthood—Prince George's County (medication only)
5001 Silver Hill Rd., Suitland, MD
301-241-0590
https://www.plannedparenthood.org/health-center/maryland/suitland/20746/
planned-parenthood--prince-george%E2%80%99s-county-4198-90230

POLITICAL, FUNDING, AND PRACTICAL SUPPORT GROUPS

NARAL Pro-Choice Maryland
8905 Fairview Rd., Suite 401, Silver Spring, MD
301-565-4154
info@prochoicemd.org

Maryland NOW
https://marylandnow.org/

Baltimore Abortion Fund
Baltimore, MD
443-297-9893
http://www.baltimoreabortionfund.org

Massachusetts (abortion is available in clinic until twenty weeks six days' gestation)

CLINICS

Four Women Health Services
150 Emory St., Attlesboro, MA
508-222-7555
http://www.fourwomen.com/

✱HealthQuarters—Beverly
100 Cummings Center, Suite 131-Q, Beverly, MA
978-705-4039
https://healthq.org/contact/beverly-ma.html

Planned Parenthood—Greater Boston Health Center
1055 Commonwealth Ave., Boston, MA
800-258-4448
https://www.plannedparenthood.org/health-center/massachusetts/boston/02215/
greater-boston-health-center-3293-90610

Reproductive Health Care Services for Women
1180 Beacon St., Suite 5B, Brookline, MA
888-410-3678
http://www.abortion-clinic-boston.com/

Women's Health Services
111 Harvard St., Brookline, MA
617-277-0009
http://womenshealthservice.com/

HealthQuarters—Haverhill
215 Summer St., Suite 16, Haverhill, MA
978-228-2291
https://healthq.org/contact/haverhill-ma.html

Merrimack Valley Women's Health Services
288 Groveland St., Haverhill, MA
978-688-7222
http://www.merrimackvalleywomenshealth.com/

HealthQuarters—Lawrence
Riverwalk Properties
280 Merrimack St., Suite 501, Lawrence, MA
978-705-6637
https://healthq.org/contact/lawrence-ma.html

North Shore Women's Center
480 Lynnfield St., Lynn, MA
781-595-4800
http://www.northshorewomenscenter.com/index.html

Planned Parenthood—Western Massachusetts Health Center
3550 Main St., Suite 201, Springfield, MA
800-258-4448
https://www.plannedparenthood.org/health-center/massachusetts/springfield/01107/
western-massachusetts-health-center-2662-90610

Planned Parenthood—Central Massachusetts Health Center
470 Pleasant St., Worcester, MA
800-258-4448
https://www.plannedparenthood.org/health-center/massachusetts/worcester/01609/
central-massachusetts-health-center-2660-90610

POLITICAL, FUNDING, AND PRACTICAL SUPPORT GROUPS

NARAL Pro-Choice Massachusetts
15 Court Sq., Suite 900, Boston, MA
617-556-8800
choice@prochoicemass.org

National Asian Pacific American Women's Forum—Boston Chapter
https://www.napawf.org/bostonchapter.html
bostonleaders@napawf.org

Planned Parenthood Advocacy Fund of Massachusetts
https://www.plannedparenthoodaction.org/planned-parenthood-advocacy-fund-
    massachusetts-inc

Massachusetts NOW
http://www.massnow.org/

Eastern Massachusetts Abortion Fund
617-354-3839
http://www.emafund.org

Jane Fund of Central Massachusetts
PO Box 562, Holden, MA
508-829-7300
http://www.janefund.org/

Abortion Rights Fund of Western Massachusetts
Amherst, MA
413-582-3532
http://arfwm.org/

Michigan (abortion is available in clinics up to twenty-four weeks' gestation)

CLINICS

Planned Parenthood—Ann Arbor Health Center
3100 Professional Dr., Ann Arbor, MI
734-973-0710
https://www.plannedparenthood.org/health-center/michigan/ann-arbor/48104/ann-
    arbor-health-center-3296-90630

Planned Parenthood—Detroit Health Center (medication only)
4229 Cass Ave., Detroit, MI
313-831-7776
https://www.plannedparenthood.org/health-center/michigan/detroit/48201/detroit-
  health-center-2890-90630

✻ Scotsdale Women's Center (medication only)
19305 W. 7 Mile Rd., Detroit, MI
313-538-2020
http://www.detroitabortioncenter.com/

✻ Summit Medical Center—Detroit Abortion Clinic
15801 W. McNichols Rd., Detroit, MI
800-482-4162
https://www.summitcenters.com/detroit-abortion-clinic/

Women's Center of Michigan—Detroit
15650 E. 8 Mile Rd., Detroit, MI
313-526-3600
http://womenscenterofmichigan.com/contact-us-in-detroit-michigan/

Eastland Women's Clinic
15921 E. 8 Mile Rd. #1, Eastpointe, MI
586-774-4190
http://eastlandwomensclinic.com/

Planned Parenthood—Flint Health Center
G-3371 Beecher Rd., Flint, MI
810-238-3631
https://www.plannedparenthood.org/health-center/michigan/flint/48532/flint-health-
  center-3298-90630

✻ Women's Center of Flint
3422 Flushing Rd., Flint, MI
810-230-1300
http://whcofmi.com/

Heritage Clinic for Women
320 Fulton St. E., Grand Rapids, MI
800-345-1393
https://www.heritageclinic.com/

Planned Parenthood—Irwin/Martin Health Center (medication only)
425 Cherry St. SE, Grand Rapids, MI
616-459-3101
https://www.plannedparenthood.org/health-center/michigan/grand-rapids/49503/
  irwin-martin-health-center-3295-90630

Planned Parenthood—Kalamazoo Health Center
4201 W. Michigan Ave., Kalamazoo, MI
269-372-1200
https://www.plannedparenthood.org/health-center/michigan/kalamazoo/49006/
kalamazoo-health-center-3299-90630

Planned Parenthood—Lansing Health Center (medication only)
300 N. Clippert, Suite 6, Lansing, MI
517-351-0550
https://www.plannedparenthood.org/health-center/michigan/lansing/48912/lansing-
health-center-2785-90630

WomenCare of Lansing
840 E. Mount Hope Ave., Suite 203, Lansing, MI
248-932-1777
http://www.womancarelansing.com/

Women's Center of Michigan—Southfield
28505 Southfield Rd., Lathrup Village, MI
248-569-7010
http://womenscenterofmichigan.com/contact-us-in-southfield-michigan/

Planned Parenthood—Marquette Health Center (medication only)
1219 N. Third St., Marquette, MI
906-225-5070
https://www.plannedparenthood.org/health-center/michigan/marquette/49855/
marquette-health-center-2605-90630

✱Women's Center of Saginaw
3141 Cabaret Trail S. #100, Saginaw, MI
989-790-1040
http://whcofmi.com/

✱Northland Family Planning Center—Southfield Abortion Clinic
24450 Evergreen Rd. #220, Southfield, MI
248-559-0590
http://northlandfamilyplanning.com/southfield

✱Northland Family Planning Center—Sterling Heights Abortion Clinic
3810 17 Mile Rd. #1, Sterling Heights, MI
586-268-1700
http://northlandfamilyplanning.com/sterling-heights

Women's Center of Michigan—Sterling Heights
11474 15 Mile Rd., Sterling Heights, MI
586-979-2190
http://womenscenterofmichigan.com/contact-us-in-southfield-michigan/

Planned Parenthood—Walker Health Center (medication only)
1135 E. Eighth St., Traverse City, MI
231-929-1844
https://www.plannedparenthood.org/health-center/michigan/traverse-city/49686/
    walker-health-center-3297-90630

Women's Center of Michigan—Warren Center
28477 Hoover Rd., Warren, MI
586-751-7247
http://womenscenterofmichigan.com/contact-us-in-warren-michigan/

West Bloomfield Michigan Abortion
6765 Orchard Lake Rd., West Bloomfield Township, MI
248-932-1777
http://womancare-abortion.com/west-bloomfield-michigan-abortion/

Women's Center of Michigan—West Bloomfield Center
6765 Orchard Lake Rd., West Bloomfield Township, MI
248-932-1777
http://womenscenterofmichigan.com/contact-us-in-west-bloomfield-michigan/

✱Northland Family Planning—Westland Abortion Clinic
35000 Ford Rd. #3, Westland, MI
734-721-4700
http://northlandfamilyplanning.com/westland

POLITICAL, FUNDING, AND PRACTICAL SUPPORT GROUPS

Reclaim
35000 Ford Rd., Suite 3, Westland, MI
https://www.reclaimproject.org/contact-us/

Planned Parenthood Advocates of Michigan
http://www.miplannedparenthood.org/

Michigan NOW
http://www.michnow.org/

In This Together (clinic escorting)
https://inthistogetherproject.com/
InThisTogetherProject@gmail.com

Michigan Women In Need Fund (MI WIN Fund)
https://www.reclaimproject.org/donorbox-abortion-funding

Fountain Street Church Choice Fund
24 Fountain St. NE, Grand Rapids, MI
http://www.fountainstreet.org/choice-fund

Jane Doe Fund
PO Box 4545, East Lansing, MI
517-336-7843

Minnesota (abortion is available in clinics until twenty-four weeks' gestation)

CLINICS

✱Women's Health Center of Duluth
32 E. 1st St. #300, Duluth, MN
800-735-7654
http://womenshealthcenterduluth.org/

Mildred Hanson MD
710 E. 24th St., Suite 403, Minneapolis, MN
877-870-1334
http://www.drmilliehanson.com/

Robbinsdale Clinic
3819 W. Broadway, Minneapolis, MN
763-533-2534
http://www.robbinsdaleclinic.com/index.htm

✱Whole Women's Health of the Twin Cities
825 S. 8th St. #1018, Minneapolis, MN
612-332-2311
https://wholewomanshealth.com/clinic/whole-womans-health-of-the-twin-cities/
#location

Planned Parenthood—St. Paul Health Center—Vandalia
671 Vandalia St., St. Paul, MN
651-698-2406
https://www.plannedparenthood.org/health-center/minnesota/st.-paul/55114/
st.-paul-health-center---vandalia-4055-90720

POLITICAL, FUNDING, AND PRACTICAL SUPPORT GROUPS

NARAL Pro-Choice Minnesota
2300 Myrtle Ave., Suite 120, Saint Paul, MN
651-602-765
info@prochoiceminnesota.org

Minnesota RCRC (Religious Council of Reproductive Choice)
PO Box 6966, Minneapolis, MN
612-870-0974
www.mnrcrc.org
info@mnrcrc.org

Planned Parenthood Minnesota Advocates
https://www.plannedparenthoodaction.org/planned-parenthood-minnesota-advocate

Minnesota NOW
https://mnnow.org/

National Asian Pacific American Women's Forum—St. Cloud Chapter
https://www.napawf.org/stcloudchapter.html
stcloudchapter@napawf.org

National Asian Pacific American Women's Forum—Twin Cities Chapter
https://www.napawf.org/twincitieschapter.html
twincitieschapter@napawf.org

HOTDISH Militia
Duluth, MN
218-727-3352

Our Justice's Abortion Assistance Fund
528 Hennepin Ave., Suite 600, Minneapolis, MN
612-825-2000, ext. 1
http://prochoiceresources.org/abortion-assistance-fund-aaf/

Mississippi (abortion is available in clinic until fifteen weeks' gestation)

CLINICS

✱Jackson Women's Health Organization
2903 North State St., Jackson, MS
601-366-2261
http://jacksonwomenshealth.com/

POLITICAL, FUNDING, AND PRACTICAL SUPPORT GROUPS

Mississippi Reproductive Freedom Fund (Mississippi)
2210 Hill Ave., Jackson, MS
769-218-9413
https://msreprofreedomfund.org/
mississippireprofreedomfund@gmail.com

Planned Parenthood Southeast Advocates
https://www.plannedparenthoodaction.org/planned-parenthood-southeast-advocates

Mississippi NOW
https://www.facebook.com/Mississippi-National-Organization-for-Women-
    59324523297/

Pink House Fund
522 Fondren Pl., Jackson, MI
769-251-0873
thepinkhousefund@gmail.com

Missouri *(abortion is available in clinic until twenty-one weeks six days' gestation)*

CLINICS

Planned Parenthood—Reproductive Health Services of PPSLR
4251 Forest Park Ave., St. Louis, MO
314-531-7526
https://www.plannedparenthood.org/health-center/missouri/st.-louis/63108/
    reproductive-health-services-of-ppslr-3302-90770

POLITICAL, FUNDING, AND PRACTICAL SUPPORT GROUPS

NARAL Pro-Choice Missouri
1210 S. Vandeventer Ave., St. Louis, MO
314-531-8616
naral@prochoicemissouri.org

ReproAction Missouri Affiliate
https://reproaction.org/take-action/?ss=40#listing

Planned Parenthood Advocates in Missouri
https://www.plannedparenthoodaction.org/planned-parenthood-advocates-missouri

Missouri NOW
https://missouri-now.org/

Gateway Women's Access Fund
PO Box 32034, St. Louis. MO
http://www.gwaf.org

Montana (abortion is available in clinic until twenty-one weeks' gestation)

CLINICS

Planned Parenthood Heights
100 West Wicks Ln., Billings, MT
406-869-5040
https://www.plannedparenthood.org/health-center/montana/billings/59105/
planned-parenthood-heights-2438-90790

Planned Parenthood—West Health Center (medication only)
1844 Broadwater #4, Billings, MT
406-656-9980
https://www.plannedparenthood.org/health-center/montana/billings/59102/
planned-parenthood-west-2441-90790

Planned Parenthood—Great Falls Health Center (medication only)
211 9th St. S., Great Falls, MT
406- 454-3431
https://www.plannedparenthood.org/health-center/montana/great-falls/59405/
planned-parenthood-great-falls-2442-90790

Planned Parenthood—Helena Health Center (medication only)
1500 Cannon St., Helena, MT
406-443-7676
https://www.plannedparenthood.org/health-center/montana/helena/59601/
planned-parenthood-helena-2443-90790

✱Blue Mountain Clinic
610 N. California St., Missoula, MT
800-727-2546
http://bluemountainclinic.org/

✱All Families Healthcare
737 Spokane Ave., Whitefish, MT
406-730-8682
https://www.allfamilieshealth.org/

POLITICAL, FUNDING, AND PRACTICAL SUPPORT GROUPS

NARAL Pro-Choice Montana
PO Box 279, Helena, MT
406-813-1680
npmtinterim@gmail.com

Planned Parenthood Advocates of Montana
https://www.plannedparenthoodaction.org/planned-parenthood-advocates-montana

Susan Wicklund Fund
PO Box 5, Livingston, MT
http://www.susanwicklundfund.org/

Nebraska (abortion is available in clinic until twenty-one weeks six days' gestation)

CLINICS

✱Abortion and Contraception Clinic of Nebraska
1002 W. Mission Ave., Bellevue, NE
402-291-4797
http://www.abortionclinics.org/clinics/bellevue-nebraska.html

Planned Parenthood—Lincoln South Health Center
5631 S. 48th St., Suite 100, Lincoln, NE
877-811-7526
https://www.plannedparenthood.org/health-center/nebraska/lincoln/68516/lincoln-south-health-center-4062-90380

Planned Parenthood—Northwest Health Center
3105 N. 93rd St., Omaha, NE
877-811-7526
https://www.plannedparenthood.org/health-center/nebraska/omaha/68134/northwest-health-center-2447-90380

POLITICAL, FUNDING, AND PRACTICAL SUPPORT GROUPS

Planned Parenthood Voters of Nebraska
https://www.plannedparenthoodaction.org/planned-parenthood-voters-nebraska

Abortion Access Fund
1002 W. Mission Ave., Bellevue, NE
800-737-3845
https://abortionaccessfund.org/

Nevada (abortion is available in clinics until twenty-four weeks' gestation)

CLINICS

A-All Women Care Abortion Clinic
7908 W. Sahara Ave., Las Vegas, NV
702-531-5400
https://lvgyn.com/

A-Z Women's Health Center
1670 E. Flamingo Rd., Suite C, Las Vegas, NV
877-892-0660
http://www.drramos.com/

Birth Control Care Center
872 E. Sahara Ave., Las Vegas, NV
800-255-7889
https://www.birthcontrolcarecenter.com/

Planned Parenthood—Las Vegas East Flamingo (medication only)
3300 E. Flamingo Rd. #25, Las Vegas, NV
702-547-9888
https://www.plannedparenthood.org/health-center/nevada/las-vegas/89121/
    las-vegas-east-flamingo-2306-90210

Planned Parenthood—Las Vegas West Charleston (medication only)
3220 W. Charleston Blvd., Las Vegas, NV
702-878-7776
https://www.plannedparenthood.org/health-center/nevada/las-vegas/89102/
    las-vegas-west-charleston-2304-90210

Safe and Sound for Women
3131 La Canada St., Suite 110, Las Vegas, NV
702-221-7233
http://www.safeandsoundforwomen.com/

West End Women's Medical Group
5915 Tyrone Rd., Reno, NV
775-827-0616
http://www.abortion.cc/

POLITICAL, FUNDING, AND PRACTICAL SUPPORT GROUPS

NARAL Pro-Choice Nevada
702-751-4219
nevada@prochoiceamerica.org

Nevada Advocates for Planned Parenthood Affiliates
https://www.plannedparenthoodaction.org/local/nevada

Nevada Now
https://www.nevadanow.org/

Planned Parenthood Advocates Mar Monte and Northern Nevada
http://www.ppactionca.org/nevada/home.html

New Hampshire (abortion is available in clinics until fifteen weeks six days' gestation, and Manchester OB-GYN will do them later in a hospital setting)

CLINICS

✳Equality Health Center
38 S. Main St., Concord, NH
855-502-3858
http://equalityhc.org/

✳Joan G. Lovering Health Center
559 Portsmouth Ave., Greenland, NH
877-436-7588
http://joangloveringhealthcenter.org/choice/

Planned Parenthood—Keene Health Center (medication only)
8 Middle St., Keene, NH
603-352-6898
https://www.plannedparenthood.org/health-center/new-hampshire/keene/03431/
    keene-health-center-2744-91770

Manchester OB/GYN Associates
150 Tarrytown Rd. Manchester, NH
603-622-3162
http://www.manchesterob.com/

Planned Parenthood—Manchester Health Center
24 Pennacook St., Manchester, NH
603-669-7321
https://www.plannedparenthood.org/health-center/new-hampshire/
    manchester/03104/manchester-health-center-2740-91770

POLITICAL, FUNDING, AND PRACTICAL SUPPORT GROUPS

Planned Parenthood New Hampshire Action Fund
https://www.plannedparenthoodaction.org/planned-parenthood-new-hampshire-
    action-fund

New Hampshire Women's Foundation
18 Low Ave., Suite 205, Concord, NH
603-226-3355
https://nhwomensfoundation.org/
info@nhwomensfoundation.org

New Jersey (abortion is available in clinic until twenty-four weeks six days' gestation)

CLINICS

Planned Parenthood—Camden Health Center (medication only)
317 Broadway, Camden, NJ
856-365-3519
https://www.plannedparenthood.org/health-center/new-jersey/camden/08103/
    camden-center-3312-90900

✱Cherry Hill Women's Center
502 Kings Hwy. N., Cherry Hill, NJ
800-877-6331
http://cherryhillwomenscenter.com/

Planned Parenthood—East Orange Health Center (medication only)
560 Dr. Martin Luther King Blvd., Suite 100, East Orange, NJ
973-674-4343
https://www.plannedparenthood.org/health-center/new-jersey/east-orange/07018/
    east-orange--health-center-2551-90920

Planned Parenthood—Elizabeth Health Center (medication only)
1171 Elizabeth Ave., Elizabeth, NJ
908-351-5384
https://www.plannedparenthood.org/health-center/new-jersey/elizabeth/07201/
elizabeth-health-center-2599-90900

Planned Parenthood—Englewood Health Center (medication only)
46 N. Van Brunt St., Englewood, NJ
201-894-0966
https://www.plannedparenthood.org/health-center/new-jersey/englewood/07631/
englewood-health-center-2946-90900

Metropolitan Medical Associates
40 Engle St., Englewood, NJ
800-932-0378
http://metropolitanmedicalassociates.com/

Planned Parenthood—Flemington Health Center (medication only)
349 Route 31, South Countryside Plaza, Bldg. B, Suite 503, Flemington, NJ
908-782-7727
https://www.plannedparenthood.org/health-center/new-jersey/flemington/08822/
flemington-health-center-2596-90900

Planned Parenthood—Freehold Health Center (medication only)
800 W. Main St., Freehold, NJ
732-431-1717
https://www.plannedparenthood.org/health-center/new-jersey/freehold/07728/
freehold-center-2683-90900

Planned Parenthood—Hackensack Health Center (medication only)
575 Main St., Hackensack, NJ
201-489-1140
https://www.plannedparenthood.org/health-center/new-jersey/hackensack/07601/
hackensack-health-center-2947-90900

Planned Parenthood—Hamilton Health Center (medication only)
2279 State Highway 33, Golden Crest Corporate Center, Suite 510, Hamilton Square, NJ
609-599-4881
https://www.plannedparenthood.org/health-center/new-jersey/hamilton-square/
08690/hamilton-health-center-2343-90900

Planned Parenthood—Montclair Health Center (medication only)
29 N. Fullerton Ave., Montclair, NJ
973-746-7116
https://www.plannedparenthood.org/health-center/new-jersey/montclair/07042/
montclair-center-2550-90920

Planned Parenthood—Morristown Health Center (medication only)
196 Speedwell Ave., Morristown, NJ
973-539-1364
https://www.plannedparenthood.org/health-center/new-jersey/morristown/07960/
morristown-health-center-3307-90900

Planned Parenthood—New Brunswick Health Center (medication only)
10B Industrial Dr., New Brunswick, NJ
732-246-2411
https://www.plannedparenthood.org/health-center/new-jersey/new-brunswick/
08901/new-brunswick-center-2684-90900

Planned Parenthood—Ironbound Health Center (medication only)
70 Adams St., Suite 13, Newark, NJ
973-465-7707
https://www.plannedparenthood.org/health-center/new-jersey/newark/07105/
ironbound-health-center-2554-90920

Planned Parenthood—Newton Health Center (medication only)
8 Moran St., Newton, NJ
973-383-5218
https://www.plannedparenthood.org/health-center/new-jersey/newton/07860/
newton-health-center-2555-90900

Planned Parenthood—Paterson Health Center (medication only)
680 Broadway, Paterson, NJ
973- 345-3883
https://www.plannedparenthood.org/health-center/new-jersey/paterson/07505/
paterson-center-2557-90920

Planned Parenthood—Perth Amboy Health Center (medication only)
450 Market St., Perth Amboy, NJ
732-442-4499
https://www.plannedparenthood.org/health-center/new-jersey/perth-amboy/08861/
perth-amboy-center-3053-90900

Planned Parenthood—Shrewsbury Health Center
69 E. Newman Springs Rd., Shrewsbury, NJ
732-842-9300
https://www.plannedparenthood.org/health-center/new-jersey/shrewsbury/07702/
shrewsbury-center-3510-90900

Planned Parenthood—Trenton Health Center
437 E. State St., Trenton, NJ
609-599-4881
https://www.plannedparenthood.org/health-center/new-jersey/trenton/08608/
trenton-health-center-3304-90900

Planned Parenthood—Washington Health Center (medication only)
66 E. Washington Ave., Washington, NJ
908-454-3000
https://www.plannedparenthood.org/health-center/new-jersey/washington/07882/
washington-health-center-2598-90900

POLITICAL, FUNDING, AND PRACTICAL SUPPORT GROUPS

Planned Parenthood Action Fund of New Jersey
https://www.plannedparenthoodaction.org/planned-parenthood-action-fund-new-
jersey-inc

New Jersey NOW
http://www.nownj.net/

The Women Centers Escort Group of New Jersey
www.thewomenscenters.com/take-action/volunteer

New Jersey Abortion Access Fund
PO Box 345, Ridgewood, NJ
http://njaaf.org/

New Mexico (abortion is available in clinics until twenty-three weeks six days' gestation, or later on an individual basis at Southwestern Women's Options)

CLINICS

Planned Parenthood—Surgical Center
701 San Mateo NE, Albuquerque, NM
505-265-9511
https://www.plannedparenthood.org/health-center/new-mexico/albuquerque/87108/
surgical-center-2956-90210

Southwestern Women's Options
522 Lomas Blvd. NE, Albuquerque, NM
505-242-7512
https://southwesternwomens.com/southwestern-womens-options-albuquerque-
new-mexico/

UNM Center for Reproductive Health
2301 Yale Blvd. SE, Suite E, Albuquerque, NM
505-925-4455
https://hsc.unm.edu/health/patient-care/family-planning-reproductive-health/index.html

Planned Parenthood—Santa Fe (medication only)
730 St. Michael's Dr., Suite 4B, Santa Fe, NM
505-982-3684
https://www.plannedparenthood.org/health-center/new-mexico/santa-fe/87505/
santa-fe-health-center-2801-90210

Hilltop Reproductive Women's Clinic
5290 McNutt Rd., Suite 106, Sunland Park, NM
575-589-3855
http://hilltopwomensreproductive.com/

POLITICAL, FUNDING, AND PRACTICAL SUPPORT GROUPS

Indigenous Women Rising
505-398-1990
https://www.iwrising.org/
indigenouswomenrising@gmail.com

Young Women United
309 Gold St. SW, Albuquerque, NM 87102
505-831-8930
https://youngwomenunited.org

Strong Families New Mexico/Forward Together
400 Gold Ave. SW, Suite 900
Albuquerque, NM
505-842-8070
https://forwardtogether.org/

Young Women United
201 N. Church, Suite 320, Las Cruces, NM
575-526-7964
https://youngwomenunited.org

New Mexico Religious Coalition for Reproductive Choice
PO Box 66433, Albuquerque, NM
505-890-4573
http://nmrcrc.org/

Planned Parenthood Votes New Mexico
https://www.plannedparenthoodaction.org/planned-parenthood-votes-new-mexico

New York (abortion is available in clinics until twenty-six weeks' gestation)

CLINICS

Planned Parenthood—Albany Health Center
855 Central Ave., Albany, NY
518-434-5678
https://www.plannedparenthood.org/health-center/new-york/albany/12206/albany-
    health-center-3336-91020

Sweet Home Medical
2550 Sweet Home Rd., Amherst, NY
716-691-1414
http://sweethomemedical.com/

Planned Parenthood—Amsterdam Health Center (medication only)
4803 State Highway/30 KEM Plaza, Amsterdam, NY
518-842-0285
https://www.plannedparenthood.org/health-center/new-york/amsterdam/12010/
    amsterdam-center-3047-91180

Planned Parenthood—Batavia Health Center (medication only)
222 W. Main St., Batavia, NY
866-600-6886
https://www.plannedparenthood.org/health-center/new-york/batavia/14020/
    batavia-health-center-2353-91040

Bronx Abortion
2070 Eastchester Rd., Bronx, NY
888-999-0640
http://www.abortionbronx.com/bronx/

✴Dr. Emily Women's Health Center
642 Southern Blvd., Bronx, NY
718-585-1010
http://dremily.com/

Planned Parenthood—The Bronx Center
349 E. 149th St., 2nd Floor, Bronx, NY
212-965-7000
https://www.plannedparenthood.org/health-center/new-york/bronx/10451/the-
    bronx-center-2524-91110

Brooklyn Abortion Clinic
14 Dekalb Ave., 4th Floor, Brooklyn, NY
718-369-1900
http://www.brooklynabortionclinic.nyc/

Planned Parenthood—Boro Hall Center
44 Court St., 6th Floor, Brooklyn, NY
212-965-7000
https://www.plannedparenthood.org/health-center/new-york/brooklyn/11201/
   boro-hall-center-2522-91110

✱Buffalo WomenServices (non-medication abortions only)
2500 Main St., Buffalo, NY
800-598-3783
http://www.buffalowomenservices.com/

Planned Parenthood—Buffalo Health Center (medication only)
2697 Main St., Buffalo, NY
866-600-6886
https://www.plannedparenthood.org/health-center/new-york/buffalo/14214/
   buffalo-health-center-3334-91040

Planned Parenthood—Canandaigua Health Center (medication only)
15 Lafayette Ave., Canandaigua, NY
866-600-6886
https://www.plannedparenthood.org/health-center/new-york/canandaigua/14424/
   canandaigua-health-center-2352-91040

Planned Parenthood—Canton Health Center (medication only)
9 Miner St., Canton, NY
315-386-8821
https://www.plannedparenthood.org/health-center/new-york/canton/13617/
   canton-center-2881-91210

Planned Parenthood—Cobleskill Health Center (medication only)
109 Legion Dr., Cobleskill, NY
518-234-3325
https://www.plannedparenthood.org/health-center/new-york/cobleskill/12043/
   cobleskill-center-2783-91180

Planned Parenthood—Corning Health Center (medication only)
135 Walnut St., Corning, NY
607-962-4686
https://www.plannedparenthood.org/health-center/new-york/corning/14830/
   corning-health-center-2345-91090

Planned Parenthood—Elmira Health Center (medication only)
755 E. Church St., Elmira, NY
607-734-3313
https://www.plannedparenthood.org/health-center/new-york/elmira/14901/elmira-health-center-2349-91090

Planned Parenthood—Glen Cove Center (medication only)
110 School St., Glen Cove, NY
516-750-2500
https://www.plannedparenthood.org/health-center/new-york/glen-cove/11542/glen-cove-center-2787-91100

Planned Parenthood—Goshen Health Center (medication only)
7 Coates Dr., Suite 4, Goshen, NY
845-562-7800
https://www.plannedparenthood.org/health-center/new-york/goshen/10924/goshen-health-center-2624-91160

Planned Parenthood—Hempstead Center
540 Fulton Ave., Hempstead, NY
516-750-2500
https://www.plannedparenthood.org/health-center/new-york/hempstead/11550/hempstead-center-3321-91100

Planned Parenthood—Hornell Health Center (medication only)
111 Seneca St., Hornell, NY
607-324-1124
https://www.plannedparenthood.org/health-center/new-york/hornell/14843/hornell-health-center-2347-91090

Planned Parenthood—Hudson Health Center (medication only)
190 Fairview Ave., Hudson, NY
518-828-4675
https://www.plannedparenthood.org/health-center/new-york/hudson/12534/hudson-health-center-2380-91020

Planned Parenthood—Huntington Center (medication only)
755 New York Ave., Huntington, NY
631-427-7154
https://www.plannedparenthood.org/health-center/new-york/huntington/11743/huntington-center-2318-91220

Planned Parenthood—Ithaca Health Center
620 W. Seneca St., Ithaca, NY
607-273-1513
https://www.plannedparenthood.org/health-center/new-york/ithaca/14850/ithaca-health-center-3333-91090

Roosevelt Women's Medical Care PC
78-13 Roosevelt Ave., Jackson Heights, NY
718-205-0234
http://www.abortionsqueens.com/

✱Choices Women's Medical Center
147-32 Jamaica Ave., Jamaica, NY
718-786-5000
http://www.choicesmedical.com/

Planned Parenthood—Johnston Center (medication only)
400 N. Perry St., Johnston, NY
518-736-1911
https://www.plannedparenthood.org/health-center/new-york/johnstown/12095/
    johnstown-center-3530-91180

✱All Women's Medical Pavilion
120-34 Queens Blvd. #420, Kew Gardens, NY
866-340-1943
http://nyabortion.com/locations/queens.shtml

Planned Parenthood—Kingston Health Center (medication only)
21 Grand St., Kingston, NY
845-562-7800
https://www.plannedparenthood.org/health-center/new-york/kingston/12401/
    kingston-health-center-2623-91160

Planned Parenthood—Massapequa Center (medication only)
35 Carmans Rd., Massapequa, NY
516-750-2500
https://www.plannedparenthood.org/health-center/new-york/massapequa/11758/
    massapequa-center-2788-91100

Planned Parenthood—Monticello Health Center (medication only)
14 Prince St., Monticello, NY
845-562-7800
https://www.plannedparenthood.org/health-center/new-york/monticello/12701/
    monticello-health-center-2615-91160

Planned Parenthood—Mount Vernon Center (medication only)
6 Gramatan Ave., 4th Floor, Mount Vernon, NY
914-668-7927
https://www.plannedparenthood.org/health-center/new-york/mt.-vernon/10550/
    mount-vernon-center-2204-91220

Planned Parenthood—New Rochelle Center
247-249 North Ave., New Rochelle, NY
914-632-4442
https://www.plannedparenthood.org/health-center/new-york/new-rochelle/10801/
   new-rochelle-center-2206-91220

Columbia Ob/Gyn Columbus Circle
1790 Broadway, New York, NY
855-75-OBGYN (855-756-2496)
http://www.columbiaobgyn.org/locations/columbiadoctors-columbus-circle

Early Options
124 E. 40th St. #702, New York, NY
212-431-8533
https://www.earlyabortionoptions.com/

✱Parkmed NYC
800 2nd Ave. #6, New York, NY
212-686-6066
https://www.parkmed.com/

Planned Parenthood—Margaret Sanger Center
26 Bleecker St., New York, NY
212-965-7000
https://www.plannedparenthood.org/health-center/new-york/new-york/10012/
   margaret-sanger-center-3325-91110

Westside Women's Medical Pavilion
1841 Broadway #1011, New York, NY
877-894-1841
http://www.nyabortion.com/locations/manhattanW.shtml

Planned Parenthood—Newburgh Health Center
136 Lake St., Suite 11, Newburgh, NY
845-562-7800
https://www.plannedparenthood.org/health-center/new-york/newburgh/12550/
   newburgh-health-center-3995-91160

Planned Parenthood—Niagara Falls Office (medication only)
750 Portage Rd., Niagara Falls, NY
866-600-6886
https://www.plannedparenthood.org/health-center/new-york/niagara-falls/14301/
   niagara-falls-office-2976-91040

Planned Parenthood—North Tonawanda Health Center (medication only)
15 Webster St., North Tonawanda, NY
866-600-6886
https://www.plannedparenthood.org/health-center/new-york/north-tonawanda/
14120/north-tonawanda-health-center-2977-91040

Planned Parenthood—Patchogue Center (medication only)
450 Waverly Ave., Suite 4, Patchogue, NY
631-475-5705
https://www.plannedparenthood.org/health-center/new-york/patchogue/11772/
patchogue-center-2317-91220

Planned Parenthood—Plattsburgh Clinic
66 Brinkerhoff St., Plattsburgh, NY
518-561-4430
https://www.plannedparenthood.org/health-center/new-york/plattsburgh/12901/
plattsburgh-clinic-3315-91210

Planned Parenthood—Poughkeepsie Health Center
17 Noxon St., Poughkeepsie, NY
845-562-7800
https://www.plannedparenthood.org/health-center/new-york/poughkeepsie/12601/
poughkeepsie-health-center-2621-91160

Planned Parenthood—Diane L. Max Health Center
21-41 45th Rd., Queens, NY
212-965-7000
https://www.plannedparenthood.org/health-center/new-york/queens/11101/
diane-l.-max-health-center-4184-91110

Planned Parenthood—Glen Falls Center
543 Bay Rd., Queensbury, NY
518-792-0994
https://www.plannedparenthood.org/health-center/new-york/glens-falls/12801/
glens-falls-center-3529-91180

New York OB/GYN Associates
92-29 Queens Blvd., Rego Park, NY
888-525-CARE (888-525-2273)
http://www.safestabortion.com/

Planned Parenthood—Riverhead Center (medication only)
877 E. Main St., Suite 100, Riverhead, NY
631-369-0230
https://www.plannedparenthood.org/health-center/new-york/riverhead/11901/
riverhead-center-2319-91220

Planned Parenthood—Greece Health Center (medication only)
2824 W. Ridge Rd., Rochester, NY
866-600-6886
https://www.plannedparenthood.org/health-center/new-york/rochester/14626/
greece-health-center-2354-91040

Planned Parenthood—Rochester Health Center
114 University Ave., Rochester, NY
866-600-6886
https://www.plannedparenthood.org/health-center/new-york/rochester/14605/
rochester-health-center-3332-91040

Planned Parenthood—Saranac Lake Clinic (medication only)
41 St. Bernard St., Saranac Lake, NY
518-891-0046
https://www.plannedparenthood.org/health-center/new-york/saranac-lake/12983/
saranac-lake-clinic-3428-91210

Planned Parenthood—Schenectady Center
1040 State St., Schenectady, NY
518-374-5353
https://www.plannedparenthood.org/health-center/new-york/schenectady/12307/
schenectady-center-4192-91180

Planned Parenthood—Smithtown Center
70 Maple Ave., Smithtown, NY
631-361-7526
https://www.plannedparenthood.org/health-center/new-york/smithtown/11787/
smithtown-center-2320-91220

Planned Parenthood—Spring Valley Center (medication only)
25 Perlman Dr., Spring Valley, NY
845-426-7577
https://www.plannedparenthood.org/health-center/new-york/spring-valley/10977/
spring-valley-center-2226-91220

Planned Parenthood—Syracuse Health Center
1120 E. Genesee St., Syracuse, NY
866-600-6886
https://www.plannedparenthood.org/health-center/new-york/syracuse/13210/
syracuse-health-center-2471-91040

Planned Parenthood—Troy Health Center (medication only)
200 Broadway, Troy, NY
518-434-5678
https://www.plannedparenthood.org/health-center/new-york/troy/12180/troy-
health-center-2780-91020

Planned Parenthood—Utica Center
1424 Genesee St., Utica, NY
315-724-6146
https://www.plannedparenthood.org/health-center/new-york/utica/13502/
utica-center-3318-91180

✱Office of Dr. Amy R. Cousins
149 Vestal Pkwy. E., Vestal, NY
800-676-9011
http://www.amycousinsmd.com/

Planned Parenthood—Watertown Center (medication only)
160 Stone St., Watertown, NY
315-788-8065
https://www.plannedparenthood.org/health-center/new-york/watertown/13601/
watertown-center-3328-91210

Planned Parenthood—West Islip Center (medication only)
180 Sunrise Hwy., West Islip, NY
631-893-0150
https://www.plannedparenthood.org/health-center/new-york/west-islip/11795/
west-islip-center-2316-91220

Planned Parenthood—West Seneca Health Center (medication only)
Wimbledon Plaza 240 Center Rd., West Seneca, NY
866-600-6886
https://www.plannedparenthood.org/health-center/new-york/west-seneca/14224/
west-seneca-health-center-2693-91040

✱All Women's Health—White Plains
222 Mamaroneck Ave., White Plains, NY
888-644-0999
http://nyabortion.com/locations/whiteplains.shtml

Planned Parenthood—White Plains Center
175 Tarrytown Rd., White Plains, NY
914-761-6566
https://www.plannedparenthood.org/health-center/new-york/white-plains/10607/
white-plains-center-2203-91220

Planned Parenthood—Yonkers Center (medication only)
20 S. Broadway, Yonkers, NY
914-965-1912
https://www.plannedparenthood.org/health-center/new-york/yonkers/10701/
yonkers-center-2202-91220

POLITICAL, FUNDING, AND PRACTICAL SUPPORT GROUPS

National Institute of Reproductive Health
14 Wall St., Suite 3B, New York, NY
212-343-0114
https://www.nirhealth.org/
nfo@nirhealth.org

New York Latina Advocacy Network (NY LAN)
http://latinainstitute.org/en/new-york

National Asian Pacific American Women's Forum—New York Chapter
https://www.napawf.org/nychapter.html
NYCChapter@napawf.org

New York State NOW
http://nownys.org/

Planned Parenthood of NYC Action Fund
https://www.plannedparenthoodaction.org/planned-parenthood-new-york-city-
  action-fund-inc

New York Coalition for Abortion Clinic Defense
https://www.facebook.com/nycacd

New York Abortion Access Fund (NYAAF)
FDR Station Box 7569, New York, NY
212-252-4757
http://www.nyaaf.org/

Access Fund of Aphrodite Medical
149 Vestal Pwky. W., Vestal, NY
607-785-4171
http://www.amycousinsmd.com/

Joan Bechhofer Fund
620 W. Seneca St., Ithaca, NY
607-273-1513, ext. 103
https://abortionfunds.org/fund/joan-bechhofer-fund/

Haven Coalition—Practical Support
http://www.havencoalition.org/
havencoalition@gmail.com

Brigid Alliance—Practical Support
https://brigidalliance.org/
info@brigidalliance.org

North Carolina (abortion is available in clinics until twenty weeks' gestation)

CLINICS

Planned Parenthood—Asheville Health Center
68 McDowell St., Asheville, NC
828-252-7928
https://www.plannedparenthood.org/health-center/north-carolina/asheville/28801/
asheville-health-center-4134-90860

Planned Parenthood—Chapel Hill Health Center
1765 Dobbins Dr., Chapel Hill, NC
919-942-7762
https://www.plannedparenthood.org/health-center/north-carolina/chapel-hill/27514/
chapel-hill-health-center-4169-90860

A Preferred Women's Health—Charlotte
3220 Latrobe Dr., Charlotte, NC
704-665-4120
http://www.apwhc.com/

✱A Woman's Choice of Charlotte
421 N. Wendover Rd., Charlotte, NC
800-637-3445
https://www.awomanschoiceinc.com/awc-charlotte/

✱Family Reproductive Health
700 E. Hebron St., Charlotte, NC
800-952-9034
http://www.familyreproductive.com/

North Durham Women's Health
400-B Crutchfield St., Durham, NC
919-908-6449
http://northdurhamwomenshealth.com/

A Hallmark Women's Clinic
1919 Gillespie St., Fayetteville, NC
800-662-0522
http://www.ahallmarkwomensclinic.com/

Planned Parenthood—Fayetteville Health Center
4551 Yadkin Rd., Fayetteville, NC
866-942-7762
https://www.plannedparenthood.org/health-center/north-carolina/fayetteville/28303/
fayetteville-health-center-4173-90860

✱A Woman's Choice of Greensboro
2425 Randleman Rd., Greensboro, NC
844-219-7668
https://www.awomanschoiceinc.com/awc-greensboro/

A Preferred Women's Health—Raleigh
1604 Jones Franklin Rd., Raleigh, NC
919-854-7888
http://www.apwhc.com/

✱A Woman's Choice of Raleigh
3305 Drake Cir., Raleigh, NC
800-540-5690
https://www.awomanschoiceinc.com/awc-raleigh

Planned Parenthood—Wilmington Health Center
1925 Tradd Ct., Wilmington, NC
910-762-5566
https://www.plannedparenthood.org/health-center/north-carolina/wilmington/
    28401/wilmington-health-center-2595-90860

Planned Parenthood—Winston-Salem Health Center
3000 Maplewood Ave., Suite 112, Winston-Salem, NC
336-768-2980
https://www.plannedparenthood.org/health-center/north-carolina/winston-salem/
    27103/winston-salem-health-center-2845-90860

POLITICAL, FUNDING, AND PRACTICAL SUPPORT GROUPS

NARAL Pro-Choice North Carolina
4711 Hope Valley Rd., Suite 4F-509, Durham, NC
919-908-9321
info@prochoicenc.org

Planned Parenthood Votes South Atlantic
https://www.plannedparenthoodaction.org/planned-parenthood-votes-south-atlantic

North Carolina NOW
https://northcarolinanow.wordpress.com/

Charlotte for Choice
https://www.facebook.com/C4CClinicEscorts/
C4CClinicEscorts@gmail.com

Carolina Abortion Fund
North Carolina
855-518-4603
http://carolinaabortionfund.org/

North Carolina Women United
PO Box 10013, Raleigh, NC
https://www.ncwu.org/contact

North Dakota (abortion is available in clinic until about sixteen weeks' gestation)

CLINICS

✱Red River Women's Clinic
512 First Ave. N., Fargo, ND
888-928-9009
https://www.redriverwomensclinic.com/

POLITICAL, FUNDING, AND PRACTICAL SUPPORT GROUPS

Planned Parenthood North Dakota Advocate
https://www.plannedparenthoodaction.org/planned-parenthood-north-dakota-advocate

North Dakota Women in Need Fund (WIN Fund)
512 First Ave. N., Fargo, ND
888-298-9009
https://www.ndwinfund.org/

Red River Clinic Escorts
https://www.redriverwomensclinic.com/volunteer
info@redriverwomensclinic.com

Ohio (abortion is available in clinic until twenty-one weeks six days' gestation)

CLINICS

Planned Parenthood—Bedford Heights Surgery Center
25350 Rockside Rd., Bedford Heights, OH
440-232-9732
https://www.plannedparenthood.org/health-center/ohio/bedford-heights/
44146/bedford-heights-surgery-center-4061-91230

Planned Parenthood—Cincinnati Surgery Center
2314 Auburn Ave., Cincinnati, OH
513-287-6488
https://www.plannedparenthood.org/health-center/ohio/cincinnati/45219/
cincinnati-surgical-center-3347-91260

＊Preterm
12000 Shaker Blvd., Cleveland, OH
877-PRETERM (877-773-8376)
https://www.preterm.org/

Founder's Women's Health Center (medication only)
1243 E. Broad St., Columbus, OH
800-282-9490
http://www.founderswhc.com/

Planned Parenthood—East Columbus Surgery Center
3255 E. Main St., Columbus, OH
614-222-3531
https://www.plannedparenthood.org/health-center/ohio/columbus/43213/
east-columbus-surgical-center-2335-91230

Northeast Ohio Women's Center
2127 State Rd., Cuyahoga Falls, OH
330-923-4009
http://northeastohioabortion.com/

Women's Med—Dayton
1401 E. Stroop Rd., Dayton, OH
800-672-6810
http://www.womensmed.com/locations/dayton-oh/

Capital Care of Toledo
1160 W. Sylvania Ave., Toledo, OH
800-282-9490
http://www.capitalcarenetwork.com/

POLITICAL, FUNDING, AND PRACTICAL SUPPORT GROUPS

New Voices for Reproductive Justice—New Voices Cleveland
12200 Fairhill Rd., Cleveland, OH
412-363-4500
info@newvoicespittsburgh.org

Restoring Our Own Through Transformation (ROOTT)
Columbus, OH
614-398-1766
https://www.roott.org/

NARAL Pro-Choice Ohio
12000 Shaker Blvd., Cleveland, OH
216-283-2180; 800-466-2725
https://prochoiceohio.org/

Ohio RCRC (Religious Council for Reproductive Choice)

PO Box 82204, Columbus, OH
614-706-3709
www.ohiorcrc.org
info@ohiorcrc.org

Planned Parenthood Advocates of Ohio
https://www.plannedparenthoodaction.org/planned-parenthood-advocates-ohio

Ohio NOW
http://ohionow.org/

Northeast Ohio Pro-Choice Action
https://www.facebook.com/neoprochoice/

Clinic Story Corps (Capital Care Clinic Escorts, Toledo)
clinicstorycorps@gmail.com

Preterm
12000 Shaker Blvd., Cleveland, OH
216-991-4000; 877-773-8376
http://www.preterm.org/

Women Have Options (WHO)
PO Box 1611, Columbus, OH
www.womenhaveoptions.org/

Oklahoma (abortion is available in clinics until thirteen weeks six days' gestation)

CLINICS

✱Trust Women South Women's Health Center Oklahoma City
1240 SW 44th St., Oklahoma City, OK
405-429-7940
https://trustwomen.org

Planned Parenthood—Central Oklahoma City Clinic (medication only)
619 NW 23rd Street, Oklahoma City, OK
405-528-2157
https://www.plannedparenthood.org/health-center/oklahoma/oklahoma-city/73103/
central-oklahoma-city-clinic-3351-90740

Reproductive Services
6136 E. 32nd Pl., Tulsa, OK
800-821-7237
http://reproductiveservices.com/

POLITICAL, FUNDING, AND PRACTICAL SUPPORT GROUPS

Oklahoma Religious Coalition for Reproductive Choice (OKRCRC)
PO Box 35194, Tulsa, OK
http://www.okrcrc.org/contact-us/

Oklahoma Call for Reproductive Justice
PO Box 892381, Oklahoma City, OK
https://ocrj.org/contact/

Planned Parenthood Great Plains Votes
http://www.ppgpvotes.org/

Roe Fund
PO Box 35194, Tulsa, OK
918-481-6444
http://www.okrcrc.org/assistance/

Oregon *(abortion is available in clinics until twenty-four weeks' gestation)*

CLINICS

Planned Parenthood—Ashland Health Center (medication only)
1532 Siskiyou Blvd., Ashland, OR
541-482-8700
https://www.plannedparenthood.org/health-center/oregon/ashland/97520/ashland-
health-center-2370-91380

Planned Parenthood—Beaverton Health Center (medication only)
12220 SW First St., Suite 200, Beaverton, OR
888-875-7820
https://www.plannedparenthood.org/health-center/oregon/beaverton/97005/
beaverton-center-2410-91400

Planned Parenthood—Bend Health Center
2330 NE Division St., Suite 7, Bend, OR
888-875-7820
https://www.plannedparenthood.org/health-center/oregon/bend/97701/bend-health-
center-2373-91400

Planned Parenthood—Eugene—Springfield Health Center
3579 Franklin Blvd., Eugene, OR
541-344-9411
https://www.plannedparenthood.org/health-center/oregon/eugene/97403/eugene-
springfield-health-center-4075-91380

Planned Parenthood—Milwaukie—Oak Grove Health Center (medication only)
14411 SE McLoughlin Blvd., Milwaukie, OR
888-875-7820
https://www.plannedparenthood.org/health-center/oregon/milwaukie/97267/
milwaukie-oak-grove-center-4195-91400

Lovejoy Surgery Center
933 NW 25th Ave., Portland, OR
800-752-6189
http://lovejoysurgicenter.com/

OHSU Center for Women's Health
808 SW Campus Dr., 7th Floor, Portland, OR
503-418-4500
http://www.ohsu.edu/xd/health/services/women/services/gynecology-and-obstetrics/
services/abortion.cfm

Planned Parenthood—NE Portland Health Center
3727 NE Martin Luther King Jr. Blvd., Portland, OR
888-875-7820
https://www.plannedparenthood.org/health-center/oregon/portland/97212/
ne-portland-center-3943-91400

Planned Parenthood—SE Portland Health Center (medication only)
3231 SE 50th Ave., Portland, OR
888-875-7820
https://www.plannedparenthood.org/health-center/oregon/portland/97206/
se-portland-center-3353-91400

Planned Parenthood—Salem Health Center
3825 Wolverine St. NE, Salem, OR
888-875-7820
https://www.plannedparenthood.org/health-center/oregon/salem/97305/
salem-center-2412-91400

POLITICAL, FUNDING, AND PRACTICAL SUPPORT GROUPS

NARAL Pro-Choice Oregon
PO Box 40472, Portland, OR
503-223-4510
info@prochoiceoregon.org

Cascades Abortion Support Collective
Portland, OR
503-610-0692
http://www.CascadesAbortionSupport.org

Planned Parenthood Advocates of Oregon
https://www.ppaoregon.org/

Oregon NOW
https://noworegon.org/

Pennsylvania (abortions are available in clinics through twenty-three weeks' gestation)

CLINICS

Planned Parenthood—Allentown Health Center
29 N. Ninth St., Allentown, PA
610-439-1033
https://www.plannedparenthood.org/health-center/pennsylvania/allentown/18101/
    allentown-medical-center-2723-91410

✷ Allentown Women's Center
31 S. Commerce Way #100, Bethlehem, PA
877-342-5292
https://allentownwomenscenter.com/

✷ Delaware County Women's Center
1 Medical Center Blvd., Alexander Silberman Center—4th Floor, Chester, PA
610-874-4361
http://delawarecountywomenscenter.com/delawarecountywomenscenter/

Planned Parenthood—Harrisburg Health Center (medication only)
1514 N. Second St., Harrisburg, PA
717-234-2468
https://www.plannedparenthood.org/health-center/pennsylvania/harrisburg/17102/
    harrisburg-medical-center-3357-91410

Planned Parenthood—Norristown Abortion Center (medication only)
1221 Powell St., Norristown, PA
610-279-6095
https://www.plannedparenthood.org/health-center/pennsylvania/norristown/19401/
    norristown-abortion-center-3952-91460

Bruce Berger, MD, and Charles Benjamin, DO
1335 W. Tabor Rd. #202, Philadelphia, PA
215-424-0222
http://www.bergerbenjamin.com/

✱PEACE (Penn Family Planning and Pregnancy Loss Center)
3400 Spruce St., 1000 Courtyard, Philadelphia, PA
215-615-5234
http://www.uphs.upenn.edu/obgyn/divisions/family.htm

✱Philadelphia Women's Center
777 Appletree St., 7th Floor, Philadelphia, PA
800-869-2330
http://philadelphiawomenscenter.com/philadelphiawomenscenter

Planned Parenthood—Far Northeast Surgical Center
2751 Comly Rd., Philadelphia, PA
215-464-2225
https://www.plannedparenthood.org/health-center/pennsylvania/philadelphia/
    19154/far-northeast-surgical-center-3441-91460

Planned Parenthood—Locust Street Surgical Center
1144 Locust St., Philadelphia, PA
215-351-5550
https://www.plannedparenthood.org/health-center/pennsylvania/philadelphia/
    19107/locust-street-surgical-center-3360-91460

✱Allegheny Reproductive Health Clinic
5910 Kirkwood St., Pittsburgh, PA
800-221-3988
http://www.alleghenyreproductive.com/

Planned Parenthood—PPWP/Women's Health Services
933 Liberty Ave., Pittsburgh, PA
412-562-1900
https://www.plannedparenthood.org/health-center/pennsylvania/pittsburgh/15222/
    ppwp-women's-health-services-3359-91470

Planned Parenthood—Reading Health Center
48 S. Fourth St., Reading, PA
610-376-8061
https://www.plannedparenthood.org/health-center/pennsylvania/reading/19602/
    reading-medical-center-2725-91410

Planned Parenthood—Warminster Medical Center
610 Louis Dr., Suite 303, Second Floor, Warminster, PA
215-957-7980
https://www.plannedparenthood.org/health-center/pennsylvania/warminster/18974/
    warminster-medical-center-2510-91410

Planned Parenthood—West Chester Surgical Center
8 S. Wayne St., West Chester, PA
610-692-1770
https://www.plannedparenthood.org/health-center/pennsylvania/west-chester/
    19382/west-chester-surgical-center-3918-91460

Planned Parenthood—York Health Center
728 S. Beaver St., York, PA
717-845-9681
https://www.plannedparenthood.org/health-center/pennsylvania/york/17401/
    york-medical-center-3786-91410

POLITICAL, FUNDING, AND PRACTICAL SUPPORT GROUPS

New Voices for Reproductive Justice—New Voices Pittsburgh
5987 Broad St., Pittsburgh, PA
412-363-4500
http://www.newvoicespittsburgh.org/
info@newvoicespittsburgh.org

New Voices for Reproductive Justice—New Voices Philadelphia
3853 Lancaster Ave., Philadelphia, PA
412-363-4500
info@newvoicespittsburgh.org

National Asian Pacific American Women's Forum—Philadelphia Chapter
https://www.napawf.org/philadelphiachapter.html

Pennsylvania RCRJ (Religious Coalition for Reproductive Justice)
717-580-6011
www.parcrj.org
parcrj@gmail.com

Planned Parenthood Pennsylvania Advocates
http://www.plannedparenthoodpa.org/

Pennsylvania NOW
http://pennsylvanianow.org/

Planned Parenthood Keystone Fund for Choice
PO Box 813, Trexlertown, PA
717-234-2479, ext. 9426
http://www.plannedparenthood.org/keystone/

Western Pennsylvania Fund for Choice
5910 Kirkwood St., Pittsburgh, PA
https://www.wpafundforchoice.org/donate/

Women's Medical Fund
PO Box 40748, Philadelphia, PA
215-564-6622
http://www.womensmedicalfund.org/

Rhode Island (abortion is available in clinics until eighteen weeks six days' gestation)

CLINICS

Planned Parenthood—Providence Health Center
175 Broad St., Providence, RI
401-421-9620
https://www.plannedparenthood.org/health-center/rhode-island/providence/02903/
    providence-health-center-3362-90220

Women's Medical Center of Rhode Island—Dr. DiOrio (medication only)
215 Toll Gate Rd. #106, Warwick, RI
401-467-9111

POLITICAL, FUNDING, AND PRACTICAL SUPPORT GROUPS

Planned Parenthood Votes Rhode Island
https://www.plannedparenthoodaction.org/planned-parenthood-votes-rhode-island

Rhode Island NOW
https://www.rinow.org/

Women's Health and Education Fund
PO Box 5863, Providence, RI
http://www.whefri.org/

South Carolina *(abortion is available in clinics until fourteen weeks' gestation)*

CLINICS

Planned Parenthood—Columbia Health Center
2712 Middleburg Dr. #107, Columbia, SC
803-256-4908
https://www.plannedparenthood.org/health-center/south-carolina/columbia/29204/
columbia-health-center-2646-90860

Greenville Women's Center
1142 Grove Rd., Greenville, SC
864-232-1584
https://www.greenvillewomensclinic.com/

Planned Parenthood—Charleston Health Center
1312 Ashley River Rd., Charleston, SC
843-628-4380
https://www.plannedparenthood.org/health-center/south-carolina/charleston/29407/
charleston-health-center-4288-90860

POLITICAL, FUNDING, AND PRACTICAL SUPPORT GROUPS

WREN
1201 Main St., Suite 320, Columbia, SC
803-939-2192
https://www.scwren.org/

Planned Parenthood Votes South Atlantic
https://www.plannedparenthoodaction.org/planned-parenthood-votes-south-atlantic

South Dakota (abortion is available in clinic until thirteen weeks six days' gestation)

CLINICS

Planned Parenthood—Sioux Falls Center
6511 W. 41st St., Sioux Falls, SD
605-361-5100
https://www.plannedparenthood.org/health-center/south-dakota/sioux-falls/57106/
sioux-falls-clinic-2738-90720

POLITICAL, FUNDING, AND PRACTICAL SUPPORT GROUPS

NARAL Pro-Choice South Dakota
605-334-5065
info@prochoicesd.org

Planned Parenthood South Dakota Advocate
https://www.plannedparenthoodaction.org/planned-parenthood-south-dakota-advocate

South Dakota NOW
https://www.facebook.com/nowsouthdakota

South Dakota Access for Every Woman
1816 S. Norton, Sioux Falls, SD
605-338-3350
http://sdaccess4everywoman.org/

Tennessee (abortion is available in clinics until seventeen weeks six days' gestation)

CLINICS

Bristol Regional Women's Center
2901 W. State St., Bristol, TN
423-968-2182
http://www.bristolregionalwomenscenter.com/

Knoxville Center for Reproductive Health
1547 W. Clinch Ave., Knoxville, TN
800-325-5357
http://kcrh.com/

Planned Parenthood—Knoxville Health Center (medication only)
710 N. Cherry St., Knoxville, TN
866-711-1717
https://www.plannedparenthood.org/health-center/tennessee/knoxville/37914/
   knoxville-health-center-2610-91560

✱Choices—Memphis Center for Reproductive Health
1726 Poplar Way, Memphis, TN
800-843-9895
https://memphischoices.org/

Planned Parenthood—Memphis Health Center
2430 Poplar Ave., Suite 100, Memphis, TN
866-711-1717
https://www.plannedparenthood.org/health-center/tennessee/memphis/38112/
   memphis-health-center-3348-91550

Planned Parenthood—Memphis Health Center near Summer and I-240 (medication
   only)
835 Virginia Run Cove, Memphis, TN
866-711-1717
https://www.plannedparenthood.org/health-center/tennessee/memphis/38122/
   memphis-health-center-near-summer-and-i240-4247-91550

Planned Parenthood—Nashville Health Center
412 Dr. D. B. Todd Jr. Blvd., Nashville, TN
615-321-7216
https://www.plannedparenthood.org/health-center/tennessee/nashville/37203/
   nashville-health-center-2716-91560

POLITICAL, FUNDING, AND PRACTICAL SUPPORT GROUPS

SisterReach
2725 Kirby Rd., Suite 15, Memphis, TN
901-614-9906
http://www.sisterreach.org

National Asian Pacific American Women's Forum—Tennessee Chapter
https://www.napawf.org/nashvillechapter.html
nashvilleleaders@napawf.org

BirthStrides
Memphis, TN
https://www.birthstrides.org/
https://www.birthstrides.org/contact.html

Tennessee Reproductive Action Fund
1750 Madison Ave. #600, Memphis, TN
866-369-8672
https://sisterreach.org/

Healthy and Free Tennessee
1726 Poplar Ave., Memphis, TN
info@healthyandfreetn.org

Tennessee Advocates for Planned Parenthood
https://www.plannedparenthoodaction.org/tennessee-advocates-planned-parenthood

Nashville NOW
https://www.facebook.com/nashvillenow2

Knoxville Abortion Doulas Collective
https://knoxabortiondoulas.org/

Texas (abortion available in clinic through twenty-one weeks six days' gestation)

CLINICS

Austin Women's Health Center
1902 S. IH 35 Frontage Rd., Austin, TX
800-252-7016
http://www.austinwomenshealth.com/

Planned Parenthood—South Austin Health Center
201 E. Ben White Blvd., Bldg. 2, Austin, TX
512-276-8000
https://www.plannedparenthood.org/health-center/texas/austin/78704/
    south-austin-health-center-2397-91620

✱Whole Women's Health of Austin
8401 N. IH 35, Suite 200, Austin, TX
512-250-1005
https://wholewomanshealth.com/clinic/whole-womans-health-of-austin/#location

Coastal Birth Control Center
1901 Morgan Ave., Corpus Christi, TX
210-614-4742
http://www.coastalbirthcontrolcenter.com/

Northpark Medical Group
8363 Meadow Rd., Dallas, TX
214-890-0015
http://www.aaronwomenscenterdallas.com/

Planned Parenthood—South Dallas Surgical Health Services Center
7989 W. Virginia Dr., Dallas, TX
214-373-1868
https://www.plannedparenthood.org/health-center/texas/dallas/75237/south-dallas-surgical-health-services-center-4149-91620

Southwestern Women's Surgery Center
8616 Greenville Ave. #101, Dallas, TX
800-727-2255
https://southwesternwomens.com/

Hilltop Women's Reproductive Clinic
500 E. Schuster Ave., Suite B, El Paso, TX
915-542- 2811
https://hilltopwomensreproductive.com/

Planned Parenthood—Southwest Fort Worth Health Center
6464 John Ryan Dr., Suite B, Fort Worth, TX
817-276-8063
https://www.plannedparenthood.org/health-center/texas/fort-worth/76132/southwest-fort-worth-health-center-4101-91620

✱Whole Women's Health of Fort Worth
3256 Lackland Rd., Fort Worth, TX
800-778-2444
http://wholewomanshealth.com/clinic/whole-womans-health-of-fort-worth/#location

Planned Parenthood—Center for Choice Ambulatory Surgical Center
4600 Gulf Fwy., Suite 300, Houston, TX
713-535-2400
https://www.plannedparenthood.org/health-center/texas/houston/77023/planned-parenthood-center-for-choice-ambulatory-surgical-center-(abortion)-2292-91650

Suburban Women's Clinic (NW Houston)
17070 Red Oak Dr., Suite 509, Houston, TX
800-233-0608
http://www.suburbanwomensclinic.com/

Suburban Women's Clinic—SW Houston
3101 Richmond Ave. #250, Houston, TX
713-526-6500
http://www.suburbanwomensclinic.com/

Texas Ambulatory Surgical Center
2505 N. Shepherd Dr., Houston, TX
713-272-6900
http://www.aaronwomenscenterhouston.com/

✱The Houston Women's Clinic
4820 San Jacinto St., Houston, TX
800-646-4483
http://houstonwomensclinic.com/

✱Whole Women's Health of McAllen
802 S. Main St., McAllen, TX
956-686-2137
http://wholewomanshealth.com/clinic/whole-womans-health-of-mcallen/#location

Alamo Women's Reproductive Services
7402 John Smith Dr. #101, San Antonio, TX
210-816-2307
http://alamowomensclinic.com/

Planned Parenthood—South Texas Health Center
2140 Babcock Rd., San Antonio, TX
210-736-2262
https://www.plannedparenthood.org/health-center/texas/san-antonio/78229/
    planned-parenthood---south-texas-medical-center-2967-91710

✱Whole Women's Health of San Antonio
4025 E. Southcross, Bldg. 5, Suite 30, San Antonio, TX
210-549-4084
http://wholewomanshealth.com/clinic/whole-womans-health-of-san-antonio/#location

POLITICAL, FUNDING, AND PRACTICAL SUPPORT GROUPS

Afiya Center
Dallas, TX
972-629-9266
https://theafiyacenter.org/
info@theafiyacenter.org

Texas Freedom Network
http://tfn.org/

Texas Latina Advocacy Network (TX LAN)
http://latinainstitute.org/en/texas

NARAL Pro-Choice Texas
PO Box 684602, Austin, TX
512-462-1661
info@prochoicetexas.org

Planned Parenthood Texas Votes
http://pptexasvotes.org/

Texas State NOW
http://nowtexas.com/

Shift (Whole Women's Health Alliance)
https://www.wholewomanshealthalliance.org/shift/

South Texans for Reproductive Justice
https://www.facebook.com/SoTX4ReproJustice/
sotx4rj@gmail.com

Frontera Fund (Rio Grande Valley)
956-307-9330
https://lafronterafund.org/

Texas Equal Access Fund (TEA Fund)
PO Box 227336, Dallas, TX
888-854-4852
http://www.teafund.org

Cicada Collective (Dallas/Fort Worth)—Practical Support
This group provides practical support such as lodging, transportation, and abortion
    doulas to North Texas abortion clinics.
940-441-3337
http://www.cicadacollective.org/ntx-abortion-support-network-ntx-asn.html
cicadacollectiventx@gmail.com

Clinic Access Support Network—Funding and Practical Support
Houston, TX
281-947-2276
http://www.clinicaccess.org

Lilith Fund
Austin, TX
877-659-4304
http://www.lilithfund.org

Stigma Relief Fund
8401 N. IH 35, Suite 1A, Austin, TX
512-250-1005
http://www.shiftstigma.org/

Fund Texas Choice—Practical Support
3903 S. Congress Ave. #41823, Austin, TX
512-900-8908; 844-900-8908
http://fundtexaschoice.org

Bridge Collective—Practical Support
Austin, TX
512-524-9822
https://thebridgecollective.org/STANDinfo

West Fund
PO Box 920088; El Paso, TX
915-213-4535 (English); 915-213-4578 (Spanish)
http://www.westfund.org/

Utah (abortion is available in clinic until twenty-one weeks six days' gestation)

CLINICS

Planned Parenthood—Metro Health Center
160 S. 1000 East, Suite 120, Salt Lake City, UT
801-257-6789
https://www.plannedparenthood.org/health-center/utah/salt-lake-city/84102/
    metro-health-center-3958-91730

Wasatch Women's Center
715 E. 3900 S. #203, Salt Lake City, UT
801-263-2111
http://www.wasatchwomenscenter.net/

POLITICAL, FUNDING, AND PRACTICAL SUPPORT GROUPS

Utah Reproductive Freedom Forum
801-746-0404
https://www.ucasa.org/rff
info@ucasa.org

The People's Justice Forum—Planned Parenthood Action Council of Utah
654 S. 900 E., Salt Lake City, UT
801-532-1586
ppac@ppau.org

Vermont (abortion is available in clinic until eighteen weeks six days' gestation)

CLINICS

Planned Parenthood—Barre Health Center (medication only)
90 Washington St., Barre, VT
802-476-6696
https://www.plannedparenthood.org/health-center/vermont/barre/05641/
barre-health-center-2654-91770

Planned Parenthood—Bennington Health Center (medication only)
194 North St., Suite 8, Bennington, VT
802-442-8166
https://www.plannedparenthood.org/health-center/vermont/bennington/05201/
bennington-health-center-2655-91770

Planned Parenthood—Burlington Health Center
183 Saint Paul St., Burlington, VT
802-863-6326
https://www.plannedparenthood.org/health-center/vermont/burlington/05401/
burlington-health-center-2650-91770

Planned Parenthood—Rutland Health Center
11 Burnham Ave., Rutland, VT
802-775-2333
https://www.plannedparenthood.org/health-center/vermont/rutland/05701/
rutland-health-center-4229-91770

Planned Parenthood—White River Junction Health Center
79 S. Main St., White River Junction, VT
802-281-6056
https://www.plannedparenthood.org/health-center/vermont/white-river-junction/
05001/white-river-junction-health-center-2745-91770

Planned Parenthood—Williston Health Center (medication only)
75 Talcott Rd., Williston, VT
802-879-4800
https://www.plannedparenthood.org/health-center/vermont/williston/05495/
williston-health-center-3317-91770

POLITICAL, FUNDING, AND PRACTICAL SUPPORT GROUPS

Planned Parenthood Vermont Action Fund
https://www.plannedparenthoodaction.org/planned-parenthood-vermont-
    action-fund

Vermont Access to Reproductive Freedom
PO Box 8452, Burlington, VT
800-491-8273
http://www.vermontaccess.org/

Virginia (abortion is available in clinic until nineteen weeks six days' gestation)

CLINICS

Annandale Women and Family Center
2839 Duke St., Alexandria, VA
703-751-4702
http://www.awfc.net/

Planned Parenthood—Charlottesville Health Center
2964 Hydraulic Rd., Charlottesville, VA
434-296-1000
https://www.plannedparenthood.org/health-center/virginia/charlottesville/22901/
    charlottesville-health-center-2815-90860

✱Whole Women's Health of Charlottesville
2321 Commonwealth Dr., Charlottesville, VA
434-973-4888
https://wholewomanshealth.com/clinic/whole-womans-health-of-charlottesville/
    #location

✱Falls Church Healthcare Center
900 S. Washington St. #300, Falls Church, VA
800-228-3561
https://fallschurchhealthcare.com/

Planned Parenthood—Hampton Health Center (medication only)
403 Yale Dr., Hampton, VA
757-826-2079
https://www.plannedparenthood.org/health-center/virginia/hampton/23666/
    hampton-health-center-4164-91750

A Tidewater Women's Health Clinic
891 Norfolk Sq., Norfolk, VA
800-490-0011
http://www.yourchoice-va.com/

A Capital Women's Health
1511 Starling Dr., Richmond, VA
804-754-1928
http://capitalwomenshealth.com/

Planned Parenthood—Richmond Health Center
201 N. Hamilton St., Richmond, VA
804-355-4358
https://www.plannedparenthood.org/health-center/virginia/richmond/23221/
    richmond-health-center-3913-91750

Planned Parenthood—Roanoke Health Center
2207 Peters Creek Rd., Roanoke, VA
540-562-3457
https://www.plannedparenthood.org/health-center/virginia/roanoke/24017/roanoke-
    health-center-2768-90860

Planned Parenthood—Virginia Beach Health Center
515 Newtown Rd., Virginia Beach, VA
757-499-7526
https://www.plannedparenthood.org/health-center/virginia/virginia-beach/23462/
    virginia-beach-health-center-4166-91750

POLITICAL, FUNDING, AND PRACTICAL SUPPORT GROUPS

Virginia Latina Advocacy Network (VA LAN)
http://latinainstitute.org/en/virginia

NARAL Pro-Choice Virginia
PO Box 1204, Alexandria, VA
571-970-2536
info@naralva.org

ReproAction Virginia Affiliate
https://reproaction.org/take-action/?ss=39#listing

Planned Parenthood Advocates of Virginia
https://www.plannedparenthoodaction.org/planned-parenthood-advocates-
    virginia-inc

Virginia NOW
http://vanow.org/

Blue Ridge Abortion Assistance Fund
PO Box 5082, Charlottesville, VA
434-963-0669

Richmond Reproductive Freedom Project
PO Box 7389, Richmond, VA
888-847-1593
http://www.rrfp.net

Washington (abortion is available in clinic until twenty-six weeks' gestation)

CLINICS

Planned Parenthood—Eastside/Bellevue Health Center
14730 NE 8th St., Bellevue, WA
800-769-0045
https://www.plannedparenthood.org/health-center/washington/bellevue/98007/
    eastside-bellevue-health-center-4151-91810

Planned Parenthood—Bellingham Health Center
1530 Ellis St., Bellingham, WA
360-734-9095
https://www.plannedparenthood.org/health-center/washington/bellingham/98225/
    bellingham-health-center-2454-91780

Planned Parenthood—Bremerton Health Center
723 NE Riddell Rd., Suite A, Bremerton, WA
800-769-0045
https://www.plannedparenthood.org/health-center/washington/bremerton/98310/
    bremerton-health-center-2461-91810

Planned Parenthood—Centralia Health Center (medication only)
1020 W. Main St., Centralia, WA
800-769-0045
https://www.plannedparenthood.org/health-center/washington/centralia/98531/
    centralia-health-center-2453-91810

Planned Parenthood—Everett Health Center
1509 32nd St., Everett, WA
800-769-0045
https://www.plannedparenthood.org/health-center/washington/everett/98201/
    everett-health-center-2994-91810

Planned Parenthood—Federal Way Health Center (medication only)
1105 S. 348th St. #B103, Federal Way, WA
800-769-0045
https://www.plannedparenthood.org/health-center/washington/federal-way/98003/
federal-way-health-center-2503-91810

Planned Parenthood—Kennewick Health Center
7426 W. Bonnie Pl., Kennewick, WA
866-904-7721
https://www.plannedparenthood.org/health-center/washington/kennewick/99336/
kennewick-health-center-2404-91850

Planned Parenthood—Kent Valley Health Center (medication only)
10056 SE 240th St. #A, Kent, WA
800-769-0045
https://www.plannedparenthood.org/health-center/washington/kent/98031/
kent-valley-health-center-2501-91810

Planned Parenthood—Lynnwood Health Center (medication only)
19505 76th Ave. W. 200, Lynnwood, WA
800-769-0045
https://www.plannedparenthood.org/health-center/washington/lynnwood/98036/
lynnwood-health-center-2996-91810

Planned Parenthood—Marysville Health Center (medication only)
10210 State Ave., Marysville, WA
800-769-0045
https://www.plannedparenthood.org/health-center/washington/marysville/98271/
marysville-health-center-2457-91810

Planned Parenthood—Mount Vernon Health Center
1805 E. Division St., Mount Vernon, WA
360-848-1744
https://www.plannedparenthood.org/health-center/washington/mt.-vernon/98274/
mt.-vernon-health-center-2843-91780

Planned Parenthood—Olympia Health Center
402 Legion Way, Suite 201, Olympia, WA
800-769-0045
https://www.plannedparenthood.org/health-center/washington/olympia/98501/
olympia-health-center-2460-91810

Planned Parenthood—Port Angeles Health Center (medication only)
426 E. 8th St., Port Angeles, WA
800-769-0045
https://www.plannedparenthood.org/health-center/washington/port-angeles/98362/
port-angeles-health-center-3972-91810

Planned Parenthood—Pullman Health Center (medication only)
1525 SE King Dr., Pullman, WA
866-904-7721
https://www.plannedparenthood.org/health-center/washington/pullman/99163/
   pullman-health-center-2793-91850

Planned Parenthood—Puyallup Health Center (medication only)
702 30th Ave. SW, Puyallup, WA
800-769-0045
https://www.plannedparenthood.org/health-center/washington/puyallup/98373/
   puyallup-health-center-2504-91810

✱Cedar River Clinics—Renton
263 Rainier Ave. S., Suite 200, Renton, WA
800-572-4223
http://www.cedarriverclinics.org/

✱All Women's Care
9730 3rd Ave. NE #200, Seattle, WA
888-94-WOMEN (96636)
http://www.awcseattle.com/

✱Cedar River Clinics—Seattle
509 Olive Way #1454, Seattle, WA
800-572-4223
http://www.cedarriverclinics.org/

Planned Parenthood—First Hill Health Center
1229 Madison St. #1040, Seattle, WA
800-769-0045
https://www.plannedparenthood.org/health-center/washington/seattle/98104/
   first-hill-health-center-4069-91810

Planned Parenthood—Seattle Health Center
2001 E. Madison St., Seattle, WA
800-769-0045
https://www.plannedparenthood.org/health-center/washington/seattle/98122/
   seattle-health-center-3309-91810

Planned Parenthood—White Center—West Seattle Health Center (medication only)
9942 8th Ave. SW, Seattle, WA
800-769-0045
https://www.plannedparenthood.org/health-center/washington/seattle/98106/
   white-center---west-seattle-health-center-4161-91810

Planned Parenthood—Shelton Health Center (medication only)
2505 Olympic Hwy. N. #400, Shelton, WA
800-769-0045
https://www.plannedparenthood.org/health-center/washington/shelton/98584/
shelton-health-center-2462-91810

✱Seattle Medical and Wellness Clinic (Trust Women Seattle)
1325 4th Ave. #1240, Seattle, WA
800-522-0606
https://trustwomen.org/clinics/seattle/home

Women's Health Care Center at UWMC—Roosevelt
4245 Roosevelt Way NE, 4th Floor, Seattle, WA
206-598-5500
http://www.uwmedicine.org/locations/womens-health-care-center-uwmc-roosevelt

Planned Parenthood—Spokane Valley Health Center (medication only)
12104 E. Main Ave., Spokane Valley, WA
866-904-7721
https://www.plannedparenthood.org/health-center/washington/spokane-valley/
99206/spokane-valley-health-center-2792-91850

All Women's Health
3711 Pacific Ave. #200, Tacoma, WA
877-471-3464
http://www.awhtacoma.com/

✱Cedar River Clinics—Tacoma
1401-A Martin Luther King Jr. Way, Tacoma, WA
800-572-4223
http://www.cedarriverclinics.org/

Planned Parenthood—Tacoma Health Center
1515 Martin Luther King Jr. Way, Tacoma, WA
800-769-0045
https://www.plannedparenthood.org/health-center/washington/tacoma/98405/
tacoma-health-center-4106-91810

Planned Parenthood—Vancouver Health Center (medication only)
11516 SE Mill Plain Blvd., Suite 2-E, Vancouver, WA
888-875-7820
https://www.plannedparenthood.org/health-center/washington/vancouver/98684/
vancouver-center-2455-91400

Planned Parenthood—Walla Walla Health Center (medication only)
828 S. First Ave., Walla Walla, WA
866-904-7721
https://www.plannedparenthood.org/health-center/washington/walla-walla/99362/
walla-walla-health-center-2405-91850

Planned Parenthood—Yakima Health Center
1117 Tieton Dr., Yakima, WA
866-904-7721
https://www.plannedparenthood.org/health-center/washington/yakima/98902/yaki-ma-health-center-3311-91850

POLITICAL, FUNDING, AND PRACTICAL SUPPORT GROUPS

NARAL Pro-Choice Washington
811 First Ave., Suite 675, Seattle, WA
206-624-1990
info@prochoicewashington.org

Full Spectrum Doulas
http://www.fullspectrumdoulas.org/
sea@fullspectrumdoulas.org

National Asian Pacific American Women's Forum—Seattle Chapter
https://www.napawf.org/seattlechapter.html
Seattlechapter@napawf.org

Planned Parenthood Votes Northwest and Hawaii
https://www.plannedparenthoodaction.org/planned-parenthood-votes-northwest-and-hawaii

Washington State NOW
https://www.facebook.com/NOWWashingtonstate

NOW Seattle
http://nowseattle.org/

Women in Need Fund
106 E. E St., Yakima, WA
800-572-4223
http://www.cedarriverclinics.org/

Northwest Abortion Access Fund
866-692-2310
http://nwaafund.org/

West Virginia (abortion is available in clinic until sixteen weeks' gestation)

CLINICS

✱Women's Health Care of West Virginia
510 Washington St., West Charleston, WV
800-642-8670
http://www.whcwva.com/

POLITICAL, FUNDING, AND PRACTICAL SUPPORT GROUPS

WV Free
PO Box 11042, Charleston, WV
304-342-9188
http://www.wvfree.org/

Planned Parenthood Votes! South Atlantic
https://www.plannedparenthoodaction.org/planned-parenthood-votes-south-atlantic

West Virginia NOW
https://www.facebook.com/WestVirginiaNOW/

WV FREE Choice Fund
PO Box 11042, Charleston, WV
304-344-9834
http://www.wvfree.org/

Wisconsin (abortion is available in clinic until twenty-one weeks six days' gestation)

CLINICS

Planned Parenthood—Madison East Clinic
3706 Orin Rd., Madison, WI
608-241-3767
https://www.plannedparenthood.org/health-center/wisconsin/madison/53704/
madison-east-2733-91860

✱Affiliated Medical Services
1428 N. Farwell Ave., Milwaukee, WI
800-498-0424
http://www.affiliatedmedicalservices.com/

Planned Parenthood—Milwaukee—Water Street Health Center
435 S. Water St., Milwaukee, WI
414-276-8777
https://www.plannedparenthood.org/health-center/wisconsin/milwaukee/53204/
milwaukee-water-street-health-center-4270-91860

POLITICAL, FUNDING, AND PRACTICAL SUPPORT GROUPS

NARAL Pro-Choice Wisconsin
612 W. Main St. #200, Madison, WI
608-287-0016
info@prochoicewisconsin.org

ReproAction Wisconsin Affiliate
https://reproaction.org/take-action/?ss=1190#listing

Planned Parenthood Advocates of Wisconsin
http://www.ppawi.org/

Wisconsin RCRC (Religious Coalition for Reproductive Choice)
PO Box 2504, Appleton, WI
920-319-4388
wi_rcrc@yahoo.com

Wisconsin NOW
http://www.nowmadison.org/

Freedom Fund
PO Box 92, Marshfield, WI
715-384-3360

Options Fund
PO Box 473, Eau Claire, WI
715-838-9991

Women's Medical Fund
PO Box 248, Madison, WI
http://wmfwisconsin.org/

Wyoming (abortion is available in clinic through the first trimester)

CLINICS

Emerg-A-Care of Jackson Hole
455 W. Broadway, Jackson Hole, WY
307-733-8002
http://emergacare.com/

POLITICAL, FUNDING, AND PRACTICAL SUPPORT GROUPS

NARAL Pro-Choice Wyoming
PO Box 271, Laramie, WY
307-742-9189
naralprochoicewy@netscape.net

Women for Women
PO Box 1472, Lander, WY
307-438-9272
http://wyomingw4w.org/

District of Columbia (abortion is available in clinic until twenty-six weeks' gestation)

CLINICS

Planned Parenthood—Carol Whitehill Moses Center
1225 4th St. NE, Washington, DC
202-347-8500
https://www.plannedparenthood.org/health-center/district-of-columbia/washington/
20002/carol-whitehill-moses-center-4221-90230

Washington Surgi-Center
2112 F St. NW, Suite 400, Washington, DC
202-659-9403
http://www.washingtonsurgi-clinic.com/

POLITICAL, FUNDING, AND PRACTICAL SUPPORT GROUPS

ReproAction—DC affiliate
https://reproaction.org/take-action/?ss=38#listing

DC Abortion Fund (DCAF)
PO Box 65061, Washington, DC
202-452-7464
http://dcabortionfund.org/
info@dcabortionfund.org (not for funding requests)

Washington Area Clinic Defense Force
PO Box 21796, Washington, DC
202-681-6577
http://www.wacdtf.org/
wacdtf@wacdtf.org

National Latina Institute for Reproductive Health—DC
http://latinainstitute.org/en/washington-dc

National Asian Pacific American Women's Forum—DC Chapter
https://www.napawf.org/dcchapter.html
napawfdc@gmail.com

DC NOW
http://www.dc-now.org/

Justice Fund DC (DC Planned Parenthood specific)
PO Box 34128, Washington, DC
202-347-8500

National Resources

Abortion Access Hackathon
https://www.abortionaccesshackathon.com/

Abortion Care Network
https://www.abortioncarenetwork.org/

Abortion Conversation Project
http://www.abortionconversationproject.org/

Advocates for Youth
http://www.advocatesforyouth.org/

ACLU Reproductive Freedom Project
https://www.aclu.org/issues/reproductive-freedom

A Is For
https://www.aisfor.org/

All* Above All
https://allaboveall.org

All Options Pregnancy Resource Center/All Options Talkline
https://alloptionsprc.org

Black Mamas Matter Alliance
https://blackmamasmatter.org

Black Women's Health Imperative
https://www.bwhi.org/

Catholics for Choice
http://www.catholicsforchoice.org/

Center for Reproductive Rights
https://www.reproductiverights.org/

Expose Fake Clinics
https://www.exposefakeclinics.com/

Feminist Majority Foundation
http://www.feminist.org/

Feminist Majority Campus Project
http://feministcampus.org/about/

If/When/How
https://www.ifwhenhow.org/

In Our Own Voice/National Black Women's Reproductive Justice Agenda
http://blackrj.org/

Interfaith Voices for Reproductive Justice
http://iv4rj.org/

Jane's Due Process
https://janesdueprocess.org/

Lady Parts Justice
https://ladypartsjusticeleague.com/

Medical Students for Choice
https://www.msfc.org/

National Abortion Federation
https://prochoice.org/

National Asian Pacific American Women's Forum (NAPAWF)
https://www.napawf.org/

NARAL
https://www.prochoiceamerica.org/

National Advocates for Pregnant Women
http://www.advocatesforpregnantwomen.org

National Clinic Access Project
http://www.feminist.org/rrights/ncapabout.asp

National Health Law Program
http://www.healthlaw.org/

National Institute for Reproductive Health
https://www.nirhealth.org/

National Latina Institute for Reproductive Health
http://latinainstitute.org/en
http://latinainstitute.org/es

National LGBTQ Task Force
http://www.thetaskforce.org/

National Network of Abortion Funds
https://abortionfunds.org/

NOW (National Organization for Women)
https://now.org/

National Partnership for Women and Families
http://www.nationalpartnership.org/

National Women's Law Center
https://nwlc.org/

Native American Women's Health Education Resource Center
http://www.nativeshop.org/

Nurses for Sexual and Reproductive Health
http://nsrh.org/

Physicians for Reproductive Health
https://prh.org/

Plan C
https://plancpills.org/home/

Planned Parenthood Federation of America
https://www.plannedparenthood.org/

Religious Coalition for Reproductive Choice
http://rcrc.org/

ReproAction
https://reproaction.org/

Reproductive Health Access Project (RHAP)
https://www.reproductiveaccess.org/

SASS (Self-Managed Abortion Safe and Supported)
https://abortionpillinfo.org/

Shout Your Abortion
https://shoutyourabortion.com

SIA Legal Team
https://www.sialegalteam.org/

SisterSong Women of Color Reproductive Justice Collective
https://www.sistersong.net/

UltraViolet
https://weareultraviolet.org/

URGE (Unite for Reproductive and Gender Equity)
http://urge.org/

VoteProChoice
https://voteprochoice.civicengine.com/

We Testify
https://wetestify.org/

Whole Women's Health Alliance (Shift)
https://www.wholewomanshealthalliance.org/outreach-education/

Women's March
https://www.joinwomensmarch.org/

Model Legislation

While activists must be working on the ground to keep abortion as accessible as we can in a post-*Roe* America, we also need to continue to fight for our rights legislatively, as well. The following two model bills are the best options for introducing change at a state level— either to codify rights in states where abortion remains legal, or to protect all people who may become pregnant and find themselves with poor birth outcomes that could put them under suspicion in states where abortion is prohibited.

Women's Equality, Dignity and Fairness Act

Summary: The Women's Equality, Dignity and Fairness Act would lay out a broad abortion rights vision including the right of women to abortion coverage in both public and private insurance, the right of clinics to operate in safety and as medically appropriate, the right of patients to receive the truth about reproductive medicine, and the right of qualified medical professionals to deliver abortion services.

Background Summary

Abortion is one of the safest and most common medical procedures in the United States. The Centers for Disease Control found that legal abortion is significantly safer than childbirth, and a study in the *American Journal of Public Health* reported that first-trimester abortion is one of the safest medical procedures in America. Approximately three in ten women will have an abortion in their lifetimes and will need access to safe, legal facilities to obtain abortion care.

Women's equality, dignity and fairness requires that women have access to abortion regardless of their economic status or source of insurance coverage. And yet, 33 states and the District of Columbia prohibit the use of state Medicaid funds for abortions, except in limited cases. Twenty-five states restrict abortion coverage in their insurance exchanges. Twenty-one states restrict abortion coverage for state employee health plans. And ten states restrict abortion coverage in standard private insurance plans.

Women's equality, dignity and fairness requires that women are able to access reproductive healthcare clinics without fear of assault. And yet, patients are stalked, threatened, and harassed. In addition to being blocked on public walkways and being called murderers, anti-choice protesters often make patients fear for their personal safety.

Women's equality, dignity and fairness requires that abortion, provided by qualified medical professionals, be accessible to all women. And yet, because of restrictive laws and physical threats, the number of abortion providers has declined in recent years. The American College of Obstetricians and Gynecologists (ACOG) recommends allowing trained advanced practice clinicians (APCs)—nurse practitioners, certified nurse-midwives and physician assistants—to perform aspiration and medication abortions, yet only a few states allow it.

Women's equality, dignity and fairness requires that reproductive health care clinics are not forced to close because of politics. And yet, 24 states have Targeted Regulation of Abortion Providers or "TRAP laws" that are intended to close abortion clinics. Most often, the restrictions dictate that abortions be performed at sites that are the functional equivalent of ambulatory surgical centers, or even hospitals, which makes the delivery of health care services prohibitively expensive. Other TRAP laws require clinicians at abortion facilities to have admitting privileges at a local hospital or mandate transfer agreements with hospitals, effectively giving hospitals veto power over whether an abortion clinic can exist.

The Women's Equality, Dignity and Fairness Act lays out a broad abortion rights vision. Abortion rights includes the right to abortion coverage in both public and private insurance, the right of clinics and clinic patients to be safe from violence, the right of women to truthful medical information, and the right of all patients to medically appropriate care.

Model Legislation

SECTION 1. SHORT TITLE
This Act shall be called the "Women's Equality, Dignity and Fairness Act."

SECTION 2. FINDINGS AND PURPOSE
(A) FINDINGS—The legislature finds that:

1) Approximately three in ten women will have an abortion in their lifetimes, and will need access to safe, legal facilities to obtain abortion care without delay.

2) Abortion is one of the safest medical procedures in the United States.

3) Women's equality, dignity and fairness requires that women have access to abortion regardless of their economic status and that no woman should have the decision to have, or not to have, an abortion made for her based on her ability or inability to afford the procedure. Since 1976, the federal government has withheld funds for abortion coverage through the Medicaid program as well as other federal health plans and programs. Seventeen states, however, have policies that include Medicaid abortion coverage because it is wrong to coerce women who cannot afford abortion to, for no other reason, carry a pregnancy to term.

4) Women's equality, dignity and fairness requires that women are able to access reproductive healthcare clinics without fear of assault. Every individual should be free to make personal health care decisions without fear of harassment and violence. Over the years, hundreds of reproductive health care facilities have experienced bombings, arsons and other attacks. Employees and physicians have been targeted, physically injured, and in some cases killed. Health care providers have been stalked, threatened, and harassed in person, on the phone, and through the mail.

5) Women's equality, dignity and fairness requires that women are given truthful science-based information about reproductive health care clinics. Some Crisis Pregnancy Centers (CPCs) use advertising to mislead women contemplating abortion into believing that their facilities offer abortion services and unbiased counseling—when the opposite is true. Because of the time-sensitive and constitutionally protected nature of the decision to terminate a pregnancy, false and misleading advertising about the services offered by CPCs is of special concern.

6) Women's equality, dignity and fairness requires that abortion, provided by qualified medical professionals, be accessible to all women. The number of abortion providers has decreased due to practice restrictions and threats of violence. The American College of Obstetricians and Gynecologists (ACOG) recommends allowing advanced practice clinicians (APCs)—nurse practitioners, certified nurse-midwives and physician assistants—to perform aspiration abortions and medication abortions. Studies show that trained APCs are fully qualified to provide aspiration and medication abortion services.

7) Women's equality, dignity and fairness requires that reproductive health care clinics are not forced to close because of politics. Today, almost 90 percent of U.S. counties lack an abortion facility. In 2015, four states had only one abortion provider, and at least ten states had three or fewer abortion providers. Clinic closures can force women to travel long distances to reach the nearest clinic, or force women to delay care as they arrange transportation, time off from work, and save additional money for travel or lodging costs. Women who face these obstacles are more likely to seek out less safe alternatives to legal abortion.

(B) PURPOSE—This law is enacted to guarantee women's equality, dignity, and fairness by ensuring the availability of abortion free from violence and political and economic obstacles.

SECTION 3. ABORTION COVERAGE EQUITY

After section XXX, the following new section XXX shall be inserted:

(A) DEFINITIONS—In this section:

1) "Abortion" means any medical treatment intended to induce the termination of a pregnancy except for the purpose of producing a live birth and any related services, including but not limited to diagnostic, counseling, referral, or follow up services.

2) "State" means the state, any state agency, and every county, city, town, municipal corporation, quasi-municipal corporation, and public institution in the state.

(B) POLICY TO COVER ABORTION

Abortion shall be covered in all types of health insurance offered, sold, or purchased in this State, including all private plans, all state-funded plans, and all state-provided benefits.

(C) RESTRICTIONS ON ABORTION CARE REPEALED

1) Section XXX [any provision of law that prohibits abortion care in private health insurance plans] is hereby repealed.

2) Section XXX [any provision of law that prohibits abortion care in state employee insurance plans] is hereby repealed.

3) Section XXX [any provision of law that prohibits abortion care in the state insurance exchange] is hereby repealed.

4) Section XXX [any provision of law that prohibits abortion care in Medicaid coverage] is hereby repealed.

5) Section XXX [any provision of law that prohibits abortion care in any other state-funded insurance program] is hereby repealed.

(D) SEVERABILITY

The provisions of this section shall be severable, and if any phrase, clause, sentence or provision is declared to be invalid or results in noncompliance with federal requirements that are a condition to the allocation of federal funds to the state, those words will not be enforced only to the extent they jeopardize federal funding or the validity of the Act.

SECTION 4. ACCOUNTABILITY FOR HARASSMENT OF WOMEN

After Section XXX, the following new section XXX shall be inserted:

(A) DEFINITIONS—In this section:

1) "Coercion" means when a person, with intent unlawfully to restrict freedom of action of another to the detriment of the other:

    a) Threatens to commit any criminal offense;

    b) Makes any scheme, plan, or pattern intended to cause a person to believe that the decision to seek reproductive or sexual health care or failure to seek reproductive health care would result in serious harm to or physical restraint against any person; or

    c) Abuses or threatens the abuse of the legal process.

2) "Entity" means a partnership, limited partnership, association of two or more individuals, or any type of corporation, whether incorporated or unincorporated.

3) "Harassment" means a knowing and willful course of conduct that is directed at a specific person, that would cause a reasonable person to be seriously alarmed or harassed, and that in fact seriously alarms or harasses the person, and that serves no legitimate purpose.

4) "Health care provider" means any person, corporation, facility or institution licensed or otherwise authorized by the state to

provide health care services, including, but not limited to, any physician, coordinated care organization, hospital, health care facility, dentist, nurse, optometrist, podiatrist, physical therapist, psychologist, chiropractor or pharmacist and an officer, employee or agent of such person acting in the course and scope of employment or agency related to health care services.

5) "Health care facility" means any office, building, or other place in which health care services are provided by a health care provider, whether or not the facility is licensed by the state.

6) "Interfering" means knowingly and intentionally pursuing a course of conduct designed to deter, prevent or delay a person from providing or referring for reproductive health care through threats, intimidation, force, coercion or misrepresentation.

7) "Intimidation" means an act or course of conduct directed at a specific person that causes fear or apprehension in such person and serves no legitimate purpose.

8) "Misrepresentation" means a false statement of substantive fact, or conduct that leads to a belief of a substantive fact material to proper understanding of the matter in hand, made with intent to deceive or mislead.

9) "Reproductive health care" means abortion, contraception, infertility treatment, prenatal care, miscarriage management, treatment for STIs, as well as counseling for all of these services.

10) "Social services office" means any office or facility in which social services are provided, or any domestic violence center, including but not limited to referral for health care services.

(B) INTERFERENCE WITH THE PROVISION OF REPRODUCTIVE HEALTH CARE PROHIBITED

1) An individual or entity may not intentionally or knowingly prevent or delay, or attempt to prevent or delay, a health care pro-

vider or health care facility's efforts to provide reproductive health care, or a social services office's efforts to refer for reproductive health care, by:

    a) Harassing, coercing or intimidating a health care provider, or interfering with the performance of a duty or the exercise of a function by an employee of a health care facility where reproductive health care is provided;

    b) Interfering with the normal course of operations of a facility that provides reproductive health care; or

    c) Harassing, coercing or intimidating patients seeking access to reproductive health care from a health care provider or facility.

2) No government official or agency may act with the intent of preventing or unnecessarily delaying a health care provider's or medical facility's efforts to provide reproductive health care, except when specifically required by law.

(C) CIVIL CAUSE OF ACTION AND INJUNCTIVE RELIEF

1) Any individual or entity who has had his, her or its ability to provide reproductive health care limited or prevented as a result of a violation of this section shall have a cause of action against the individual or entity that engaged in that conduct. Any health care provider, entity or facility that has experienced a violation of this section may bring an action for compensatory damages and/or for injunctive relief for the purpose of stopping or preventing violations or threatened violations of this section, or to determine the applicability of this section to actions or threatened future actions. Such individual or entity may bring an action for statutory damages as permitted under this section, which in the event of a violation of the Act shall be fifteen thousand dollars ($15,000) per violation.

2) For all violations of this section, the plaintiff may recover reasonable attorneys' fees and costs.

3) Any plaintiff bringing a claim under this section shall be entitled to proceed under a pseudonym upon providing the court with affidavit asserting the harm that could arise to the plaintiff and/or his or her family or home if his or her identity is not concealed. The plaintiff shall be entitled to a presumption from the court that identification poses a risk of retaliatory physical or mental harm to the requesting party and to innocent nonparties. In a suit to which this section applies, only the following persons are entitled to know the true identifying information about the plaintiff: the judge and any court personnel working with the judge on the action in question; a party to the action; the attorney representing a party to the action; and a person authorized by a written order of a court specific to that person. The court shall order that no person shall divulge that information to anyone without a written order of the court, and a court shall hold a person who violates the order in contempt.

4) Any plaintiff bringing a claim under this section shall be presumed entitled to a protective order from the court prohibiting discovery regarding the following facts and any other associated facts that the plaintiff alleges will endanger him or herself or his or her family: the plaintiff's residential and work addresses, phone numbers and e-mail addresses, any information about the plaintiff's children, parents, or other family members including their names, ages, where they attend school, their phone numbers and e-mail addresses, any information about contractors with whom the plaintiff works; and any other identifying information. If the defendant or defendants believe that the above information is relevant to the defense's claims, defendant shall make a motion for discovery of that information under court seal. The court shall allow the information to be discovered only if the information is relevant to the

defense's claims, and only under seal with all non-relevant information redacted by plaintiff before it is provided to the court.

SECTION 5. CRISIS PREGNANCY CENTER FRAUD

After section XXX, the following new section XXX shall be inserted:

(A) DEFINITIONS—In this section:

1) "Abortion" means any medical treatment intended to induce the termination of a pregnancy except for the purpose of producing a live birth.

2) "Client" means an individual who is inquiring about or seeking services at a pregnancy services center.

3) "Emergency contraception" means any drug or device approved by the U.S. Food and Drug Administration that prevents pregnancy after sexual intercourse.

4) "Health information" means any oral or written information in any form or medium that relates to health insurance and/or the past, present or future physical or mental health or condition of a client.

5) "Limited services pregnancy center" means a pregnancy services center that does not directly provide, or provide referrals to clients, for abortions or emergency contraception.

6) "Pregnancy services center" means a facility, including a mobile facility, where the primary purpose is to provide services to women who are or may be pregnant, and that either offers obstetric ultrasounds, obstetric sonograms or prenatal care to pregnant women, or has the appearance of a medical facility. A pregnancy service center has the appearance of a medical facility if two or more of the following factors are present:

    a) The facility offers pregnancy testing and/or pregnancy diagnosis;

    b) The facility has staff or volunteers who wear medical attire or uniforms;

c) The facility contains one or more examination tables;

d) The facility contains a private or semi-private room or area containing medical supplies and/or medical instruments;

e) The facility has staff or volunteers who collect health information from clients; or

f) The facility is located on the same premises as a state-licensed medical facility or provider or shares facility space with a state-licensed medical provider.

6) "Premises" means land and improvements or appurtenances or any part thereof.

(B) UNLAWFUL FRAUD

It is unlawful fraud for any limited services pregnancy center to disseminate or cause to be disseminated before the public in [insert jurisdiction], or to disseminate before the public anywhere from [insert jurisdiction], any advertising about the services performed at that center if the management of the center knows or, by the exercise of reasonable care, ought to know is untrue or clearly designed to mislead the public about the nature of services provided. Advertising includes representations made directly to consumers; marketing practices; communication in any print medium such as newspapers, magazines, mailers or handouts; any broadcast medium such as television or radio; or over the Internet such as through websites and web ads.

[Bill drafting note: A particular state might use language that is similar to any existing Unfair and Deceptive Trade Practices Act.]

(C) ENFORCEMENT

1) The [insert appropriate authority] may enforce the provisions of this section through a civil action in any court of competent jurisdiction. Before filing an action under this section, [insert appropriate

authority] shall give written notice of the violation to the limited services pregnancy center. The written notice shall indicate that the limited services pregnancy center has ten (10) days in which to correct the false, misleading, or deceptive advertising. If the limited services pregnancy center has not responded to the written notice within ten (10) days or refuses to correct the false, misleading, or deceptive advertising within that period, [insert appropriate authority] may file a civil action.

2) [Insert appropriate authority] may apply to any court of competent jurisdiction for injunctive relief compelling compliance with any provision of this section and correcting the effects of the false, misleading, or deceptive advertising. Such an injunction may require a limited services pregnancy center to:

a) Pay for and disseminate appropriate corrective advertising in the same form as the false, misleading, or deceptive advertising.

b) Post a notice on its premises, in a location clearly noticeable from the waiting area, examination area, or both, stating:

i. Whether there is a licensed medical doctor, registered nurse, or other licensed medical practitioner on staff at the center; and

ii. Whether abortion, emergency contraception, or referrals for abortion or emergency contraception are available at the center.

c) Any other narrowly tailored relief that the court deems necessary to remedy the adverse effects of the false, misleading, or deceptive advertising on women seeking pregnancy-related services.

3) Upon a finding by a court of competent jurisdiction that a limited services pregnancy center has violated this section, [juris-

diction] shall be entitled to recover civil penalties from each and every party responsible for the violation of not less than [$500] and not more than [$5,000] per violation. In addition, if the [jurisdiction] prevails it shall be entitled to reasonable attorney's fees and costs pursuant to order of the court.

4) Nothing in this section shall be interpreted as restricting, precluding or otherwise limiting a separate or concurrent criminal prosecution under the [insert relevant law]. Jeopardy shall not attach as a result of any court action to enforce the provisions of this section.

[Bill drafting note: Because of the sensitivity of First Amendment issues and the fact that abortion opponents often file suit over the First Amendment, Findings should be carefully crafted to describe the problem in your own jurisdiction.]

SECTION 6. QUALIFIED PROVIDERS OF ABORTION

(A) DEFINITIONS—In this section:

1) "Aspiration abortion" means medical treatment intended to induce the termination of a pregnancy by dilating the cervix and using suction to remove the fetus and related pregnancy material from the uterus.

2) "Certified nurse-midwife" means a person licensed under [insert relevant provision].

3) "Medication abortion" means the use of medication intended to terminate a pregnancy so that it does not result in a live birth.

4) "Nurse practitioner" means a person licensed under [insert relevant provision].

5) "Physician assistant" means a person licensed under [insert relevant provision].

(B) QUALIFIED PROVIDERS TO INCLUDE NURSE PRAC-TITIONERS AND NURSE-MIDWIVES

1) A nurse practitioner or a certified nurse-midwife is authorized to prescribe and supervise medication abortions and to perform an aspiration abortion if he or she has successfully completed training and achieved clinical competency and adheres to standardized procedures approved by the [insert relevant board governing nurse practitioners and certified nurse-midwives].

2) It is unprofessional conduct for any nurse practitioner or certified nurse-midwife to prescribe or supervise an aspiration or medication abortion without prior successful completion of training and validation of clinical competency.

3) The [insert relevant board governing nurse practitioners and certified nurse-midwives] shall issue rules for training, clinical competency, and standardized procedures for medication abortion and aspiration abortion.

(C) QUALIFIED PROVIDERS INCLUDE PHYSICIAN ASSISTANTS

1) A physician assistant is authorized to prescribe and supervise medication abortions and to perform an aspiration abortion if he or she has successfully completed training and achieved clinical competency and adheres to standardized procedures approved by the [insert relevant board governing physician assistants].

2) It is unprofessional conduct for any physician assistant to prescribe or supervise an aspiration or medication abortion without prior successful completion of training and validation of clinical competency.

3) The [insert relevant board governing physician assistants] shall issue rules for training, clinical competency, and standardized procedures for medication abortion and aspiration abortion.

[Bill drafting note: You will have to consult with local advocates and the affected healthcare professional associations before writing this bill. Healthcare regulatory schemes often differ from state to state. In addition, there are various ways to achieve the same goal, depending on the wording of your state's "physician-only" provision (that is, existing statutory language that an abortion can be performed only by a physician):

a) A few states have used regulatory processes and a few have used Attorney General opinions to allow APCs to practice despite so-called "physician-only" laws. These non-legislative avenues might be possible in your state.

b) Depending on the state, you might simply repeal the "physician-only" provision; the underlying statutory and regulatory scheme might be sufficient to allow APCs to handle both aspiration and medication abortions.

c) Alternatively, by inserting definitions of APCs or by using current definitions in state law, you might amend the existing "physician-only" provision to add APCs, making it a physician *and* APCs only law. Unless you add additional restrictions, this approach would cover both aspiration and medication abortions.]

SECTION 7. REPEAL OF TARGETED REGULATION OF ABORTION PROVIDERS

1) Section XXX [any provision of law that singles out abortion facilities or personnel for requirements that are more burdensome than those imposed on facilities that provide medically comparable procedures] is hereby repealed.

2) Section XXX [any provision of law that is the proximate cause of the closure of an abortion facility or facilities and which has not been proven by clear and convincing evidence necessary to prevent a bona fide threat to patient safety] is hereby repealed.

3) Section XXX [any provision that includes onerous licensing standards comparable or equivalent to the standards of ambulatory surgical centers e.g. procedure room size, corridor width, required minimum distance from hospital, transfer agreement with hospitals] is hereby repealed.

4) Section XXX [any provision that includes onerous requirements on clinicians that perform abortions e.g. admitting privileges] is hereby repealed.

SECTION 8. REPEAL WAITING PERIODS AND MANDATORY BIASED COUNSELING

1) Section XXX [any provision of law that requires a waiting period before an abortion is performed] is hereby repealed.

2) Section XXX [any provision of law that necessitates multiple trips to a clinic for reasons other than medical necessity] is hereby repealed.

3) Section XXX [any provision of law that necessitates an ultrasound or sonogram for reasons other than medical necessity] is hereby repealed.

SECTION 9. SEVERABILITY

The provisions of this Act shall be severable, and if any phrase, clause, sentence or provision is declared to be invalid or is preempted by federal law or regulation, the validity of the remainder of this Act shall not be affected.

SECTION 10. EFFECTIVE DATE

This Act shall take effect on July 1, 20XX.

Pregnant Women's Dignity Act

Summary: The Pregnant Women's Dignity Act would protect women who suffer a pregnancy loss from investigation by law enforcement, judicial or administrative authorities.

Background Summary

Law enforcement authorities are investigating and prosecuting women who have lost a pregnancy. In recent years, 38 states have enacted so-called "fetal homicide" laws. Although legislators generally approved these bills to prosecute people who commit a crime against a pregnant woman, they are now being used to punish women who suffer a pregnancy loss, based on the idea that they might have intentionally or negligently caused it.

The National Advocates for Pregnant Women have documented hundreds of such cases. For example:

In Iowa, a pregnant woman who fell down a flight of stairs was reported to the police after seeking help at a hospital. She was arrested for attempted fetal homicide.

In Utah, a woman gave birth to twins; one was stillborn. Health care providers believed that the stillbirth was the result of the woman's decision to delay having a cesarean. She was arrested on charges of fetal homicide.

In Louisiana, a woman who went to the hospital for unexplained vaginal bleeding was imprisoned for over a year based on charges of second-degree murder before medical records revealed she had suffered a miscarriage at 11 to 15 weeks of pregnancy.

In South Carolina, a woman who was eight months pregnant attempted suicide by jumping out a window. She survived despite suffering severe injuries but because she lost the pregnancy, she was arrested and jailed for the crime of homicide by child abuse.

In Mississippi, a girl became pregnant at age 15 and lost her baby in a stillbirth. Prosecutors charged her with a "depraved heart murder" after they discovered she had used cocaine, although there was "no evidence that drug abuse had anything to do with the baby's death."

In the United States, approximately one million known pregnancies end in miscarriage or stillbirth each year and it is inconceivable that any one could be the subject of criminal investigation. As many as 15 to 20 percent of known pregnancies end in miscarriage and, in addition, approximately 26,000 end in stillbirth and 19,000 in neonatal deaths.

Government investigations of women who lose a pregnancy are not worth the trauma they inflict. Such investigations will deter women from seeking medical care after they've experienced a pregnancy loss and undermine the crucial doctor-patient relationship as health care providers are pressured to collect evidence against their patients.

Model Legislation

SECTION 1. SHORT TITLE
This Act shall be called the "Pregnant Women's Dignity Act."

SECTION 2. FINDINGS AND PURPOSE

(A) FINDINGS—The legislature finds that:

1) The argument that "life begins at conception" has been used to justify police powers in response to pregnancy loss, including law enforcement investigation, arrest and prosecution.

2) In the United States, approximately one million known pregnancies per year end as a result of miscarriage and stillbirth.

3) As many as 15 to 20 percent of all pregnancies end in miscarriage. An additional one percent of pregnancies—approximately 26,000 per year—end in stillbirth and 19,000 end in neonatal deaths.

4) The actual number of pregnancies lost is likely to be substantially higher because many occur before women even know they are pregnant.

5) Some law enforcement authorities have begun investigations of women on the suspicion that they did something to intentionally or negligently end their pregnancies.

6) In countries where abortion is largely criminalized, such as in El Salvador, there are an increasing number of cases involving bedside interrogations and prosecutions of women who have lost their pregnancies.

7) Because it is difficult to distinguish between pregnancy loss that results from abortion and pregnancy loss that results from miscarriage and stillbirth, women subject to investigation have an extremely difficult time defending themselves.

8) Government investigations of women who lose their pregnancies inflict trauma on those who are already suffering and represent a profound disruption of the women's family life and their ability to care for the children they already have.

9) Such government investigations will deter women from seeking medical care after they've experienced a pregnancy loss.

10) Such government investigations will undermine the crucial doctor-patient relationship as health care providers are pressured to collect evidence against their patients.

(B) PURPOSE—This law is enacted to ensure that women who experience pregnancy losses are not subjected to government investigation.

SECTION 3. PROTECTION OF WOMEN WHO LOSE A PREGNANCY

After section XXX, the following new section XXX shall be inserted:

(A) DEFINITIONS—In this section:

1) "Pregnancy outcome" means the result of a pregnancy,

including miscarriage, abortion, stillbirth, neonatal death, and the birth of a child who survives.

2) "State" means the state and every county, city, town, municipal corporation, quasi-municipal corporation, and public institution of higher education in the state.

(B) POLICY AGAINST INVESTIGATION OF WOMEN WHO LOSE A PREGNANCY

1) It shall be the policy of this State to prohibit government authorities from investigating women based on their pregnancy outcomes.

2) No police agency or sheriff's office shall initiate a criminal investigation based on a woman's pregnancy outcome.

3) No state judicial authority shall authorize a search warrant or a subpoena for health records related to a woman's pregnancy outcome, or compel a woman or a medical professional to testify about a woman's pregnancy outcome.

4) No state social services agency shall initiate an investigation of a woman based upon that woman's pregnancy outcome.

5) No person who is a mandatory reporter under [state law that designates certain people like social workers, teachers and doctors as mandatory reporters of child abuse or neglect] shall be required, expected or encouraged to inform child welfare authorities about a woman's pregnancy outcome.

SECTION 4. REPEAL
The following sections are hereby repealed: [list existing provisions inconsistent with this Act].

SECTION 5. EFFECTIVE DATE
This Act shall take effect on July 1, 20XX.

Permissions

Abortion Desert Image (page 12): Cartwright AF, Karunaratne M, Barr-Walker J, Johns NE, Upadhyay UD. Identifying National Availability of Abortion Care and Distance From Major US Cities: Systematic Online Search. *J Med Internet Res* 2018;20(5):e186 DOI: 10.2196/jmir.9717 PMID: 29759954

Post-Roe desert (page 12)—Derivative, Robin Marty

How to use birth control pills as emergency contraception (page *33–35*) from *A Womb of One's Own*, https://wombofonesown.wordpress.com. Reprinted with permission.

Model legislation for state legislatures (page 44) from Public Leadership Institute, http://publicleadershipinstitute.org/model-bills/reproductive-rights/29-model-bills-playbook-abortion-rights/. Reprinted with permission.

Instructions for finding abortion pills (page 115–116) from www.Abortionpillinfo.org. Reprinted with permission.

Abortion pill report card and study information (page 116–118) from Plan C website, www.plancpills.org. Reprinted with permission.

Information and images on how to induce a miscarriage with medications (page 118–125 on) from Women Help Women, Self-Managed Abortion: Safe and Supported, https://womenhelp.org/en/page/408/how-should-I-take-the-pills; https://womenhelp.org/en/page/623/how-to-use-misoprostol-for-abortion-graphic-instructions; https://consult.womenhelp.org/en/page/417/what-to-do-in-%20case-of-emergency Reprinted with permission.

Del Em image (page 135) from Women's Health Specialists, www.womenshealthspecialists.org/self-help/menstrual-extraction/. Reprinted with permission.

How to perform a menstrual evacuation (page 136–138) from the Skeptic Files Message board, originally from *Womenpower—Do It Yourself Abortion—Time's Up!*, http://www.skepticfiles.org/atheist2/selfabor.htm. Reprinted with permission.

How to perform a manual vacuum aspiration (page 139–142) from Médecins Sans Frontières, https://medicalguidelines.msf.org/viewport/EONC/english/9-5-manual-vacuum-aspiration-mva-20316948.html. Reprinted with permission.

Abortion tools picture (page 142) courtesy of author.

Notes

1 Arit John, "Arizona GOPer Resigns After Calling for Forced Sterilization of Women on Medicaid," *Atlantic*, September 15, 2014, https://www.theatlantic.com/politics/archive/2014/09/arizona-goper-resigns-after-calling-for-forced-sterilization-of-women-on-medicaid/380191/.

2 "Henry Hyde Quotes," AZ Quotes, https://www.azquotes.com/author/29083-Henry_Hyde.

3 Sarah Torre, "Hyde Amendment Turns 40: More Than 2 Million Lives Saved," *Daily Signal*, October 5, 2016, https://www.dailysignal.com/2016/10/05/hyde-amendment-turns-40-more-than-2-million-lives-saved/.

4 Michael J. New, "Hyde @ 40: Analyzing the Impact of the Hyde Amendment," Charlotte Lozier Institute, September 27, 2016, https://lozierinstitute.org/hydeat40/.

5 Michelle Garcia, "In Many States the End of Roe v. Wade Is Already Here," Vox.com, July 9, 2018, https://www.vox.com/2018/7/3/17526222/abortion-states-access-roe-v-wade-kennedy.

6 Robin Marty, "The Long Road to a Safe and Legal Abortion," *Slate*, October 20, 2014, https://slate.com/human-interest/2014/10/abortion-clinic-crisis-women-of-texas-could-have-to-drive-up-to-600-miles-to-end-a-pregnancy.html.

7 "Abortion in Latin America and the Caribbean," Guttmacher Institute, March 2018, https://www.guttmacher.org/fact-sheet/abortion-latin-america-and-caribbean.

8 "North Carolina Motorcycle Abortion Bill Passes State House," *Huffington Post*, July 11, 2013, https://www.huffingtonpost.com/2013/07/11/north-carolina-motorcycle-abortion_n_3582006.html.

9 "What If Roe Fell," Center for Reproductive Rights, accessed August 1, 2018, https://www.reproductiverights.org/what-if-roe-fell.

10 "Which Kind of Emergency Contraception Should I Use?," Planned Parenthood, accessed August 27, 2018, https://www.plannedparenthood.org/learn/morning-after-pill-emergency-contraception/which-kind-emergency-contraception-should-i-use.

11 "Unintended Pregnancy in the United States," Guttmacher Institute, September 2016, https://www.guttmacher.org/fact-sheet/unintended-pregnancy-united-states.

12 "Beyond the Beltway," Power to Decide, August 2018, https://powertodecide.org/system/files/resources/primary-download/extended-supply-contraception.pdf.

13 Jane Doe, *A Womb of One's Own*, June 30, 2014, accessed August 11, 2018, https://wombofonesown.wordpress.com/2014/06/30/a-womb-of-ones-own-complete-text-basic-edition/.

14 "ACOG Practice Bulletin," American College of Obstetricians and Gynecologists,

November 2017, https://www.acog.org/Clinical-Guidance-and-Publications/Practice-Bulletins/Committee-on-Practice-Bulletins-Gynecology/Long-Acting-Reversible-Contraception-Implants-and-Intrauterine-Devices.

15   Safe and Sound for Women Pricing, Las Vegas, NV, accessed September 16, 2018, http://www.safeandsoundforwomen.com/you-should-know/.

16   Ronnie Cohen, "Denial of Abortion Leads to Economic Hardship for Low-Income Women," Reuters, January 18, 2018, https://www.reuters.com/article/us-health-abortion-hardship/denial-of-abortion-leads-to-economic-hardship-for-low-income-women-idUSKBN1F731Z.

17   Hannah Smothers, "People Are Urging Women to Start Saving an Emergency Abortion Fund," *Cosmopolitan*, November 10, 2016, https://www.cosmopolitan.com/sex-love/a8274910/people-are-urging-women-to-start-saving-an-emergency-abortion-fund/.

18   Perry Stein, "Proposed Zoning Changes Would Restrict Abortion Clinics in Manassas," *Washington Post*, April 27, 2015, https://www.washingtonpost.com/local/virginia-politics/proposed-zoning-changes-would-restrict-abortion-clinics-in-manassas/2015/04/27/8a28df92-ece9-11e4-8666-a1d756d0218e_story.html?utm_term=.8aae66c2bd2a.

19   " 'It Was Just One Thing After Another': An Abortion Provider on His Four-Month Ordeal to Reopen the Only Clinic in Northern Alabama," *Slate*, October 28, 2014, http://www.slate.com/articles/double_x/doublex/2014/10/dalton_johnson_on_reopening_an_abortion_clinic_in_alabama.html.

20   "Whole Woman's Health Officially Announces South Bend Abortion Clinic Plans," WNDU News, October 30, 2017, https://www.wndu.com/content/news/Whole-Womans-Health-officially-announces-South-Bend-abortion-clinic-plans-454149003.html.

21   Jeff Parrot, "South Bend Council Allows Anti-Abortion Group to Open Site Next to Proposed Abortion Clinic," *South Bend Tribune*, April 24, 2018, https://www.southbendtribune.com/news/local/south-bend-council-allows-anti-abortion-group-to-open-site/article_f516f3b8-3e60-5bd9-9889-3b6ee69e606e.html.

22   Mariella Mosthof, "John Oliver's Segment About Crisis Pregnancy Centers on 'Last Week Tonight' Sheds Light on Their Misleading Tactics," *Romper*, April 8, 2018, https://www.romper.com/p/john-olivers-segment-about-crisis-pregnancy-centers-on-last-week-tonight-sheds-light-on-their-misleading-tactics-8728576.

23   "Characteristics of U.S. Abortion Patients in 2014 and Changes Since 2008," Guttmacher Institute, May 2016, https://www.guttmacher.org/report/characteristics-us-abortion-patients-2014.

24   Willie Parker, MD, "Dr. Willie Parker: The South Is 'Ground Zero' in the Abortion Fight," *Glamour*, April 5, 2018, https://www.glamour.com/story/dr-willie-parker-the-south-is-ground-zero-in-the-abortion-access-fight.

25   Jody Steinauer, "Want to Protect the Right to Abortion? Train More People to Perform Them," *New York Times*, August 29, 2018, https://www.nytimes.com/2018/08/29/opinion/abortion-provider-training-roe.html.

26   "Reproductive Justice," SisterSong.net, accessed September 4, 2018, https://www.sistersong.net/reproductive-justice/.

27   Philip Bump, "Trump Celebrates Winning 52 Percent of Women in 2016—Which Is Only How He Did Among Whites," *Washington Post*, March 10, 2018, https://www.washingtonpost.com/news/politics/wp/2018/03/10/trump-celebrates-winning-

52-percent-of-women-in-2016-which-is-only-how-he-did-among-whites/?utm_
term=.3c4c64110e5a.

28   Tamar Auber, "Protesters Pound on Doors of Supreme Court: 'Kavanaugh Has Hot to
Ho,'" Mediaite.com, October 6, 2018, https://www.mediaite.com/tv/protesters-pound-on-
doors-of-supreme-court-kavanaugh-has-got-to-go/.

29   Erin Matson, "When It Comes to Abortion Rights, Civil Disobedience Could Be the Only
Option," *Teen Vogue*, August 16, 2018, https://www.teenvogue.com/story/when-it-comes-
to-abortion-rights-civil-disobedience-could-be-the-only-option.

30   David DeKok, "Mom Ann Whalen Sentenced to Prison for Giving Daughter Abortion
Pills," Reuters, September 6, 2014, https://www.huffingtonpost.com/2014/09/07/ann-
whalen-abortion-daughter_n_5777120.html.

31   Tara Culp-Ressler, "Over 60 Pro-Choice Activists Arrested for Protesting North
Carolina's Radical Abortion Restrictions," ThinkProgress, July 9, 2013, https://
thinkprogress.org/over-60-pro-choice-activists-arrested-for-protesting-north-carolinas-
radical-abortion-restrictions-cc00133de6d3/.

32   "Rachel Sadon, "Kavanaugh Confirmed Amidst Day of Protests and More Than 150
Arrests in D.C.," *DCist*, October 6, 2018, https://dcist.com/story/18/10/06/kavanaugh-
confirmation-protests/.

33   H. S. Seo, "125 Women Take 'Abortion Pill' in Protest of Anti-Abortion Law," Korea
BizWire, August 27, 2018, http://koreabizwire.com/125-women-take-abortion-pill-in-
protest-of-anti-abortion-law/123240.

34   Molly Redden, "New Website Offers US Women Help to Perform Their Own Abortions,"
Guardian, April 27, 2017, https://www.theguardian.com/world/2017/apr/27/abortion-
website-women-help-women.

35   "Abortifacient Herbs," Sister Zeus, accessed August 11, 2018, http://www.sisterzeus.com/
Abortif.htm.

36   David Brennan, "Woman Dies After Using Parsley to Induce Miscarriage, First Death
Since Argentina Senate Rejected Abortion Bill," *Newsweek*, August 15, 2018, https://
www.newsweek.com/woman-dies-after-using-parsley-induce-miscarriage-first-death-
argentina-1073864.

37   Abigail R. A. Aiken et al., "Self Reported Outcomes and Adverse Events After Medical
Abortion through Online Telemedicine: Population Based Study in the Republic of
Ireland and Northern Ireland," *BMJ*, May 16, 2017, https://www.bmj.com/content/357/
bmj.j2011.

38   *When Self-Induced Abortion Is a Crime: Laws That Put Women at Risk*, National
Institute for Reproductive Health, June 2017, https://www.nirhealth.org/wp-content/
uploads/2017/06/Self-Abortion-White-Paper-Final.pdf.

39   DeKok, "Mom Ann Whalen Sentenced."

40   "Roe's Unfinished Promise: Decriminalizing Abortion Once and for All," SIA Legal
Team, accessed August 8, 2018, https://www.sialegalteam.org/roes-unfinished-promise.

41   Nellie Gilles, Sarah Kramer, and Joe Richman, "Before 'Roe v. Wade,' the Women of
'Jane' Provided Abortions for the Women of Chicago," NPR, January 19, 2018, https://
www.npr.org/2018/01/19/578620266/before-roe-v-wade-the-women-of-jane-provided-
abortions-for-the-women-of-chicago.

42   Kate Manning, "Leeches, Lye and Spanish Fly," *New York Times*, January 21, 2013,
https://www.nytimes.com/2013/01/22/opinion/leeches-lye-and-spanish-fly.html.

43   Daniella Silva, "Anna Yocca, Tennessee Woman in Coat-Hanger Attempted Abortion Case, Released from Jail a Year Later," NBC News, January 11, 2017, https://www. nbcnews.com/news/us-news/anna-yocca-tennessee-woman-coat-hanger-attempted-abortion-case-released-n705416.

44   "Building a Del Em," *Reproductive Right Blog*, accessed August 11, 2010, http://the-reproductive-right.blogspot.com/p/building-del-em.html.

45   Emily Bazelon, "A Mother in Jail for Helping Her Daughter Have an Abortion," *New York Times Magazine*, September 22, 2014, https://www.nytimes.com/2014/09/22/magazine/a-mother-in-jail-for-helping-her-daughter-have-an-abortion.html.

46   Lisa Ryan, "How to Plan an Abortion in the Surveillance State," *Cut*, January 25, 2017, https://www.thecut.com/2017/01/how-to-safely-research-and-learn-about-abortion.html.

47   "What to Do If Your Phone Is Seized by the Police," ACLU Freedom of the Press Foundation, June 27, 2018, accessed August 11, 2018, https://freedom.press/training/mobile-security-for-activists-and-journalists/.

48   Mark Yates, "Three Reasons to Never Use Fingerprint Locks on Phones," AVG Signal, July 12, 2016, https://www.avg.com/en/signal/3-reasons-to-never-use-fingerprint-locks.

49   "Surveillance Self-Defense: Communicating with Others," Electronic Frontier Foundation, accessed August 11, 2018, https://ssd.eff.org/en/module/communicating-others.

50   Russell Brandom, "Police Are Using DNA Testing to Track Down a Fetus's Mother," *Verge*, May 10, 2018, https://www.theverge.com/2018/5/10/17340666/dna-testing-georgia-fetus-codis-abortion-genetics-investigation.

51   Tina Moore, Georgett Roberts, and Aaron Feis, "Teen Who Left Fetus on Plane May Have Had Botched Abortion," *New York Post*, August 8, 2018, https://nypost.com/2018/08/08/teen-who-left-fetus-on-plane-may-have-had-botched-abortion/.

52   *A Womb of One's Own.*

53   Theodore Schleifer, "Anti-Abortion Group Claims Credit for Planned Parenthood Hacking," CNN, July 27, 2015, https://www.cnn.com/2015/07/27/politics/planned-parenthood-hacked/index.html.

54   Sara Ashley O'Brien, "Abortion Funds Band Together to Sue Cyberattackers," CNN, March 29, 2018, https://money.cnn.com/2018/03/29/technology/abortion-fundraiser-cyberattack-lawsuit/index.html.

Index